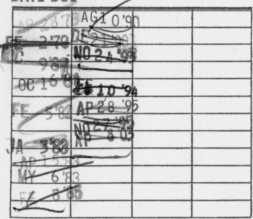

Last Home for the Aged

Critical Implications of Institutionalization

Sheldon S. Tobin

Morton A. Lieberman

Last Home
for the Aged

 Jossey-Bass Publishers
San Francisco · Washington · London · 1976

LAST HOME FOR THE AGED
Critical Implications of Institutionalization
by Sheldon S. Tobin and Morton A. Lieberman

Library of Congress Catalogue Card Number LC 76-11941

International Standard Book Number ISBN 0-87589-280-9

Manufactured in the United States of America

JACKET DESIGN BY WILLI BAUM

FIRST EDITION

Code 7608

*The Jossey-Bass
Behavioral Science Series*

Preface

Conventional wisdom has it that long-term care settings profoundly affect older people both psychologically and physically. Life in an institutional setting is assumed to result in severe consequences for the elderly. Yet something other than institutional life itself may account for a portrait that encompasses disorientation, withdrawal, hopelessness, and gross distortions in the content of the self-concept. May it be, we asked ourselves, that much of the portrait is sketched in prior to entering and living in these settings? Also, independent of the setting, is not the very discontinuity of moving from one environment to another particularly onerous for the elderly? If so, then might not explanations other than institutional life itself be equally valid in explaining "institutional" effects?

With these types of questions in mind we began our exploration of effects and their causes during and through the process of becoming institutionalized in what is considered to be the best type of contemporary long-term care institutions—the sectarian home for the aged. By studying older people who enter the better settings, we were able to isolate irreducible effects of the institutionalization process.

In the first chapter, we describe how we approached the problem. At a theoretical level, we offer various explanations for "institutional" effects. At an investigatory level, we delineate our research design, in which eighty-five older people were followed with in-depth interviews from before to after admission to homes for the aged. At a phenomenological level, we provide a portrait of community elderly—the "old old" who are most vulnerable and for whom institutional care may soon become the preferred way to cope with life changes.

Chapters Two, Three, and Four are on effects and their causes during three phases in the process: before admission, shortly after admission, and through the first year after admission. Chapter Two focuses on the many psychological differences between elderly people in the predecision phase and in the anticipatory institutionalization phase. Three case studies are used to illustrate these changes and also to identify causal factors, as well as to examine psychological experiences that underly changes and how these people coped with their experiences. Chapter Three presents the ensuing changes—again using the dimensions of functional capacity, affective responsiveness, emotional states and self-perceptions—from before to shortly after admission. The shifts in loss meanings and interpersonal relations are also examined and one of the cases is used to illustrate the changes from before to after admission. Next, in Chapter Four, changes throughout the institutionalization process are examined within the context of survivorship through the first year after admission. Vulnerability to environmental discontinuity is discussed. Another of the three cases is used to illustrate both adaptation through the first year as well as psychological characteristics associated with resisting the severe stress associated with entering and living in the institutional environment.

The fifth and final chapter focuses explicitly on the implications of our findings for direct practitioners, as well as for planners and policymakers. The explanations for what others have labeled "institutional effects" form the basis for discussions of early intervention, including services to prevent premature institutionalization, selection for and matching of would-be residents in institutional environments, managing the anticipatory crisis, and preparation for admission. Institutional life as a cause of effects is then reexamined. Finally, the chapter considers emerging institutional forms and the potential for developing innovative institutions within a viable long-term care system of social health care for the elderly.

Our effort was made possible by a major grant from the National Institute of Child Health and Human Development, HD-0364, to Morton Lieberman. That institute also provided the opportunity to Lieberman to devote himself to full-time research through a Research Career Development Award. Support for Sheldon Tobin during the time of writing this manuscript has largely come from the Administration on Aging, in the form of training and research grants. The inestimable support of the School of Social Service Administration and the Committee on Human Development of the University of Chicago is gratefully acknowledged.

A less visible source of support was a training grant from the National Institute of Child and Human Development to Bernice Neugarten as principal investigator. Bernice Neugarten has had a profound effect on both our lives—as colleague, cherished friend, and guide to the intellectual excitement of discovery. In this instance, the training grant permitted us to use our project as a research training laboratory for our many students. Because, in turn, of the productivity and contributions of the students, this book to a significant extent represents the synthesis of their masters' theses and doctoral dissertations. These students are: David Chiriboga, Gloria Edelhart, Elizabeth Etigson, Kristin Glasser, Mitchell Goodman, James Gorney, Herbert Haberland, Joseph Kuypers, David Miller, Alan Pincus, Valencia Prock, Virginia Revere, Arthur Rosner, Diana Slaughter, Darrel Slover, and Barbara Turner. Also inestimable was the contribution of our research assistants, particularly Anne Coplan, Roland Kaufman, Naomi Kistin, and Dorothy Stern. A special contribution was made by the interviewers who in most ways are more knowledgeable than us about the process that we are reporting: Rosalie Guttman, Charlotte Lindon, Dorothy Palfi, Joan Rosner, Adeline Shagam, and Patricia VanCleve.

Juanita Denson is to be deeply thanked for her persever-
ence and skill in translating illegible script into understandable
text through countless revisions. A special debt is owed to
Grace Lieberman, content editor, who transformed pages of
pedantry into readable prose. To Arnold Levin and Powell Lawton, readers of earlier drafts who provided the necessary encouragement and the perceptive criticisms that helped to sharpen
this book's focus, likewise an acknowledgement of our debt.

We owe special thanks to the innumerable staff of the
three Jewish Federation homes in Chicago for their cooperation—or, more appropriately, collaboration—in our studies.
Foremost was one of the directors, Jerome Hammerman, whose
intellectual stimulation outlives his untimely death. Murray
Berg and Jacob Gold, the directors of the other two homes, as
well as Jerome Grunes, psychiatric consultant to one of the
homes and clinical mentor of Sheldon Tobin, were of truly inestimable help. It is to the credit of the few singled out, as well
as all the other staff, that they ran the risk of being blamed for
institutional effects. These people demonstrated an impressive
commitment to discover with us effects and their causes so as to
benefit not only their residential populations but also the
elderly populations of all institutions.

Lastly, but most importantly, we are grateful to the elderly people who not only gave generously of their time but who
also were our teachers. They taught us what it is like to become
a resident in the last home for the aged—a future any one of us
may share.

It is to those with whom we presently share our lives that
we dedicate this book, particularly to our wives Maureen Tobin
and Grace Lieberman, who taught us the *art of living*.

Chicago, Illinois   Sheldon S. Tobin
July 1976   Morton A. Lieberman

Contents

Last Home
for the Aged

Critical Implications
of Institutionalization

❦ 1 ❦

What Do Institutions Do to the Old?

To live to an advanced old age may indeed be a blessing; but it may also be a curse. Living through the eighth and ninth decade of life can bring both personal deterioration and social losses. When less drastic efforts to adapt to these misfortunes fail, the elderly person and his or her family are often forced toward the more drastic solution of seeking institutional care. With each advancing year, the older person becomes increasingly aware that a catastrophic illness or a major loss in the social support system may necessitate this usually dreaded possibility.

Because American society has had a custodial orientation toward the needy aged, the institutional care facility has unfortunately been one of the most accessible sources of medical services for aged persons, especially those in the lower-middle-income and poverty groups (Blenkner, 1969). Furthermore, because of the limited number of alternative services, the elderly are forced to seek an institutional setting even when all they require is select services offered as part of institutional care (Brody, 1969). Home health care may be required for those who need the assurance of medical care and surveillance, whereas day care (day hospital) may be required for others whose

daily medical and social needs are greater. Because these services
are not readily available, the elderly fear becoming clients in the
present service system, with its emphasis on institutional care,
and many aged persons who cling to independent living do so
with little or no direct service and with consequent accelerated
deterioration.

The one of six or so older Americans who need and could
benefit from social and health services are largely among the
oldest of the old, those above 75 or 80 years of age. The
younger old people, of course, also have unmet needs, especially
for income, but generally do not need extensive social and
health services to remain independent. The elderly who are
most in jeopardy are the very old who have a minimum of social
supports. Not surprisingly, they tend to be elderly women
(beyond the age of 75, there are almost three women for every
man) and they are likely to be widows. The older person who
never married and has no close relatives, in particular, cannot
escape the fear of eventually having to seek institutional care.
But the never married are not alone in this fear. Most of the
elderly do have children and do interact with them frequently,
but these elderly also fear the possibility of ending their years in
an institution. Not only do the elderly live close to their children—60 percent live within walking distance of at least one
child (Adams, 1968; Shanas, Townsend, Wedderburn, Friis,
Milhøj, and Stehouwer, 1968), and only 7 percent of blue-collar
children live more than 2 hours by car (Komarovsky,
1964)—but also two of three older people among the grand-
parent generation are given help by younger generations (Hill,
Foote, Aldous, Carlson, and MacDonald, 1970). It is to the next
youngest generation that grandparents—and particularly elderly
widows—turn for household management, care in illness, and
assistance when institutional care appears necessary (Troll,
1975). Yet to survive until the eighth or ninth—and increasingly
until the tenth—decade of life means that one's children are
themselves likely to be quite old and unable to meet the needs
of their dependent parents. Although these "elderly" children
may be dedicated and responsible, their parents fear that their
own personal deterioration or changes in their social support

system will be beyond the scope of their families to handle. Families, although rarely preferring that their elderly member be provided for in institutions, sometimes are unable to avoid seeking institutional care for their older family members. Often, in fact, families wait too long before seeking professional advice that might have been helpful if it had been offered before the family had no alternative to an institutional setting.

In the next 20 years or so, the likelihood is that we will have a much greater number of the very old and, thus, many more very old parents who will be dependent on elderly children, many of whom will be themselves too debilitated or too pressed with financial or other responsibilities for their own adult children to add care for an aged, deteriorating parent to their own burdens. If the typical age of those now seeking institutional care is in the lower 80s, we can expect it to rise to the late 80s in the next generation of the elderly. Regardless of what efforts are made to prevent premature institutionalization, a significant percentage among the very old will require institutional care. Noninstitutional congregate settings facilitate independent living for many, but the percentage among the very old who will need institutional care will most likely not become less than the current 5 percent or so, a percentage that represents an absolute figure of about one million Americans. Currently, the elderly in long-term care institutions average 82 years of age, and in many institutions 20 percent or more of the residential population is 90 years of age or over. Although almost 5 percent of those 65 years of age and over reside in institutions, of those between 65 and 75 years of age less than 2 percent reside in institutions. This percentage rises to 7 percent for those 75 to 85 and to more than 16 percent for those 85 and over (Office of Nursing Home Affairs, 1975). It is indeed the oldest of the old who are cared for in long-term care institutions!

Elderly people who enter long-term care institutions do so to assure survival by retarding further deterioration, maintaining residual capacities, and restoring lost functioning. These varied therapeutic goals are certainly congruent with a residential setting that has as a purpose the provision of health care within a structured social environment. Yet long-term care institutions for the aged have been charged with creating an "institutional personality syndrome" in older people. The literature is replete with descriptions of the institutionalized elderly as disoriented and disorganized, withdrawn and apathetic, depressed and hopeless. These characteristics are frequently ascribed to the singular effects of institutional life. Townsend (1962, pp. 328-329) succinctly summarizes the general view:

> *In the institution, people live communally with a minimum of privacy and yet their relationships with each other are slender. Many subsist in a kind of defensive shell of isolation. Their mobility is restricted, and they have little access to a general society. The social experiences are limited, and the staff lead a rather separate existence from them. They are subtly oriented toward a system in which they submit to orderly routine, noncreative occupation, and cannot exercise as much self-determination. They are deprived of intimate family relationships and can rarely find substitutes which seem to be more than a pale imitation of those enjoyed by most people in a general community. The result for the individual seems fairly often to be a gradual process of depersonalization. He has too little opportunity to develop the talents he possesses and they atrophy through disuse. He may become resigned and depressed and may display no interest in the future or in things not immediately personal. He sometimes becomes apathetic, talks little, and lacks initiative. His personal habits and toilet may deteriorate. Occasionally he seems to withdraw into a private world of fantasy. In some of the smaller and more humanely administered institutions, these various characteristics seem to be less frequently found, but they are still present.*

The institution, in other words, is perceived as a coercive force often causing more incapacity than it cures. Although this accusation has been directed at a variety of human caretaking institutions, a more recent focus has been on long-term care institutions for the elderly, including geriatric wards of state mental hospitals, domiciliaries of the Veterans Administration (VA), proprietary nursing homes, and nonprofit homes for the aged. It was the British version of nonprofit institutions that received Townsend's attention and that he implicates as having deleterious effects because of their "dehumanizing" and "depersonalizing environments." Because the nonprofit homes tend to be the best of the contemporary long-term care institutions for the aged in the United States, it is difficult to avoid the implication that even the finest institutions cause the deleterious sequelae commonly referred to as *institutional effects.*

Nonprofit homes for the aged, however, are not the most common of long-term care institutions. Long-term care institutions also include long-term mental hospitals, in which half the residential populations are likely to be elderly; geriatric and chronic disease hospitals; and nursing and personal care homes. In the third group of facilities live more than 80 percent of the institutionalized elderly. However, 75 percent of these facilities are proprietary nursing homes (run for profit), which have increased by a third in the past 10 years and are the target of the many recent investigations of nursing home abuses. Of the other two types of nursing and personal care homes, less than 10 percent are government sponsored (domiciliaries of the Veterans Administration and county homes) and 20 percent are nonprofit homes, of which half are sponsored by a religious group (sectarian homes). Nursing and personal care homes, in addition to being classified by auspice or ownership, are also classified by level of care, such as skilled versus intermediate nursing care. (For the preceding and additional statistics, see Office of Nursing Home Affairs, 1975.) The nonprofit homes with a range of care levels are the facilities most similar to those studied by Townsend.

If indeed it is true that unavoidable deleterious effects follow entering and living in the best of long-term care institutions —then it is imperative that institutions be used differently, that new forms of institutional care be developed, and, most importantly, that other forms of caretaking arrangements be considered. Home health care and day care services become indispensable alternatives to institutional care for all elderly people. On the other hand, if it is possible to develop humane, long-term care institutions that produce minimal unwelcomed effects, then such care should be available for those elderly whose needs are difficult to meet through alternative arrangements. Surely the potential of quality institutional care should not be denied to very old people who may be both physically frail and mentally confused and whose families are unable to care for them in a community environment.

The conventional view, as well as the prevailing view sustained by prior research, is that caretaking institutions have deleterious effects on the psychological well-being and physical survival of the very young as well as the very old. The evidence for institutional effects on the old has usually been generated, however, by contrasting community and institutionalized elderly, as Townsend did. Yet there are other explanations of why institutionalized elderly are different from their peers in the community. Institutionalized elderly, for example, may be a very select group among all the elderly. Not all the elderly enter long-term care institutions. Those who do may be of a particular personality type or have a particular set of social or physical problems. Even if there were no selection bias, however, the unpleasant aspects of the process of becoming institutionalized —deciding to apply for admission, waiting for acceptance by the institution, and then awaiting admission—may also be sufficient to account for the decrements observed in institutionalized elderly when they are compared with their peers who have remained in the community. When community elderly are compared with institutionalized elderly, however, information on the status of the latter *as they underwent* the process of becoming institutionalized is essential if the effects of the process are to be isolated from the effects of institutional context. Once the older person and his family decide that "it's time" (to go to a home), the older person may begin to experience a sense of loss stemming from feelings of separation and rejection. These feelings become inseparable from the fear or even dread of the impending institutionalization. Before the actual event of entering the institution, therefore, adverse changes that have been attributed to the effects of the institutional environment may actually have already begun. Another source of such effects may be the environmental discontinuity involved in the process of relocation from familiar to an unfamiliar environment. This process itself may be associated with severe consequences, particularly for old people.

Each of these possible sources of explanation for the portrait of institutionalized elderly will shortly be considered in greater detail. The review of these explanations of effects is an important background for subsequent chapters, because a major aim of the present research has been to address the question of what effects or what proportion of effects observed in institutionalized populations of the old may be attributed to selection biases, to the institutionalization process, to environmental discontinuity, and to institutional life itself. (See reviews by Lieberman, 1969, and Kasl, 1972, in which similar questions are raised.)

The Traditional View

If, indeed, such causes as these come readily to mind to explain the debilitation and accelerated death rates that so consistently distinguish the institutionalized old from their peers who live in the community, one is immediately motivated to ask why there has been such a general trend to infer that these effects are attributable solely to the institutional milieu. The answer to this question would appear to lie in two factors—the history of, and the method of inquiry on institutionalized populations.

The earliest report of the effects of institutional living on the very young was in 1756 by Hanway, an English philanthropist, who found that 50 percent of infants in a particular foundling home died before their second birthday (1957). He added that death rates in foundling homes of 60 to 70 percent were not unusual, as contrasted to a death rate of 13 to 15 percent for children under 2 years of age from similar backgrounds who lived at home. He attributed the high or excess mortality to deficient institutional care: "Many children instead of being nourished with care by the fostering hand or breast of a wholesome country nurse are thrust into the impure air of a workhouse, into the hands of some careless, worthless young female or decrepit old woman and inevitably lost . . . ."

It was not until the 1940s, when Spitz (1945) studied infants over time, that attention was turned to effects less dramatic than mortality, although he also was concerned about marasmus (infant death consequent to apathy and depression). Observations of two groups of infants, one group reared in a foundling home and the other in a nursery, revealed a not uncommon downward spiral that eventually developed into depression and, for some, marasmus. This spiral was more frequent in the foundling home than in the nursery. Spitz attributed these differences between the two institutions to maternal and sensory deprivation. The syndrome that he identified, and that now has become generally accepted, includes withdrawal and cognitive disorganization as well as depression. As stated by Bowlby (1952, p. 15) in his now classic review:

> *The child's development is almost always retarded—physically, intellectually, and socially—and symptoms of physical and mental illness may appear. Such evidence is disquieting, but skeptics may question whether the retardation is permanent and whether the symptoms of illness may not be easily overcome. The retrospective and follow-up studies make it clear that such optimism is not always justified and that some children are gravely damaged for life. This is a somber conclusion that must now be regarded as established.*

The effect of institutions on adult patients of mental institutions has also received much attention. Reviewing the many studies on the effects of mental and other institutions, Sommer and Osmond (1961) classified institutional effects into six general symptoms: (1) deindividuation, a reduced capacity for thought and action as a result of dependence on the institution;

(2) disculturation, the acquisition of institutional values and attitudes unsuited to the previous or preadmission environment; (3) emotional, social, and physical damage to the resident from losses of status, security, and so on; (4) estrangement from the consequences of technological and other changes in the outside world; (5) isolation through loss of contact with the outside world; and (6) stimulus deprivation, a result of the senses being deadened by prolonged institutionalization. This classification was based on findings of studies that usually compared short- and long-stay patients. As Sommer and Osmond caution, selective discharge of the better-functioning patients could very well have led to an overestimation of institutional effects. The studies rarely follow a sample from before admission through the first year after admission.

The classification itself is a useful one, grouping several individual effects under general headings. The first symptom category, deindividuation, for example, includes increased dependency, decreased self-assertion, accepting of authority, and inability to make decisions. These behaviors within deindividuation, as well as the many other behaviors scattered among the other five categories, are found, Sommer and Osmond add, in all total institutions, among staff as well as inmates, and in animals in zoos.

The symptoms of institutionalized young children and mental patients are not unlike the symptoms identified in studies of the elderly residing in homes for the aged, domiciliaries, and nursing homes. A review of these studies (Lieberman, 1969) suggests that institutionalized elderly people share the following characteristics: poor adjustment; depression and unhappiness; intellectual ineffectiveness because of increased rigidity and low energy (but not necessarily intellectual incompetence); negative self-image; feelings of personal insignificance and impotence; and a view of self as old. Residents tend to be docile and submissive, to show a low range of interests and activities, and to live in the past rather than the future. They are withdrawn and unresponsive in relationship to others. There is some suggestion that they have increased anxiety, which at times has as a focus their own death (see, for example, Ames,

Learned, Metraux, and Walker, 1954; Chalfen, 1956; Coe, 1965; Davidson and Kruglov, 1952; Dörken, 1951; Eicker, 1959; Fink, 1957; Fox, 1950; Lakin, 1960; Laverty, 1950; Lepkowski, 1956; Lieberman and Lakin, 1963; Mason, 1954; Pan, 1948; Pollack, Karp, Kahn, and Goldfarb, 1962; Shrut, 1958; Swenson, 1961; Tuckman and Lorge, 1952). Other investigators (Blenkner, Bloom, and Nielsen, 1971; Camargo and Preston, 1945; Kay, Norris, and Post, 1956; Lieberman, 1961; Roth, 1955; Whittier and Williams, 1956) have reported marked increases in mortality rates for aged persons entering mental institutions or homes for the aged.

These studies clearly demonstrate that aged persons residing in a variety of institutional settings are psychologically worse off and likely to die sooner than aged persons living in the community. But these studies share two crucial methodological weaknesses that the investigation described in the present volume was launched to correct. First, they have not established that the institutionalized populations that were studied were comparable to aged people living in the community, differing only in respect to where they lived. Without such information, all of this research is worthless in determining whether life in the institution induced the negative effects. Differences between institutional and community residents do not of themselves mean that institutionalization is the essential variable that created the differences. Second, the earlier studies have examined institutionalized residents only *after* they were institutionalized. They do not, in other words, provide a longitudinal view of institutionalized individuals prior to and after the experience that has been assumed to be the stressor. Thus they do not unequivocally demonstrate that the characteristics of institutional life itself, and not other factors associated with the process of becoming institutionalized, some of which may well have been introduced *before* the individuals have even entered the institution, induce these deleterious effects.

The Total Institution

The most compelling statement of reasons for the effects of these institutions has been offered by Goffman (1961) in his characterization of the "total institution." He has argued that these environments dehumanize their inhabitants. The process of dehumanization has been referred to by Goffman (1961), in his study of inmates of mental hospitals, as a *moral career*, in which the moral aspects of the process of becoming a mental patient refer to the "regular sequences of changes that career entails in the person's self and in his framework of imagery for judging himself and others" (p. 128). According to Goffman, because the interaction with others within the institutional setting strips the inmate of a previous identity, the experience is a "deselfing" one, or to use his more dramatic phrase "a mortification of the self."

The type of institution that has this potential for harmful effects has been labeled by Goffman (1961) as the *total institution*. He emphasizes that a basic characteristic of total institutions is the breakdown in the barrier between sleep, play, and work, so that all three of these activities of everyday life take place in the same setting with the same people. He uses four characteristics for the classification of an institution as a total one. First, all activities are conducted in the same place and under the same authority. Second, each phase of the resident's daily activity is carried on in the immediate company of a large batch of others, all of whom are treated alike and are required to do the same thing together. Third, all phases of the day's activities are tightly scheduled, with one activity leading at a prearranged time into the next, and the whole sequence of activities is imposed from above by a system of explicit formal rulings and is enforced by a body of officials. Fourth, the various enforced activities are brought together into a single rational plan, purportedly designed to fulfill the official aims of the institution.

Goffman has developed a classification of five general types of total institutions in modern society. The first type includes those places that care for persons who are perceived to be both incapable and harmless, such as homes for the aged and homes for the indigent. Goffman has suggested that the use of the appellation "home" connotes society's effort to offer a replacement for the care and protection typically found in the consanguineal family in Western civilization. A second type of total institution includes those places that care for people who are perceived as being incapable of looking after themselves, and who are also perceived as a threat to the community, such as mental hospitals and leprosaria. A third type of total institution, such as jails and concentration camps, has been developed to protect the community against those seen as potentially dangerous. The fourth type of total institution includes places that are established to pursue some worklike task, such as army barracks and boarding schools. The final type includes institutions designed as retreats from the world, especially those that serve as training institutions for religious organizations, such as monasteries and convents.

Common to all these types of institutions is not only congregate living, but also the split between residents and supervisory staff. This division is rather clear in institutions that care for people who are unable to care for themselves, especially when the institution employs an array of skilled medical and health-related practitioners. Total institutions of a medical orientation are clearly both residential communities and bureaucracies that have a mission and a goal to care for the residents. The home for the aged is this type of total institution and, because of its totality, the home for the aged must be assumed, by the terms of Goffman's analysis, to exert a deleterious effect on its residents.

Goffman's criteria of totality have encouraged others to assess the degree of totality of various institutions for the aged. Coe (1965), for example, contrasted the effects of three institutional environments of different degrees of totality, in which components of totality included the lack of privacy, rigidity of scheduling, limitations on access to personal property, and the use of force by staff. By these criteria, the nonprofit sectarian homes tend to be less total than state mental hospitals or commercial nursing homes. Sectarian homes for the aged, for example, try to permit privacy by not having large wards, but neither do they usually have single rooms. More often, because there are two or four people to a bedroom, there is a limit on privacy, making it mandatory to adjust to roommates. Meal schedules may be rigid, but there are many activities permitting flexibility in the resident's scheduling of daily events. Residents are allowed to bring in personal property, such as clothes or a television set, but obviously cannot bring in their own beds or other large furniture. The staff is expected not to use physical force, and any abuse of residents is grounds for dismissal.

Bennett (1963) developed a more extensive list of criteria for the totality of institutions for the aged. Related to high totality were permanent residence in the institution, activities oriented to the institution, formal provision for dissemination of normative information, provisions for continual observation by staff of behavior of residents, standardized rewards and punishments, removal of most personal property, inability to make decisions about use of personal property, involuntary recruitment, and congregate residential living. The criteria generated by Coe and Bennett permit an analysis of the degree of totality of varied institutions for the aged. Using these indicators of totality, it is generally true that sectarian homes are less total than other long-term care institutions for the aged, such as state mental hospitals and nursing homes. There are, for example, efforts to individualize "rewards and punishments"; some activities are scheduled for groups and others are open to choice; some decisions are made by residents; and patterns of recruitment are ostensibly voluntary.

In addition to degree of totality, other, related dimensions have been assumed to have effects on residents. Pincus (1968) and Kosberg and Tobin (1972), for example, add the dimension of "resource-rich" versus "resource-poor." The sectarian homes studied in the present case have extraordinarily good physical and medical resources, as well as high staff/patient ratios. Townsend (1962) used ratings of adequacy of the physical facility, staffing, and services as components of his assessment of the quality of care in 173 institutions. Lieberman, Tobin, and Slover (1969) explored the psychological characteristics of twenty-seven institutional environments in terms of such dimensions as individuation of care and the extent to which the care was dependency producing.

While it is possible to discriminate among long-term care institutions for the aged in terms of the degree of totality or of what appears to be "goodness" or "badness," few studies have been undertaken to examine adverse effects among environments that differ on the degree of totality. An exception is the study in which Coe (1965) found that higher institutional totality was related to more withdrawal and depersonalization. However, because all total institutions share characteristics that may adversely influence their residents, these common characteristics may be more salient in producing negative influences than are those characteristics that differentiate one institution from another. Certainly this interpretation of the literature is a sensible one—considering that the negative characteristics associated with institutionalized elderly have been noted in residents in the best of contemporary long-term care institutions, the sectarian homes for the aged, as well as in those of lesser repute.

Biases Caused by Selection

Another explanation that has been offered in the literature for the typical portrait of institutionalized elderly is that a particular type of older person seeks institutional care. In this explanation, the institution is not seen as causing deleterious changes. Rather, this view holds that people admitted to institutions are either characterized by the typical institutional portrait prior to their entering the institution or that they have characteristics that sensitize them to respond negatively to living in institutions. Thus, differences that are found between older people living in the community and those residing in institutions are not considered an effect of institutional life but of population differences. Because psychological studies of institutionalization have invariably employed cross-sectional designs —in which investigators have inferred, rather than demonstrated, "institutional effects" from their comparisons of community and institutional residents—this explanation can not be discounted.

Since the turn of the century, the proportion of aged people residing in institutions has steadily increased. This trend, coupled with increased longevity has meant that institutions have been used more and more to cope with major incapacitating physical or mental illnesses. It would be reasonable to conclude, therefore, that aged people residing in institutions are physically and mentally different from those who live in the community. Studies of particular samples of institutionalized aged, however, in contrast to simple population statistics, show that significant proportions of the elderly residing in institutions do not differ physically or mentally from their community counterparts. Gitlitz (1956, 1957) using morbidity, mortality, and psychiatric disorder statistics from a large home for the aged, suggests that the incidence of specific types of morbidity may not differ from their incidence among the community aged. These apparent discrepancies between population statistics and studies carried out on particular small samples stem to some extent from the underestimation of psychiatric and physical morbidity in community samples and the relative overestimation in the institutional samples because of better or more intensive diagnostic techniques used among the latter.

The occurrence of physical illness among the institutionalized aged takes on added significance because of the suggestive evidence (Birren, 1959; Coe, 1965) that physical illness, even at preclinical levels, affects psychological status. If it could be shown that pathological psychological characteristics attributed to institutionalization were significantly related to physical illness, the evidence for selective factors would be appreciably strengthened. To date, there is no strong empirical evidence demonstrating this relationship.

Also supporting the view that selection biases account for the institutional portrait are the statistics on community elderly who have functional status comparable to institutionalized elderly. For almost every person over 65 years of age who enters an institution, for example, there are two other elderly (8 percent) who live in the community who are essentially homebound, with one of four of these homebound elderly bedridden; and there are close to two others (6 percent) who are quickly approaching this status (Shanas and others, 1968). In all, about one of six of the community elderly need protective services to maintain or restore functioning (see, for example, Hall, Mathiasen, and Ross, 1973). Thus it would appear that considerations other than physical and mental status determine who will enter a long-term care institution. It may indeed be those older people who have the psychological attributes that are characteristic of institutionalized elderly who enter these institutions.

Who come to institutions and why they come is an exceedingly complex question that no single study answers. Several studies bear directly on the question, but, unfortunately, most (Bortner, 1962; Fogel, Swepston, Zintek, Vernier, Fitzgerald, Marnocha, and Weschler, 1956; and Webb, 1959) represent highly specialized populations among the institutionalized aged (VA domiciliaries). Although using different methods, these investigators attribute psychological differences between institutionalized and community aged to selection processes. For example, Webb (1959) found that the type of individual who applies to and resides in such institutions differs in socioeconomic background as well as in personality, being characterized by rigidity, stereotyped thinking, apathy, resignation, egocentricity, passivity, and strong needs for love, affection, and care. Many of the factors identifying the persons who apply also identify institutionalized populations. Lowenthal (1964), investigating pathways to mental institutions among the aged, found that a low level of supportive interpersonal relationships differentiated those who entered from those who did not enter such institutions. Such studies, although few in number and covering a limited range of institutions, point to an association between entering an institution and certain psychological or social characteristics.

A selection bias is obviously in evidence when the characteristics of elderly who select institutional care as a solution already have psychological characteristics that are like those of institutional residents. A more subtle type of bias exists when these characteristics are not present but when other characteristics are present that sensitize people to the negative effects once they are living in an institutional environment. Goldfarb (1969), for example, argues that a particular personality type, the dependent personality, is more likely to seek institutional care. If this type of person, in addition, is more likely to react adversely to living in an institution, then the portrait of institutionalized elderly is a product of selection bias in interaction with institutional life. Beyond the attributes that sensitize older people to the effects of institutional life, we must also consider that a self-selection process is operating in which the older people who seek institutional care are those who are deteriorating more rapidly than others. These older people would be closer to becoming morbibund and dying, independent of their entering and living in the institution. For them, becoming institutionalized only hastens the terminal process (see Palmore and Jeffers, 1971, for a collection of articles on predictors of survival among the elderly).

Population survey data can at best be suggestive; they cannot offer positive evidence that selection plays a role. Other studies, focused more directly on the selection issue, are limited in number and scope. There are, however, sufficient data to indicate that the differences between institutionalized and noninstitutionalized aged are significantly influenced by the factor of selection. Institutionalized aged share some characteristics because of *who* they are and not *where* they are. On the other hand, the evidence for selection is not sufficient to explain all of the noxious effects associated with living in an institution.

Preadmission Effects

A quite different explanation, independent of selection bias, suggests that the factors that cause noxious effects are set into motion by the process of becoming institutionalized, prior to actually entering and living in the institution. In this explanation, the older person before admission may be similar in psychological characteristics to institutional residents but not because he or she is inherently like them and inherently different from community residents. Rather, this view holds that any older person who decides to meet his or her needs through an institutional solution may be so changed by the forces set in motion in the process that he or she comes to approximate institutionalized elderly in his or her psychology before entering the institutional environment.

This explanation has heretofore received little attention.

Its clarification requires study designs that compare older
people before admission to matched community samples; or,
better yet, that follow individuals from before a decision to
seek institutional care through the decision-making process and
through the period of awaiting admission so that one may track
changes in cognitive function, affective responsiveness, emotional life, and so forth.

The losses associated with moving to an institution may be
experienced before the actual move. Separation may become
final after entering and living in the institution, but discussions
of the move and application to a home can certainly lead to
feelings of separation from and rejection by family members
who have been involved in the decision (see, for example,
Hacker and Gaitz, 1969). Indeed, separation is the main explanation for the effects of acute hospitals on young children and
for the finding of Spitz (1945) that, among young children who
enter long-term care institutions, those with the best mothering
before the move are most likely to show the greatest effects of
hospitalization. That is, children with the best mothering, because they have the most to lose from the separation, suffer the
most adverse consequences when placed in a new environment.
(For a review of the effects when children enter hospitals see
Vernon, Foley, Sipowicz, and Schulman, 1965.)

Several investigators who have examined attitudes of the
aged toward institutional care have found meanings of loss associated with such a move. Kleemier (1961), for example, suggested that older people exhibit a generalized negative feeling
toward all special settings for the elderly. Montgomery (1965),
who studied rural elderly, found a consistent desire to remain in
their present residence and equated this desire with highly-
valued independence. Shanas (1961) found that older people
associated moving to institutions with loss of independence,
rejection by children, and a prelude to death.

To see the move to a long-term care institution as a prelude to death is not unrealistic, given the age of older people
who enter these institutions and given the fact that an old-age
home will probably be the setting where death will occur for
many of the longevous, frail, and deteriorated elderly. By

examining obituary notices, Kastenbaum and Candy (1973) estimated that living beyond 65 years of age is associated with a one to four chance of spending the final period of life in a long-term care institution.

Possibly, to have serious negative effects, moves must have meanings of loss. The absence of these meanings can be used to explain why, according to Carp's (1967) study of elderly persons moving into apartment dwellings, these persons indicated an increase in satisfaction and adjustment. Similarly, the absence of massive death rates or increased psychological or physical disability following "therapeutic" moves of elderly mentally ill from mental hospitals to nursing homes, boarding houses, or homes for the aged may be explained by the absence of anticipated loss. Such moves have been shown to depart from the general expectation that relocation of the elderly is associated with increased mortality and morbidity, as reflected, for example, in the population studied by Stotsky (1967), where those who received preparation for the move, thus possibly experiencing less anticipated loss and perceived loss after the move, had more favorable outcomes than those who did not receive preparation.

Environmental Discontinuity

The degree of discontinuity between the new and old environments suggests a fourth condition that may explain the noxious effects observed to follow institutionalization and that does not focus explicitly on the nature of the institutional environment. A number of investigators have studied the effects of radical environmental changes on the psychological well-being and physical survival of the aged. Many of these studies have involved changes from community living to life in an institution; others have studied relocation from one institutional setting to another. Some have investigated environmental changes that involve movement from one community setting to another. These studies are particularly relevant to the consideration of negative change among those living in institutional settings. They suggest that disruption of life caused by *moving* into an

institution may create many of the effects attributed to *living* in
an institutional setting. The majority of these studies (Aldrich
and Mendkoff, 1963; Blenkner, 1967; Goldfarb, Shahinian, and
Turner, 1966; Jasnau, 1967; Lieberman, 1961) showed that
changing the environment of elderly persons sharply accelerates
death rates.

In most real-life situations the effects of environmental discontinuity are impossible to disentangle from those of loss.
Fried (1963), for example, uses fragmentation of space and loss
of group identity to explain serious depressive reactions to
forced relocation of the elderly under urban renewal. Similarly
Friedsam (1961), in studying reactions to a tornado, found that
changed living patterns created profound psychological distress
that was particularly destructive for the elderly. In its purest
form, environmental discontinuity as a cause of negative effects
is present when anticipated loss is not associated with the move.
This was the case in the "culture shock" that was experienced
by young people in the Peace Corps. These youth volunteered
for service, welcomed the opportunity to serve in a foreign culture, and were appraised that they might experience culture
shock. Yet the strangeness of the alien culture, the inability to
use established modes of interaction and the absence of familiar
social supports still interacted to produce disorientation, anxiety, depression, and anomie (Foster, 1962).

Effects in this framework are thus seen as a function of the
difference between the two environments. The larger the difference between the new and old environment—with expectations
being equal—the greater the possibility that the elderly person
will need to develop adaptive responses often beyond his capacity. In this light, the effect of an institution can be viewed less
as a product of its quality or characteristics than of the degree
to which it forces the person to make new or overtaxing adaptive responses. It is possible that some of the current trends
aimed at "deinstitutionalizing" institutions, for example, making them more open to the outside community, less congregate,
and so forth, are effective because they permit the use of prior
and less demanding adaptive responses.

Effects Throughout the Process

These four sources of explanation for the portrait of the institutionalized older person are not necessarily mutually exclusive. There may be various selection biases that determine the type of older person who seeks and receives institutional care. This select group of would-be residents may also react to seeking and anticipating institutional care in ways that make them appear similar to those already institutionalized. The move from community living to institutional residence is a major environmental discontinuity that causes a major disequilibrium independently or in combination with any or all of the other three factors. After entering and living in the institution, "true institutional effects" may ensue.

The gray portrait, which has been attributed to actually living in an institutional environment, can thus be understood as the end stage of a process that begins well before entering and living in these facilities. The earliest period in the process even precedes the decision to seek institutional care when older people and their families are aware that this type of solution could become necessary either if deteriorative changes were to occur in their elderly family members or if the intimate support system of the elderly family member could no longer provide certain resources that allowed the person to maintain community status. Another identifiable period follows the decision to seek institutional care and another when the person is waiting entrance into the institution. Following the decision to seek care is a period of variable length until the actual entering and living in the new environment. During this period residents-to-be are confronted with leaving their familiar environment for a foreign one that most likely will be their last home. After entering, there is an immediate reaction, often taking the form of extreme confusion or severe withdrawal, which slowly subsides as the older person adjusts to the demands of the setting. During the first 2 months after entering the home, the resident is in an initial adjustment phase and by the end of the year has either adapted to the institution and survived intact or has deteriorated or died.

Each of these periods, as well as the transition from one period to another, may be associated with its own set of adaptive demands, meanings, coping styles, and effects. Each period may constitute a unique situation that demands different forms of adaptation. Essentially, this model is the one used to understand stress effects and has been most ambitiously elaborated by Lazarus (1966). In his schema, an event must elicit an appraisal of threat, of potential harm to be a stressor. Real-life situations, as contrasted with the laboratory situation developed by Lazarus, consist of many stressful events and meanings with one predominant threat, which can be labeled the *focal concern*. This focal concern evokes further appraisals about ways of dealing with the event and its meanings. Conscious, as well as less conscious, coping maneuvers shape the form of behavior that gets expressed. When studying people in stress situations, what the observer sees is a combination of coping and the consequences of coping. Consequences that are judged to be maladaptive are labeled *stress reactions*. In the context of the institutionalization process, these maladaptive reactions to stress become synonymous with negative effects, encompassing cognitive dysfunction, modifications in affective responsivity, painful emotional states, distortions in the self-system and, of course, morbidity and mortality.

This model is useful in understanding negative characteristics that are generated before entrance into the institution, but after a decision to become institutionalized is made. While awaiting admission, the older person is confronted with anticipation of the impending event of actually entering and living in the institution. In this period of anticipating institutionalization, what is observed is the individual coping with the meaning of the events that have led to becoming a resident-to-be and with the losses associated with leaving the community and independent status. What gets substituted is the in-limbo status of being neither an independent-living community elderly person nor an institutionalized older person.

On entering the institution, the old person is confronted with another situation that demands appraisal and coping. The loss of familiar support, the strangeness of the foreign environment, and the identification with other elderly who are frail and deteriorating become a reality. A new set of behaviors come into evidence, and among these behaviors there will be some that can be labeled *effects*. The decrements that arise after the initial impact of the first month are the true "institutional effects" that can be attributed to institutional life itself. A singular challenge is to determine which among the many effects attributed to institutional life are actually institutional effects. Possible ameliorative effects that result from the assurance of care or of being able to adjust to the formerly feared environment are also necessary to consider.

After the initial adjustment phase, the older person becomes part of the residential community, and other psychological changes may ensue. Systematic study of these changes in a total sample followed over time is impossible because of losses from morbidity and death. Only the most intact survive the first year after admission. Study of the differences between the debilitated or dead and the intact survivors, however, allow us to address another set of issues, including prediction of severe consequent outcomes. That is, attributes assessed before admission that are associated with later deterioration and death are predictors (or covariates) of these outcomes. For preinstitutional attributes actually to be predictors of vulnerability to entering and living in the institution, however, they must be shown not to be associated with survival (associated with the same outcomes) for elderly who were not institutionalized during the intervening period. Preinstitutional attributes that are not generally associated with survival but that are associated with severe outcomes where institutionalization intervenes are attributes that sensitize older people to the deleterious effects of living in the institution and that suggest which aspects of the institution may be stressful. Institutional causes for severe outcomes can also be inferred from the types of initial reactions associated with consequent deterioration and death.

The study of changes in the institutionalized old becomes, therefore, the sorting out of the effects of institutional life from other sources associated with the institutionalizing process. To accomplish this allocation of causal factors, it is necessary either to contrast matched samples at fairly close periods in the process of becoming institutionalized or to follow the same people over time. Both of these methods have been employed in the present investigation. At each contact, respondents were evaluated on four major psychological dimensions that have been used to characterize institutionalized elderly people: cognitive functioning, affective responsiveness, emotional states, and self-perception. The pattern of changes in these dimensions allows isolation of the effects of the institutionalization process and also reveals general coping styles. When these data are added to other data, such as the meaning of loss, it is possible to work back from reactions or effects to coping behaviors appropriate to the nature of situational demands that have initiated the psychological disequilibrium. Stated another way, concentrating on assessing effects, supplemented by other data, permits identification of the situational elements that have led to inadequate coping behaviors that, in turn, have been followed by negative effects.

The Research Design

Having established our research objectives, we selected a sample from people that were about to enter the best of long-term care facilities. We will first discuss how we gathered the sample, the intervals between events (applying, application, accepted, entering) and interviews, the homes the sample persons entered, the rationale and selection of measures of effects, the data gathered, and the interviewers employed to gather the data. Then we will discuss how we gathered two additional samples and matched institutional and community samples. The introduction to the community sample forms the background for the last section of this chapter, a portrait of community elderly. The status and attitudes of the very old—particularly of those elderly who would apply to the homes—establishes a baseline for the study of institutional effects.

The Study Sample. The 100 persons who constituted the study sample were first interviewed when on a waiting list to enter one of three sectarian homes for the aged. The interviews were conducted during a 2½-year period, from March 1964 through October 1966. The first 35 of the 100 respondents had been on the waiting list of one of the homes before the interviewing began, while the remaining 65 were contacted as they were added to the waiting list of all three homes. Because of the long period of initial data collection, some respondents were being seen for their first waiting-list interview while others had already responded to the two follow-up interviews, having entered one of the homes a year before. The final 1-year follow-up interview was completed in February 1968. In all, therefore, 4 years was needed to collect 100 waiting-list respondents and to follow up the 85 respondents who had entered one of the three homes during the first year after admission.

The 100 respondents in the study sample do not include all the aged persons admitted to the three homes during the period the sample was gathered. Rather, they represent a select sample of the total population of elderly persons admitted to these homes during this period. The bias toward a more adequate sample of elderly people can be clarified by examining the selection of the initial 35 cases who were on the waiting list of two of the three homes. At that time, these two homes had records of persons who had been accepted for residence in the home and who were then waiting admission. At one home these potential residents were divided into two groups, "urgent" and "not urgent" (or "deferred"). At the other home, there were no official categories, but priorities were set on the basis of the need for protective care. From February 1, 1964, to June 1, 1964, there were 45 individuals on the waiting list for the first home and 53 for the second home. In both institutions, the administrative staff anticipated that several individuals would be admitted to the home in less than 3 months. These individuals were not included in the sample because of the short time available for interviewing. To those who were expected not to be admitted within 3 months, the administrator of each home sent a letter explaining briefly the nature of the study and requesting cooperation. In a few days, this letter was followed by another from the study project director inviting participation, and after a week or so the potential respondent was called by the interviewer for an appointment.

Of a total 98 potential respondents in the waiting-list pool

for the homes, 35 completed the interviews. Nineteen refused
to take part in the study after the initial contact making comments such as: "I don't want to talk about myself," or "I don't
want to be bothered." An additional 26 individuals were excluded because they were physically too ill to be interviewed or
because they had serious limitations in vision, hearing, or communication. In 8 situations a relative intervened, usually a
daughter, stating that the respondent was "too confused," "too
nervous," or "too sick" to be interviewed. Seven respondents
were admitted to the home before they could be interviewed, 2
individuals lived outside the state, and 1 individual died. If the
latter 10 are considered as available for interviewing, then of a
total of 88 potential respondents, the 35 respondents represent
a selection rate of 40 percent. Of those not selected for the
study, there was an equal division between those elderly persons
who were not cooperative and those who had physical deficits
of enough severity to limit their participation as interviewees.

Applicants to the three homes were processed by staff in a
central family-service screening agency that determined the
appropriateness of the request for institutional care. If the caseworker at the screening agency assessed the person as unable to
maintain himself (or most likely, herself) in the community,
application to one of the homes was recommended to the person and his family. The applicant was free to choose one of the
three homes, each of which were placed quite far from one
another in the city. One of the three, therefore, was often close
to the neighborhood in which the respondent had been living,
while the other two were at great distance from the homes of
relatives and friends. After the person or his family made a
choice from among the three homes, the caseworker made a
referral to the social service department at that home. The
home was then visited by the person and family to gather information and impressions, and the applicant was interviewed by
the intake caseworker at the home, as well as by the consultant
psychiatrist, medical personnel, or other staff if additional data
were needed for evaluation. If the staff at the home approved
the admission (a decision usually related to the absence of
psychosis or terminal illness and to the appropriateness of cus-

todial care for the applicant), the application was submitted to a board committee for final approval. The typical interval between application and placement on the waiting list was about 6 weeks. Those applicants who needed immediate custodial care usually entered a nursing home until space was available in the home. When a space became available, the applicant had the option to defer admission until a later date, which often helped those still living in the community to live more comfortably, knowing that the home remained a viable alternative in case of further physical deterioration or social disruptions. Most applicants, however, preferred immediate admission. The period from application to admission was typically 7 months. The range, however, was rather large, from less than 1 month to over 2 years after our interview. The more confused aged on the waiting list, who could not respond coherently to lengthy and comprehensive interview questions and tasks, were excluded from the study sample. Generally, therefore, the study sample was composed of elderly people who were more psychologically intact than those who were entering nursing homes or state mental hospitals for long-term or permanent care.

Most of the respondents in the study sample had grown up in Eastern Europe and emigrated to American cities early in their adult life. Only 24 were born in the United States. Of the other 76 respondents, 69 were born in eastern Europe and 7 in western Europe. The average educational level was less than 8 years of formal school. The typical occupation of the men or the husbands of the women had been as small shopkeepers or unskilled tradesmen. While most had reared a rather successful generation of children, they themselves had suffered both the hardships that necessitated emigration in the first place and the stresses of adapting to American society with little education or financial security.

The 85 aged persons who entered the homes averaged 78 years of age; the youngest was 63 and the oldest, 91. Congruent with the sex distribution among the general population of the very old, 60 (or 71 percent) were women and only 25 (or 29 percent) were men. Of the 76 (89 percent) who had married, 14 had a living spouse at the time the study began; most of the remaining 62 had been widowed in recent years, although a few had been divorced or separated many years before.

About one of three (30) respondents did not have any living children, whereas most (60) had two or more living children. About one of three (35) did not have any living siblings. About one of three respondents (31) were living alone when first interviewed on the waiting list; about one half (49) were living in the community with others, either with another unrelated older person (2) or one or more family members other than spouse (34), or with spouse (13); and one of five (20) were living in a nursing home while awaiting admission.

Intervals in Assessment. Of the 100 aged persons who were interviewed while they were on the waiting list for one of three homes, 85 actually entered one of the homes. Of the 15 who did not enter during the period of the study, 6 withdrew their applications, 5 preferred to delay admission until a later date, and 4 died while on the waiting list. As shown in Table 1, the 85 respondents were first assessed after they had been accepted for admission to a home and while they were still on the waiting list (Time 1, approximately 4 months before admission to one of three homes), and then again approximately 2 months (Time 2), and 12 months (Time 3) after admission. None of these applicants was unable to tolerate several hours of interview and tasks when on the waiting list.

Table 1. Intervals of Time Passed (in Months) in
Becoming an Institutionalized Person

Interval	Number in Sample	Range	Mean	Standard Deviation	Median
Application–Approval	85	0-4	1.5	.8	.8
Approval–Time 1 (WL) Interview	85	0-18	3.6	3.8	2.7
Time 1 Interview–Admission	85	0-27	3.3	3.9	4.2
Admission–Time 2 Interview	81	1-9	3.0	1.1	2.3
Time 2 Interview–Time 3 Interview	56	6-17	11.0	2.8	10.2
Application–Time 1 Interview	85	1-20	5.0	4.2	3.0
Time 1 Interview–Time 2 Interview	81	1-15	6.1	3.3	5.2
Time 1 Interview–Time 3 Interview	56	10-26	16.8	4.0	15.2
Admission–Time 3 Interview	56	10-21	14.3	3.0	13.2

The waiting-list interview was typically gathered 3½ months after the respondent had applied for admission to the home and 4 months before admission. Of the 85 respondents who entered one of the three homes, all but 7 responded to the complete interview 2 months after admission. Thus for 78 respondents the necessary interview data were available to study the change from preadmission to 8 weeks after institutionalization. Of the original 85, 45 were interviewed 1 year after admission. Of the remaining 40, 13 had died, 13 were too ill to be interviewed, and 14 refused.

Although the 85 applicants entered three different sectarian homes, the similarities between the homes made it possible to consider them as one setting—a voluntary, sectarian home for the aged. The three homes were located in a large midwestern city and are operated by the same sectarian social agency. The smallest of the three had a maximum capacity of 142 residents and the largest, 286. Most (47) of the respondents in the sample of 85 aged persons were admitted to the third home, which had a capacity of 236.

The homes tended to draw their residents from the same general population, and those already living in them shared the same social characteristics as those in the study sample awaiting admission. The breadwinner had usually been an unskilled tradesman or small businessman. The homes were remarkably similar in mean age of residents, percentage of females, and percentage of residents on old-age assistance. Furthermore, the general level of health of the residents appeared comparable across the three homes. After conducting a survey of the three homes, S. Kaplan (1966, p. 91) concluded:

> *The only generalization that can be safely made about the differences among the residents of the three homes is that no overall differential pattern can be observed. On various measures of sensory impairment, help needed in activities of daily living, and mental impairment there is no uniformity in how the homes compared with each other. From the survey data, there is no basis for saying that the residents of*

one home on the whole are either sicker or healthier
than the residents of the other homes.

The majority of the residents in each home lived two in a room. There were no large dormitories or wards in any of the three homes. The largest rooms, containing four beds, were usually on the infirmary floor and used for acutely ill residents. There were a limited number of single rooms in each home. Residents were allowed to keep personal possessions in their rooms and to keep the doors to their rooms closed if they wished. They were free to leave their rooms or the building as they chose as long as their health permitted.

The homes were similar in their facilities. Each had a large central dining room and one or more dining rooms for residents who needed special help in eating. Each home had a large auditorium, several day rooms, a sheltered workshop, occupational and physical therapy facilities, and up-to-date medical facilities. Each home also had an infirmary, and while the residents may at times have been temporarily transferred to a hospital for special care, only very rarely did a resident have to be transferred to a state mental hospital because of uncontrollable disruptive behavior. Again, only rarely was a resident discharged to the community, so that the three homes were in fact almost invariably homes for the rest of their residents' lives.

All three homes were similar in meeting high professional and legal standards for accreditation and licensing. All had a full complement of medical and paramedical staff, including full-time social workers and consulting psychologists and psychiatrists. Each also had a recreational director who ran a wide range of programs from mass activities to small interest groups. Each home maintained a resident organization and a synagogue, each with its own officers. Opportunities were made available for residents to perform small jobs around the home. The similarities in high professional and legal standards placed all three in the forefront of modern geriatric institutions.

Confirmation for the similarities among the three homes was offered by Pincus (1968) who attempted to highlight the differences among the homes by adapting a framework originally developed by Kleemier (1961). The Pincus analysis clarified the similarities of the homes in their excellence of physical care and orientation toward the social needs of residents. The homes did show some minor differences on the four dimensions Pincus developed: public-private, structured-unstructured, resource-sparse/resource-rich, and integrated-isolated. The public-private dimension refers to how much the environment allows the resident to establish and maintain a personal domain that is not open to public view or use and into which the institution will not transgress. The structured-unstructured dimension refers to how much the resident must adjust his life to imposed rules, discipline, and the various means of social control exercised in the institution. The resource-sparse/resource-rich dimension refers to how much the environment provides opportunities to engage in a variety of work and leisure activities and to participate in social interaction with other residents and staff in a variety of social roles. The isolated-integrated dimension refers to how much the environment affords opportunities for communication and interaction with the larger heterogeneous community (people and places) in which the institution is located.

To explore the differences among the homes on these four dimensions, Pincus analyzed interviewer comments and evaluations, observed the homes personally and developed and analyzed a Home Descriptive Questionnaire that was administered to staff of the homes. These three procedures revealed only scattered significant differences among the three homes on the four dimensions, suggesting only minor dissimilarities. For example, on the public-private dimension, one of the homes ranked higher because there was a slightly larger percentage of single rooms, but in this home there was less personalization of the available physical space than in the other two homes. While two homes seemed similar in amount of privacy, the third home was more crowded but did have the advantage of freer access to the outdoors. On the structured-unstructured dimension, the physical plants did not differentiate the homes, nor did the number or types of rules and regulations and programs. The largest of the homes did appear, however, to have more rules. On the resource dimension, the only difference was that in the largest home there was less coordinated staff effort to get residents involved in activities. In the isolated-integrated dimension, differences found were related to location. That is, because the largest and smallest homes were located in lower-class black neighborhoods there was less use of the surrounding community by their residents than there was by the residents of the third home.

The minor differences among the three homes evidenced in all three of Pincus' analyses demonstrated that for the purpose of the present investigation of the psychological process of institutionalization the three homes could be treated as homogeneous.

The Measurement of Effects. The theoretical considerations that guided the selection of measures were largely suggested by the review of the effects of institutions on young children, mental patients, and older people. Four psychological areas emerged as most critical in the study of effects. The effects of transitions were assessed in four areas: cognitive functioning, affective responsiveness, emotional states, and self-perception. Each area is briefly reviewed here, introducing the particular studies that have elucidated the importance of these areas to the study of institutionalized elderly (invariably when community and institutional samples were compared).

The area of cognitive functioning includes disorientation in time and place, a decrease in perceptual accuracy or acuity, cognitive disorganization, and an increase in rigidity. Much like culture shock (Foster, 1962), which causes a period of acute disorganization when moving from a familiar cultural setting to a foreign one, the move into an institutional environment for the aged person has been characterized as a disorienting and disorganizing experience. One approach to the assessment of this variable has been through the use of the Rorschach Inkblot Test (Ames and others, 1954; Ames, 1960; Davidson and Kruglov, 1952; Klopfer, 1946). In these studies, the investigators have focused on the cognitive organization of the responses to the inkblots and have reported differences between institutionalized and community aged on several cognitive variables. The findings suggest that entering and living in an institutional environment adversely affects the organization of cognitive processes. The manifestation of this disorganization takes several forms, including disorientation, misperception, and rigidity. To tap one or another aspects of cognitive adequacy, several instruments were used in the present study, each tailor-made. The Rorschach Inkblot Test was not used because of its threatening nature to the very old, because they cannot readily recognize the dark and blurred shapes. Older people are often quick to blame their failing eyesight for the lack of recognition. They often become very agitated; any assurance that objects are seen by others only stirs up further panic. An instructional set that includes the type of objects often seen usually leads to their searching for these objects in all ten inkblots.

The six variables that were assessed encompassed orientation in time and place, orientation to the immediate present, learning and retention, cognitive organization, perceptual organization and accuracy, and the capacity to vary responses.

In the area of affective responsiveness, reduced response is commonly considered to reflect an active withdrawal from an impinging, potentially destructive environment. To verify this impression of reduced emotional responsiveness among institutionalized aged, Webb (1959) compared aged male veterans in VA domiciliary housing to a sample of community persons of comparable age, education, vocational background, and social status. Significant differences between the two were found, the aged institutionalized in the domiciliary showing more apathy. A lessened responsiveness was also in evidence in the Rorschach studies. Our assessment of this area was through two measures: the range of affects incorporated into stories told in response to five Murray Thematic Apperception Test (TAT) cards and the willingness to introspect about inner feelings.

A range of emotional states has been discussed in the literature on infants and children in child care institutions, as well as on state mental hospital inmates and the aged institutionalized. In the literature on the aged in institutions, two studies relate to the more manifest level of unhappiness and dissatisfaction, often under the general rubric of adjustment (Pan, 1948; Rosenthal, 1942). Rosenthal looked at the adjustment of 23 residents in a home for the aged, comparing this group with Levisohn's (1942) middle-class aged sample living with their families. Rosenthal's sample was characterized by a state of resignation and unhappiness. Pan (1948) compared 116 women over 60 years of age living in 12 institutions with 1,804 community aged persons from the Cavan, Burgess, Havighurst, and Goldhamer sample (1949). Pan's institutionalized sample obtained lower adjustment scores in such areas as satisfaction and interest in life, attitude toward the past, companionship, and participation in activities.

Few investigators have assessed emotional states other than through self-reports of global levels of satisfaction or feelings of well-being. Two other types of variables that were thought to merit attention especially for an old population were hope and anxiety-depression. Prior to the present investigation, hope had not been studied as a variable that may be adversely affected by institutionalization (see the review by Haberland, 1972). Anxiety and depression as consequences of the transition to institutional living have been inferred from a variety of measures but have not been the focus of the studies in which they have been in evidence. Institutionalization is generally considered to raise anxiety and to increase depressive affect but it is necessary to demonstrate more explicitly, through repeat measurements, that these adverse states are changes specifically associated with institutional residence.

Two different approaches were used to measure the dimension of self-perception: perceived capacity for self-care and the general presentation of self.

The measurement of change in the perceived capacity for self-care was approached by assuming that elderly people have many chronic diseases that may impede functioning. One task of the aged persons, therefore, is to transcend these bodily deficits and to maintain physical integration. It is not uncommon to attempt to accomplish this task by employing mechanisms such as denial or counterphobic maneuvers. When these mechanisms appear in extreme forms in younger persons, we tend to think of such mechanisms as indices of psychopathology. But for elderly persons such mechanisms are clearly less psyopathological because they facilitate the maintenance of functioning. Giving in to the underlying deficits may quickly lead to decompensation and death. From the perspective of the need to transcend physical deficits in aging, an environment that does not encourage full use of potential may cause irreversible deterioration. Kahn (1971) has referred to the excessive disability produced in residents of institutions for the aged that discourage use of individual physical and psychological potential.

This excessive disability would be expected to show in an aged person's perception of his or her own capacity for self-care. In becoming an institutionalized person, he would be expected in time to perceive himself as less able to take care of his daily personal needs. This self-perception by the aged resident facilitates the adoption of the patient role, as has been described for inmates of mental hospitals (Goffman, 1961). Because most residents in homes for the aged are in their late 70s or 80s, unless they are motivated to use residual capacities to care for themselves, they are likely not to do so and consequently to perceive themselves as less able to do so.

Tuckman and Lorge (1953) compared an institutionalized sample of aged persons to community aged, using the Cornell Medical Index, to investigate the degree to which the institution encouraged increased perception of individual deficiencies. Because the institutional sample reported fewer symptoms of physical illness, these investigators concluded that institutional care and protection tended to reduce the number of complaints. This finding has received scant attention and the general view of researchers and practitioners has been that entering and living in an institution for the aged increases the number of complaints and the perception of a decreased capacity for self-care.

The literature regarding the self-system of the aged in institutions suggests that when they are compared to elderly people in the community, the self-concept of the institutionalized aged is marked by lower self-worth, lower self-esteem, more self-degradation, and lower feelings of power to cope with the outside world (Lakin, 1960; Lieberman and Lakin, 1963; Lepkowski, 1956; Mason, 1954; Newman, 1964; Pan, 1948; Pollack,

Karp, Kahn, and Goldfarb, 1962; Webb, 1959). A few investigators, however, have not found this negative self-view to be
associated with institutionalization. Lepkowski (1956), for
example, in his study of institutionalized aged, did not find
lowered self-esteem. Newman (1964) also found that institutionalization did not necessarily lower the individual's self-
esteem, but that self-esteem covaried with the amount of social
interaction. Kahana and Coe (1969), studying the self-concept
of institutionalized, found that residents had "well differentiated self-conceptions, making frequent mention of past and
present social roles" (p. 67).

Unfortunately, in all these studies, two dimensions related
to self-perception were not differentiated. First, there is self-
esteem, which is considered to decline after institutionalization.
And second, the content of the self-image is assumed to change
so that the person cannot maintain a consistent self-image. It
was necessary, as is made clear in the discussion of assessments
throughout this volume, to assess changes on both of these variables as discrete components within the dimension of the self-
concept to disentangle what presently appear to be inconsist-
encies in observable changes. A third dimension of the self that
we also assessed was the adequacy of examples to support the
content of the self-image.

Measures. The measures used to assess changes over time
represent only a fraction of the assessments that were made.
Other measures, such as those that will be referred to in Chapter
Four, which were used only for the prediction of vulnerability,
will be explained more fully in a forthcoming book (Lieberman
and Tobin, in press). Standardized measures will be reviewed
only briefly, in the next chapter, where the community control
sample and the sample on the waiting list are contrasted. The
Appendix at the end of this book focuses on the measures developed specifically for the present study, such as the measures
of anxiety and depression based on Gottschalk's system for
verbal behavior (Gottschalk, Springer, and Gleser, 1961) but
here adapted for use with the sentence completion test and the
several measures related to the self based on the Leary (1957)
system using a task—the self-sort instrument—developed specifi-

cally for the present study. Also included in the Appendix is the measure of focal concern using as data reconstruction of the earliest memory.

The Data.   A basic interview, consisting of sixteen structured tasks and nine focused interview guides was developed to gather the data for the assessment of change. The interview was administered in four to six sessions of 2 to 3 hours each, and took from 12 to 16 hours to complete. The interviewer also made six types of personal assessments after the interview was completed. Additional data were gathered as needed. On followup after institutionalization, for example, a page was added that required the interviewing of two staff members concerning the respondent's adaptation to the home.

The selection of tasks, as well as the construction of focused interview guides, was guided by the desire to assess a wide range of dimensions through more than one source of data. For some variables, existing standardized instruments and rating scales were used; for others, new instruments were created for this aged sample.

The development of such an extensive battery of assessment techniques necessitated several procedures of special importance because of the age of the study population—for example, the development of special instructional sets and the establishment of a sequence for the administration of tasks that assured the respondent of success and comfort early in the interview sessions. Respondents in this sample were unfamiliar with "test-taking" procedures and were also frightened of being evaluated, especially because they were aware of their own cognitive deficits. Respondents needed constant reassurance from the interviewer to allay anxiety that they were not being evaluated for admission to the home. Also, it helped to have a sequence of tasks.

Two main techniques were used to achieve standardization: (1) the respondent was asked to repeat each set of instructions to the interviewer, and (2) the type of responses wanted were demonstrated. For example, to assure scorable responses to the Thematic Apperception Test (TAT), the respondent was shown a trial card and told that there was no right or wrong story. He or she was then read two different stories to the card, and finally, the instructions were repeated if the respondent still did not understand the procedure.

After the initial pretest of the basic battery, many of the structured tasks were modified and several tasks were discarded because useful data could not be elicited from the aged persons in the sample. Once some tasks were modified and others discarded, instructional sets developed for each task, and the questions determined for the focused interview, the entire battery was again pretested, with the forms for the interviewers' assessments added.

The finally established sequence was based on such factors as the need to let respondents know at the first session that "tests" were part of the interview. During the first session, testing was introduced with a relatively easy task. Change of pace was accomplished through balancing tests and interview questions. The second session was organized so that the respondent could "play out a theme" relating to the review and evaluation of his life. More open-ended interview questions, designed to collect more intimate data, were asked in later sessions, after the development of good rapport and a cooperative relationship.

The Interviewers. The six women who administered the bulk of the interviews were selected because they had characteristics found to be important during the pretesting of the interview schedule with an institutional control sample. Interviewers were selected who were mature women from 30 to 40 years old, who had a professional orientation toward the work, and who were able to deal with old and sometimes sick people without becoming depressed. Three were psychiatric nurses, one a psychologist, one a professional writer, and one an interviewer of several years' experience. Of the total 362 full interviews, 348 were completed by these six interviewers; the remaining 16 were gathered by graduate students who were writing dissertations based on the study data.

Two types of analyses were undertaken to assure that a systematic bias did not exist among the interviewers. Ten waiting-list interviews done by each interviewer were compared for style of respondent/interviewer interaction. Each interviewer also completed an extensive questionnaire related to their reasons for working on the study and their attitudes towards the respondents. These analyses revealed remarkable consistency among interviewers supporting a high comparability of data across interviewers.

The Institutional Sample.   Selected residents in two of the three homes were included in the institutional sample. On December 1, 1966, the resident population at one home was 243 and at the other, 132. For each institution, a list was compiled of all residents who were in the old-age home from 1 to 3 years, January 1, 1961, to December 31, 1963. A total of 141 had been residents for this period of time. The 1- to 3-year residency period was used not only to maximize the individual's opportunity to make an adjustment to institutional living but also to minimize the possibility of major physical and mental debilitating changes occurring in the resident's condition since his preinstitutional state. In addition, three general criteria were used for selection of the institutional sample:

1. The resident could walk and give himself personal care.

2. Communication with the resident was possible.

3. Evaluation by the staff of the institution that the resident had not undergone major debilitating physical or mental changes since institutionalization.

The aim was to select only those institutional residents who could, in terms of self-care and mental functioning, live in the community.

This sample was similar to the other two on the many demographic variables: for example, 75 percent were women; the average age was 81 years and the range in age was 67 to 90; and the average education was less than grammar school (5.9 years) with a range of 0 to 14. Thus the procedures used to gather the three samples did indeed generate three samples that were alike on the many demographic measures assessed.

The Community Sample.   The community sample is of

special importance because these elderly people were in an earlier phase relative to the problems that direct old people towards institutionalization. The contrasts between them and respondents in the primary sample when on the waiting list elucidates the effects of the transition from this earlier period to the anticipatory institutionalization period. To be similar to the waiting-list sample, the sample of community elderly had to average 80 years of age, had to be single (never married, or else widowed), had to be predominantly female, had to be ambulatory, had to be of the educational and ethnic background, and had to be in similar financial circumstances. Because the community sample was gathered at the same time as the primary sample, but after the institutional control sample, the primary matching was with the latter sample.

As a means of tapping a group of community residents who shared the characteristics of those applying and those already living in the homes, respondents in the institutionalized sample were requested, at their first interview session, to give the names of their friends. It was thought that friends would be of the same cultural background and socioeconomic status as the residents. The plan did not work. The residents in the homes typically responded: "All my friends have died or left the city"; "Have no friends now. They have either died or moved away. Last time I heard from a friend was last year"; or "I don't know anybody."

The responses were negative from the few friends who were referred. For example, a letter sent to a friend was returned, as the friend no longer lived at that address. Several of the people referred were not well and "did not feel up to it." A different approach was needed. A review of the intake records in the homes disclosed that a majority of the women had been members of a variety of organizations prior to institutionalization—sisterhoods, senior citizen groups, and volunteer health and welfare organizations. On the other hand, the male residents seemed to have very few organizational affiliations prior to institutionalization. This information led to the decision to use two approaches to obtain a community sample.

First, with the cooperation of the sectarian community

centers in which many of the residents had been active, a brief description of the study was given to members of two senior citizen groups, to invite their participation. The two senior groups were quite similar in cultural background to the institutional sample in that a majority of the members were born in Eastern Europe. The response from the two senior groups showed motivation to participate in the study, many of the members expressing a wish to contribute to research on aging, but at the same time asking: "Why should the university be interested in me?"

An attempt was made to limit the volunteers from the two senior groups to women, to more closely approximate the ratio of women to men in the institutional sample. As these group members were interviewed, they, in turn, were requested to name friends who would be eligible for the study. An introductory letter was sent to each person referred in this way, followed in a few days by a telephone call for an appointment.

In sharp contrast to the institutional sample, only a few of the community respondents were unable to give the names of friends, and many gave the names of more than one friend. One 89-year-old woman gave the names, addresses, and telephone numbers of ten friends. Even after the quota for the community sample had been reached, several community respondents called to give the names of additional friends.

Locating aged men, especially men who lived alone, to approximate the living situations of several of the male respondents prior to their institutionalization, proved to be more problematic than obtaining the women respondents. Several managers of residential hotels located near one of the homes were contacted by telephone and letter, but they were reluctant to give the names of their tenants. Finally, through the cooperation of a colleague who lived in one such residential hotel, the names of several elderly single and widowed men were obtained. A letter introducing the study was sent to each of these men and followed in a few days by a telephone call for an appointment. There were no refusals from the four elderly men contacted by this method.

In order to obtain a sample of 40 community respondents,

57 individuals were contacted. Ten did not meet the selection criteria either because they were married, under the age of 70, or, in one case, already institutionalized. Seven individuals met the criteria but refused, saying: "I'm too busy," "I don't feel up to it," "I'm going to be out of town."

This procedure generated a community sample that was very similar to the waiting-list sample, as well as to the institutionalized sample, on all demographic variables. The average age of the group was 80, with an age range from 70 to 92 years of age; there were 34 women and 6 men; all were unattached, 6 who had never married and 34 who were widowed; and only 10 had been born in the United States. More than half of the women had been married to men who were proprietors of small businesses such as tailor shops, dry-goods stores, delicatessens, and grocery shops. Women who had never married tended to be either professional women or skilled bookkeepers or secretaries. As is true in the general population of elderly, the average education level was eight grades (slightly more than the study and institutionalized samples because the community sample included a few high school graduates and 4 college graduates; the distribution in the lower grade levels, however, was comparable in all three samples).

The community sample, like the other samples, usually had children. The average was two children; only 7 had no children and 15 had three or more children. The average community respondent had two siblings; 13 had none and 11 had three or more. Thus 80 percent had children and 50 percent had living siblings. The majority of the community respondents interacted with these family members; 35 had children or siblings or both who lived within a 20-mile radius and with whom they had weekly contact either in person, or by telephone or letter. The typical pattern was to live alone (50 percent) and to visit frequently with family. When they lived with family members, as 17 did, most (13) lived with a daughter and, in turn, most (11) with a married daughter. On these many demographic variables, not only was the community sample like the people in the sample who were followed from preadmission through entering and living in the institution, but they were also like the general population of the very old, in being predominantly foreign-born, widowed women who lived alone but who had frequent contact with their children and siblings.

Portrait of the Community Elderly

If the findings resound in agreement regarding decrements observed in the institutional old, they are equally robust in demonstrating that, on the whole, even the very aged who live in the community in the United States look remarkably well able to function (see, for example, Cumming and Henry, 1961; and Twente, 1970.) The characteristics of the group of forty community elderly are representative of what has generally been observed when such populations have been studied.

Mental and Physical Status. The criteria used for selecting the sample determined to a large extent that the people in the sample were in good mental and physical health for people of their age. Because the homes do not accept applicants who have psychiatric disorders or are terminally ill, and because those on the waiting list who were not sufficiently lucid to respond to a lengthy interview were further screened out, the matched community sample could not include the most disoriented or debilitated elderly who lived in the community. The sample was thus composed of older people of relatively sound mind and body who could care for themselves fairly well.

Although able to care for themselves, they—like other older people—reported a great many physical symptoms. Two of five, for example, gave self-reports of dizziness and general malaise; one of seven reported weakness of limbs; and many reported sleep problems, loss of appetite, constipation, headaches, nausea, nervousness, and so forth. The degree of physical problems was even more striking for self-reports on diseases. Eye problems (one of two), arthritis (one of three), and high or low blood pressure (one of four) led the list. One of seven or more reported heart, gastrointestinal, hearing, or lung problems. Only one of five reported none of these diseases and two of three reported two or more diseases. These statistics (that are no way different from the study sample) suggest the presence of a great deal of disease.

The reasons for their longevity, as well as for the presence

of identifiable diseases and deficits, are explained by Isaacs,
Livingstone, and Neville (1972, pp. 75, 77) in their book, so
aptly titled *Survival of the Unfittest*:

> *Finally, let us briefly consider, why do the unfit
> survive? Why do they survive unfit? The reason is be-
> cause lethal disease is treatable and non-lethal disease
> is not. Many of the once-fatal maladies of the elderly,
> such as pneumonia and fractured neck of femur, are
> effectively cured by modern medicine, while the non-
> lethal diseases of the brain, the heart and circulation,
> the muscles and joints, the vision and hearing, exert
> their baneful effects unchecked, or only partially re-
> lieved. For some of these non-lethal but socially
> intensely disruptive diseases, most notably 'senile
> dementia,' medicine has yet to find not merely a
> cure, not merely a means of prevention, but a basic
> understanding of its cause. For other diseases of the
> aged, such as atherosclerosis, some progress is being
> made towards developing methods of prevention, but
> it seems likely that these measures will have to be
> applied early in life if the effects of the disease on
> function in old age are to be avoided. In yet other
> diseases which cripple in late life, such as rheumatoid
> arthritis, effective methods of treatment are available,
> but they require early diagnosis and elaborate surgical
> treatment; the economic and administrative problems
> of bringing the right treatment to the right patient at
> the right time are so great that an effective solution
> seems equally remote. In a few other diseases of the
> very old impressive advances are being made, but
> ironically the greatest progress is in the ever-improv-
> ing organization of medical and social services in late
> life, which promote the Survival of the Unfittest.
> Man's strength and intellect decline while his capacity
> to survive increases. Man has learned to outlive the
> vigour of his body and the wisdom of his brain, but
> he has not yet learned how to provide, from the*

society which he has created, for the new needs of those who survive unfit.

Survival is indeed an issue for the very old. How do the very old survive? How do they live? Obviously, they live with a great deal of uncertainty. What will happen to them and when are unknown. Thus their task becomes the maintenance of functioning in spite of both "event uncertainty" and "time uncertainty." Indeed, respondents in the community sample were able to transcend physical impairment and retain functional capacity. If a central task of aging is to transcend bodily deterioration, then it can be said that respondents in the community sample were in fact accomplishing this task. For some, the deficits were simply ignored; for others, the deficits became challenges that were vigorously met and overcome. One example of the latter was an obese woman with a weak heart, heavily medicated with digitalis, who several times a day trudged up and down from her third-floor apartment whenever she wished to go out. The interviewer, when arriving upstairs huffing and puffing, was greeted with a loud laugh and a few chosen words on how she must keep herself in better shape.

Psychological Status.   In general, what is the psychological status of the very old people who are living independently in the community? As in other studies of older people who live in the community, the very old in the present sample were doing surprisingly well at the time they were studied. Assessments on the dimensions used to tap effects revealed efficient cognitive functioning, responsiveness to affects, positive emotional states, and viable self-systems.

Their cognitive functioning was not at all constricted. They were oriented in time and place, accurate in their perceptions, and cognitively organized. Affectively, they were responsive to their own inner life and were able to shift in affective expression when situations warranted such a shift. They are characterized by good emotional tone, including relatively high feelings of well-being and hopefulness, and of minimal anxiety and depression. They perceived themselves as adequate in their capacity for self-care, had quite high self-esteem, and were able to use their present environment for the maintenance of their self-concept. They tended toward feelings of dominance and affiliation in relationships with others. Their portrait as a group suggested a high degree of competence in coping with life circumstances, although, to be sure, with a great deal of physical deficit.

Adverse Life Changes.   Their rather sound psychological status may reflect the absence of adverse life changes. Possibly, unlike other very old people, they had not experienced recent adversity. To assess the types and amount of adverse change among the sample, eight types of changes that might happen to people who are very old were identified: illness, insufficient funds for need, move of significant others, death of significant others, relationship deterioration, homemaking incapacity, neighborhood deterioration, and relocation. Each of the eight types was assessed to determine whether a substantial change had occurred in the preceding 3 years.

The scoring for each of the eight types of changes will be reviewed, as well as the number and percentage in the community sample who showed these significant adverse changes.

A change in physical status, or illness, was considered to have occurred if, during the past 3 years, there had been an illness requiring a physician's care, and if the illness had caused a change in the respondents life-style. Such changes had occurred for three of five (or 62 percent) of the community sample during the past 3 years. Changes included increased dizziness, increased difficulty in ambulation because of arthritis, hospitalization for colitis, more lung and circulatory difficulties, and so forth.

Change resulting in insufficient funds was considered to have occurred if the respondent reported an increase in financial stress, usually as a difficulty in meeting financial needs at present or in the immediate future. Included were increasing difficulty living on social security payments that were the only source of income, savings recently exhausted and more dependent on children for money, inability to afford apartment rent when roommate moved out, and so forth. Comments such as "it is difficult to manage on eighty dollars a month—many dogs live a better life than the aged," or "enjoyed Golden Agers but quit because it was too expensive," were considered indicative of economic adversity. Only three (or 8 percent) reported this type of adverse change.

Two changes, move of and death of significant others, may be considered together. No one in the community sample had experienced a move by a significant other during the past 3 years. An impressive number, however, had lost a significant other (sixteen, or 40 percent). Five had become widowed, three for the second time; two had lost children and two a niece or nephew who was like a child to them; four, a brother or sister; one, a close brother-in-law; and two, sons-in-law. In all, six of the sixteen had lost a child or child-surrogate who was one generation younger and to whom they were very attached.

The change called *relationship deterioration* refers to a relationship to a significant other that had appreciably changed for the worse. Seven (or 18 percent) reported such a change during the preceding 3 years. For example, an 83-year-old widow reported that her son-in-law, with whom she now lived, would not talk to her: "I don't do nothing to him and he hates me." A 76-year-old widow, also living with a daughter and her family, who used to spend summers with another daughter reported, of this second daughter, "now she comes to visit me a couple times a year." A 77-year-old widow who lived alone reported that her relationship with her daughter had changed following the daughter's major surgery and her son-in-law's heart attack. And an 84-year-old widow who lived with her son reported that her relationship to him had changed after his recent remarriage: "After all it's their home. I'm living with them. Before my son lived with me. Now it's different."

A change in homemaking capacity was considered to have occurred if the respondent perceived a substantial decrease in the capacity for cleaning, cooking, sleeping, grooming and so forth. Examples of responses were, "Getting harder to look after myself"; "I can no longer see to cook, or order groceries or dial the telephone"; and "Not sure of getting one hot meal a day—it's no fun cooking for yourself—I don't eat as good as I should." Of the forty, only four (or 10 percent) felt a significant decrease in their homemaking capacity.

A change related to neighborhood deterioration was considered to have occurred if the respondent perceived, and was distressed by, a deterioration in the neighborhood because of changes in socioeconomic composition. None of the community respondents reported this type of change.

A large number of the respondents had moved from one location to another within the last 3 years (13, or 32 percent). Six moves were of individuals who were living alone at both times, four of whom were either forced to move by urban renewal or because their apartment hotel closed down. Of the other two who remained living alone, one moved to be closer to two sisters who shared an apartment and the other to another neighborhood because the original neighborhood had changed 10 years before. Four others moved to their own apartments after their spouses died. Two moved when their children who they were living with moved and one moved into a daughter's apartment after her daughter's divorce.

Overall, eight of nine (or 88 percent) in this sample of forty elderly persons had undergone an adverse change in one or more of the eight areas, and half had experienced adverse changes in two or more areas within the preceding 3 years. As noted earlier, the primary changes were in physical status (62 percent), but half also had suffered a change in one or more aspects of social relationships and close to half (42 percent) had experienced a substantial change related to living arrangements.

Although generally the community respondents had undergone a great many adverse changes, none had actively sought institutional care. Many had discussed various living arrangements with their families, including the possibility of applying to one of the homes under study. For the present, however, this alternative was discounted and for those living in a two- or three-generation household this arrangement was their preference, in spite of intergenerational conflicts. Some of these very old people who lived with younger family members, as well as many who lived alone, were aware that their intimate support system was precarious, invariably made more precarious by the death or illness of responsible others, and, for some, by the need to change living arrangements.

In sum, these very old people were in a stage of predecision regarding the seeking of institutional care. Various other solutions short of institutional care had been considered and some changes had been made to assure community living. This attempt to ensure community living was most clear in the changes in living arrangements. For some the move was into a child's home; for others it was a move to an apartment that was closer to children after the death of a spouse; and for others it was a move to an apartment closer to siblings. Independent of living arrangements, the community respondents had frequent visits with family members and kept in close touch by phone. The family absorbed the disruptions in events. Changes had occurred and other changes were expected to occur but the time had not yet come when institutional care was seen as the only alternative.

Attitudes Toward Institutional Care.   Although many adverse changes had occurred in the past few years, none of the respondents in the community sample had sought institutional care. What were the attitudes of respondents in the community sample toward institutions? Before discussing the attitudes of our respondents, let us review what two other investigators have found. From her study of rural elderly, Twente (1970, pp. 61-62) reported:

> *Of all the moves to other housing, the one most dreaded is that to an institution. The older person who needs institutional care often resists leaving his home in order to postpone the time when he is admitted to a 'place within four walls.' Sometimes it seems he hopes to be able to live with a son or daughter instead. Aging men and women may refer to the time when they themselves took care of their own parents. They dread the prospect of institutional care because some see it as the end of what little independence they have. Certainly what remained of freedom is likely to vanish once a person is inside institutional walls.*

Similar sentiments are offered by others. In a national

survey, Shanas (1962) found that only 3 percent of the sample
of elderly 65 years and over preferred institutional living arrangements. Her summary of why older people feel the way
they do about nursing homes and homes for the aged is the generally accepted one (pp. 102-103):

> *Almost all older people view the move to a*
> *home for the aged or to a nursing home with fear and*
> *hostility . . . . All old people—without exception—*
> *believe that the move to an institution is the prelude*
> *to death . . . . [The old person] sees the move to an*
> *institution as a decisive change in living arrangements,*
> *the last change he will experience before he dies . . . .*
> *Finally, no matter what the extenuating circum-*
> *stances, the older person who has children interprets*
> *the move to an institution as rejection by his family.*

To assess the fear of becoming institutionalized among the
community sample, an interview guide was developed that consisted of a precoded questionnaire and a series of open-ended
questions (Kuypers, 1969). Because at the time this interview
guide was developed most of the respondents had already been
interviewed, these data were gathered from the fourteen community respondents, who had not yet been interviewed. This
guide was designed to strip away progressively the more manifest defensive attitudes and to obtain the more latent attitudes
regarding the seeking of institutional care and the perception of
the homes that they would apply to if institutional care were
sought.

Often older people are reluctant to voice concern regarding
their future. Heyman and Jeffers (1965) reported, for example,
that as many as one of two people over 60 years of age (50
percent of a sample of 180 with a median age of 72) expressed
no concern about their future. One of four said he or she had
no plans of any kind in the event of a long-term illness; two of
three indicated that some financial plans had been made; and
only about one in twelve had specific plans for housing or nursing care. Similar findings regarding an apparent lack of concern

about the future were also published in the *Edmonton Senior Resident Survey Reports* (James, 1964). Heyman and Jeffers conclude that: "Although the mechanism of denial may have been present, the lack of expressed concern over long term illness appears to be based chiefly on security these elderly persons found in family life, religion, a stable environment, financial resources and their relative good health at the time of the study" (p. 153). These authors thus offer one explanation for the lack of readiness to plan for future crises—because most older people live in stable life situations, they feel there is no need to worry or fret about the future.

There are obviously other explanations for the findings of Heyman and Jeffers. Possibly older people fear talking about an uncertain future that may include a long period of debilitation and dependency before death. Independent of uncertainties regarding the future, the community respondents in the present study had a rather positive appraisal of the institutions to which they would eventually apply. They felt that old-age homes were necessary, that the staff in the homes met the needs of the residents, that a resident could maintain self-respect, and that the home provided companionship. Less positive were their perceptions of the homes as "friendly places" or not friendly, and their doubts about whether the resident could overcome a boring existence. People who went into the homes were perceived as different from themselves: such people could not turn to their family for support and could not take care of themselves. If these supports were to diminish or vanish for themselves and if there were a lessening of ability for self-care, then they themselves would be different. If they themselves were no longer independent, autonomous, and self-sufficient, the home would become a necessary alternative. Then they would obey the rules, as others had done before them, and adjust to the institution. For these others, who lacked social supports and who could not care for themselves, and for themselves, if such changes should overtake them, they felt it was not "a mistake" to enter the home. Most felt that if they had to go into a home they would not lose their sense of self-worth. Such sentiments were expressed in the answer to our questions.

The focused interview that followed the questionnaire, however, revealed more latent attitudes toward entering an institution. When the interviewers probed feelings about living in the home, all fourteen communicated that they would make the transition if they absolutely had to, although the home had rigid rules and regulations and offered a life with little privacy. For twelve of the fourteen, entering the home was anticipated as a calamity. One respondent said, "I'd have to give up everything. It's a new life. If, God forbid, I became helpless, that would be my only reason. And I hope and pray that day will never come." For another respondent, the home was "an institution" and "an institution means a place where people are sent—a home, a hospital, it could even be a jail!" A third respondent said:

> Most of them go there before they have to. Their children don't want them. They have no money. They're weaker. Their mates are dead. They have no choice. They play cards, look at TV, sit and look out of the window, read newspapers; listen to sermons, lecturers, debates. They have entertainment.
>
> I know everything's regimented. You have to be up at a certain time. You have to have a bath at a certain time. Meals are at a certain time. Then there are times when you're free and you can go to the sun parlors and talk or laugh with your friends. I wouldn't like it. If I have to, because of deterioration, I would make up my mind that that's my fate. I think it's a place to die.

These types of responses support earlier findings that institutionalization is a dreaded event. The possibility is suppressed but is easily brought to consciousness when probed by the interviewer. If events necessitated a decision, events that made self-care extremely difficult and made significant others less accessible, then the sectarian home would be the first choice. It may be giving up "everything," to be in an institution "like a jail," or to go there as "a place to die," but friends have gone into the home and have survived—and survival can be uppermost in the thoughts of the extremely vulnerable very old.

Personality Types. Because the community sample was a rather homogeneous group of foreign-born elderly, it was possible that one or another personality type might dominate. Also, of course, it was important to determine whether the primary sample was of this same personality type. If the primary sample, for example, was composed of one type of person and the community sample of several, there would be an indication of a selection bias related to who seeks institutional care. But the findings are very clear. There was a wide range of personality types in both the community and primary sample. One measure (a dimension generated by the Self-Sort Task), for example, revealed wide and equivalent spreads on such divergent personality dimensions as managerial-autocratic, aggressive-sadistic, rebellious-distrustful, self-effacing/masochistic, and cooperative-overconventional. On two overall personality dimensions (dominant-submissive and affiliative-hostile), there were similar wide spreads within the two samples, and the two samples did not differ one from another. The community sample, as well as the sample on the waiting list, much like the general population of the very old, contained a variety of different personality types. Thus, it is not a single type of person or a few specific types who seek institutional care when they are old. Stated another way, factors other than personality type must be used to explain why some older people and not others apply for admission to the homes. In turn, differences on measures of psychological status between the community sample and the waiting list sample cannot simply be explained by selection bias. On the contrary, any differences would have to be interpreted as a result of the process of becoming an older person on the waiting list.

Loss Meaning. Many losses had occurred in the lives of these older people, a great many in the recent past, and further changes could bring about the need to seek institutional care. Yet, on the surface, this sample of community respondents was functioning admirably well. Possibly there were more subtle issues of loss that dominated their lives. To determine if there was such a dominant meaning attached to the losses they had experienced, a measure of the experience of loss was developed that could determine whether the meaning of loss clustered around separation, physical deterioration, or death. The measure was related to the reconstruction of the respondent's earliest memory.

Was one or another loss theme dominant? No! Three of five respondents (60.5 percent) did not introduce themes of loss. Only three introduced themes of interpersonal loss, eight of injury, and none of death. The community sample apparently was not focused on losses. Real-life losses may have been ubiquitous in their lives, but they were apparently not experienced as central or critical for everyday functioning.

2

Anticipating Institutionalization

The older person awaiting entrance to a nursing home has arrived at this juncture after several steps. He or she has had to make the hard decision to seek institutional care, has had to apply for admission and wait to learn if his or her application has been accepted. Once accepted, then, it is no surprise that the person's psychological status reflects the stress of undergoing this process, as well as of anticipating the impending event of actually moving into the institution. The net effect of the admission process and of the anticipation of the change in life-style can be explored by contrasting the psychological status of the study sample when on the waiting list to the matched community sample.

The Psychological Contrast:
Predecision and Awaiting Admission

Comparisons of the old people who were awaiting institutionalization with those who were living in the community revealed marked differences between the two groups in cognitive functioning, affective response, emotional state, and self-perceptions (see Tables 2 and 3). Moreover, as Table 3 illustrates, the

Table 2. A Comparison of the Community and Waiting-List Samples

Area of Psychological Functioning	Community Sample (N = 35)	Waiting-List Sample (N = 100)
Cognitive functioning	No constriction: oriented in time and place, perceptual accuracy, and cognitively organized[a]	Constriction: minimal disorientation and disorganization[a]
Affective responsiveness	Responsiveness to emotional life[c]	Constriction in emotional responsiveness[c]
Emotional state	Relatively high feeling of well-being[c] Hopefulness[c] Minimal anxiety and depression[c]	Moderate feeling of well-being[c] Limited hopefulness[c] Anxious and depressed[c]
Self-perception	Perception of adequacy in self-care Quite high self-esteem[c] Use of present environment for maintenance of self-concept[b] Feelings of both dominance[a] and affiliation	Perception of adequacy in self-care Lower self-esteem[b] High distortion and conviction used for maintenance of self-concept[b] Feelings of diminished dominance,[a] but not of diminished affiliation

[a] $p \leqslant .05$
[b] $p \leqslant .01$
[c] $p \leqslant .001$

psychological status of the study sample while on the waiting list was not unlike the psychological status generally descriptive of aged persons who live in institutions: slight cognitive disorganization; constriction in affective response; less than optimal feelings of well-being, limited hope, and heightened anxiety and depression; diminished self-esteem; distortions in the evidence provided to support self-concept; and a perception of oneself as having little capacity to dominate in interaction with others. Measure by measure, the differences between the study population and the community control population added up to make the following portrait.

Cognitive Functioning. Because cognitive adequacy (or its converse, cognitive impairment) was conceptualized as a complex of functions rather than as a single, static entity, six

Table 3. Comparisons Between Waiting-List Sample and the Two Control Samples: Community and Institutionalized Samples (Analysis of Variance, Using Age and Sex as Covariates)

Area of Psychological Functioning	Mean			Contrast			
	Community (N = 35)	Waiting List (N = 100)	Institution-alized (N = 37)	Community vs Waiting List		Waiting List vs Institutionalized	
				F	P	F	P
Cognitive functioning							
Orientation (MSQ)	.7	1.3	1.7	.44	—	1.29	—
Time estimate (60 seconds)	23.2	21.8	26.4	.84	—	7.57	.007
Retention (Paired Word Learning)	7.6	12.6	16.2	30.63	.0001	23.14	.0001
Organization (BGT)	27.3	34.5	35.2	3.79	.05	.02	—
Perceptual accuracy (TAT)	27.9	21.8	22.1	20.11	.0001	.21	—
Originality (Reitman)	10.2	9.4	9.9	10.83	.0007	3.68	.05
Signs of cognitive inadequacy	.5	1.4	1.0	5.12	.02	4.42	.04
Affective responsiveness							
Range of affects	5.8	4.3	5.2	21.54	.0001	6.03	.01
Willingness to introspect	3.4	2.1	1.8	35.26	.0001	.03	—
Emotional states							
Well-being	19.2	15.8	16.8	15.86	.0002	.36	—
Hope	.7	-.9	-.4	15.37	.0002	1.89	—
Anxiety	15.3	19.8	16.2	6.16	.01	1.22	—
Depression	7.6	13.9	12.3	17.01	.0001	.39	—
Self-perception							
Perception—self-care inadequacy	.8	2.3	2.7	.86	—	.05	—
Self-esteem	23.2	19.2	18.3	15.82	.0002	2.31	—
Adequacy	3.9	-.83	1.8	8.50	.004	5.89	.02
Dominance	.34	-.21	.31	3.75	.05	4.72	.03
Affiliation	.08	.16	.09	.21	—	2.43	—

different variables were selected for assessment: (1) orientation in time and place; (2) orientation in the immediate present; (3) learning and retention; (4) cognitive organization; (5) perceptual organization and accuracy; and (6) the capacity to vary responses (originality versus rigidity). While each task represents a different approach to cognitive functioning, the various measures are associated with each other.

The ten-question Mental Status Questionnaire or MSQ (Kahn, Pollack, and Goldfarb, 1961), which requires answering such questions as the name of "this place," "today's date," name of the President of the United States, and so on, was used to tap the respondent's orientation in time and place. The difference in scores, while favoring the community sample, was not statistically significant (community mean = .7, waiting-list mean = 1.3).

The ability to estimate the passage of 1 minute (60 seconds) was used to assess orientation to the immediate present. Both samples grossly underestimated the number of seconds, with neither group differentiating itself from the other in this capacity.

The Inglis (1959) Paired Word Association Learning Test was adopted to gain a measure of learning retention. The respondent was asked to listen to three pairs of words. He was told that the first word in each pair (the stimulus word) would be presented again and that he would be asked to respond with the second word (the response word). Each time the respondent was presented with the first word and could recall the second word, the pair of words was repeated by the interviewer. The number of times the pair of words had to be repeated was counted as the number of errors on the task.

The two samples were significantly different on this task. The community sample averaged only 7.6 errors as compared to 12.6 errors for the waiting-list sample ($p = .0001$). The largest difference between the two samples was attributable to the difference in the percentages of fast learning. For example, 40 percent of the community sample learned the paired word with 3 or less errors as compared to 17 percent of the waiting-list sample. Conversely, 83 percent of the waiting-list sample made four or more errors, while only 60 percent of the community respondents made four or fewer errors in attempting to recall the response words.

Of the original set of eight designs that Bender (1938) developed for the Bender Gestalt Test (BGT), we used three to assess organization in visual motor dysfunction (Designs 1, 3, and 8). With the designs in full view, the respondent was asked to copy all three on a single 8½-by-11 (inches) sheet of paper. The organization of each reproduced design was then scored separately by the Pascal and Suttell (1951) system, which establishes scores for deviations from the actual design. Higher scores thus reflect greater distortion. The waiting-list sample reproduced designs that were appreciably more disorganized than those of the community group (p = .05, community mean = 27.3, waiting-list mean = 34.5).

The differences between the two samples are illustrated in Figure 1 reproductions. The total possible score was 60: a maximum of 10 from complete distortion of the first design, 20 from the second, and 30 from the third. The various types of errors in copying the designs, as well as the maximum points subtracted for each type of error, were as follows. For Design 1, maximum points subtracted were: wavy line (2), dots or dashes (3), circles (8), number of dots (2 for each added or subtracted), double row (8), workover (2), and second attempt (3 for each attempt). For Design 3, maximum points subtracted were: asymmetry (3), dots, dashes, circles (3), number of dots (2), extra row (8), blunting (8), distortion (8 each), workover (2), second attempt (3 for each attempt), and part missing (8). For Design 8, maximum points subtracted were: ends not joined (8), angles extra (3), angles missing (3), extra dots or dashes (3), double line (1 for each), distortion (8 for each), guide lines (2), workover (2), second attempt (3 for each), and part missing (8).

The first example reproduced in Figure 1, which received a low composite score of 12, shows a rather accurate reproduction of each of the three designs. On Design 1, there was a score (subtraction) of 2 (for wavy line); on Design 3, a score of 5 (3 for circles and 2 for workover); and, on Design 8, a score of 5 (2 for workover and 3 for second attempt).

The second example received a score of 28, which is close

Figure 1. Illustrations of Copying of the Bender Gestalt Designs
(Copied by Hand)

Example 1 (Scored 12)   Example 2 (Scored 28)

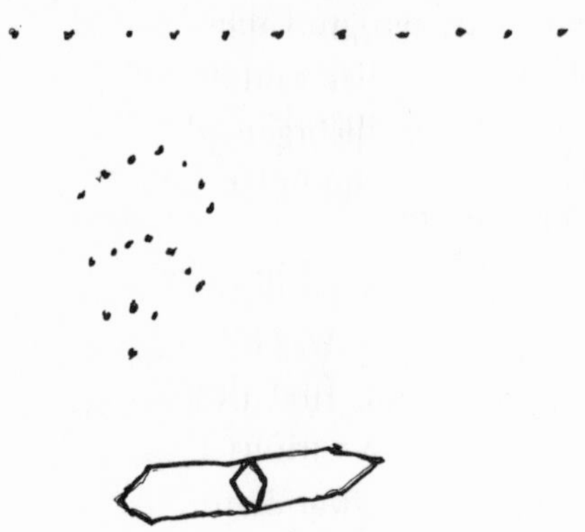

Example 3 (Scored 36)    Example 4 (Scored 50)

to the mean for the community sample; whereas the third sample received a score of 36, which is close to the mean for the waiting-list sample. In both these examples, the general form of the reproduction tends to be accurate, except for the highly distorted design in the third example. Example 4, scored 50, shows gross distortion: the first design is rather accurate (and only two points were subtracted for being a wavy line), but the second design is almost completely inaccurate (scored 18), and the third design is totally inaccurate (scored the maximum, 30).

The stories told to five of the Murray Thematic Apperception Test (TAT) cards were scored by the Dana (1959) system, yielding a measure of perceptual accuracy. The five cards were:

1. A young boy contemplating a violin resting on a table in front of him.

2. A family farm scene with a younger woman in the forefront looking off in the distance and an older woman in the background.

6BM. A short elderly woman standing with her back to a tall young man, who is looking downward with a perplexed expression.

7BM. A younger and an older man facing each other. Only their heads, which are fairly close together, are shown.

17BM. A naked man in the posture of climbing up or down a rope.

Two subscores, one of perceptual organization and another of perceptual range, were summed to obtain a total score of perceptual accuracy. In scoring perceptual organization, each story was given 1 point for each of seven elements included in the story: card description, present behavior, past events, future events, feeling, thoughts, and outcome. For each story there was thus a possible range of scores from 0 to 7, and for all five stories from 0 to 35. To get at perceptual range, each story was scored for the presence of responses to three or four selected stimulus properties with a possible total of 16 for all five stories. Higher scores for both subscores, therefore, reflect greater accuracy, and the possible range for the total score—the sum of the two subscores—is 0 to 51.

The difference between the waiting-list and community samples on this task was highly significant (p = .0001, waiting-list mean = 21.8, community mean = 27.9). The following are two TAT protocols, one from the community group, which received a score of 28, and one from the waiting-list group, which received a score of 21. The protocols illustrate dramatically the differences between the two samples in perceptual accuracy.

EXAMPLE 1. A TAT from the Community Sample (Score = 28;
interviewer's comments in italics)

Card 1. *(Entered into TAT experience wholeheartedly and seemed to enjoy it).* Violin. He's think of this violin. He's thinking maybe I could or will play the violin. But he doesn't know whether he can play. *(How will it turn out?)* Maybe he will play. *(Ha?)* Or maybe he doesn't like to play—he looks so sad. Maybe he'll play it. He's thinking about it.

Card 2. "Beautiful—beautiful—that is nice—a farm—he makes the furrows here—he makes corn or potatoes. I used to help on the farm. The mother here *(respondent pointed)*—the mother is looking for the daughter. The daughter is going to school. This is in the mountains—little hills there. I don't know what the mother thinks of the daughter. It is a nice horse. *(How will it turn out?)* I don't understand it too much. The daughter doesn't like the farm. She wants to leave to go to school. The mother can't say anything. *(How will it turn out?)* She will study. The mother looks like she is very sad. She thinks the daughter should take care of the farm but the daughter wants to go to school. The daughter will go away."

Card 6BM. "Mother and son. Oh, the son has trouble. It looks like the mother is sad. Maybe he'll go away and leave the mother. He has trouble—he has trouble. I don't know, he has told the mother something *(?)* I don't know, maybe he stole something. He doesn't look like that though. But the mother is sad, but he is not satisfied and he will go away. *(How will it turn out?)* He may be good. *(How so?)* A mother is a mother—a mother forgives. He is a nice fellow, but something is wrong. I think he'll go away."

Card 7BM. "What is this? Father and son. Both look—I cannot explain. He *(points to lower figure)* looks so much younger—not so good, not so friendly—maybe somebody died? He looks growlish—so sad—no—maybe the mother died. I don't know. *(How will it turn out?)* I don't know what it is. The older man looks sad too. Maybe they have trouble together, but I don't think so. Maybe it will be good—but I cannot say. Both are thinking. Father is sad, and so is the son."

Card 17BM. "Oy! He's a—maybe he's in the circus—he turns—makes something—have nothing on—I don't know what to think of him. Maybe he's going up? I don't know. He has a funny face. He's a comic act—He's a—I don't know—I don't like him (laughs). If he goes up, he has to come down too. Circus boy—something like that."

EXAMPLE 2. A TAT Protocol from the Waiting-List Sample (Score = 21; interviewer's comments in italics)

Card 1. "Well, this youngster seems to be a little discouraged about something. He's troubled—that's all. *(Respondent handed back card. I gave it to her again. "Tell me more.")* He has a violin in front of him. It may be his music that's troubling him, I don't know. *(What happens to him?)* I have no idea. *(Make it up.)* Maybe he will be disappointed. *(Will he?)* Maybe it will come out all right in the end. *(Will it?)* Maybe."

Card 2. "Oh, this is a beautiful picture. This girl seems to be a student. She's very attractive. The other woman? I don't know what she is thinking. She's a different type.

She's also very nice-looking. The man is working in a field. He's very strong. It's a beautiful country. They have a beautiful home. *(What will happen?)* This girl seems very determined. She has that determined look. *(What about?)* She's holding a book—maybe about her studies. I don't know. *(Tell me more.)* This woman here seems very serene. The man is very interested in his work, I believe. That's a beautiful field there."

Card 6BM. "She's a very pleasant-looking woman and he's a very troubled young man—he is troubled-looking, really troubled. I don't know where they are. He's troubled about something. *(What is he troubled about?)* I don't know, but it troubles him terribly. He'll have to face the consequences." *(Respondent smiled.)*

Card 7BM. "This is a very studious sincere older man. He is saying something to the younger man that the younger man is troubled about. I have no idea where they're at or what's going to happen. They too will have to face the consequences."

Card 17BM. "Here's a circus performer. It looks like he's enjoying his work. He makes me think of . . . have you ever watched Don Ameche in "Circuses in Foreign Countries"? It's very interesting. He enjoys it, but I don't know what is going to happen. *(Make it up.)* I can't, I don't know."

The twelve Reitman stick figures (Reitman and Robertson, 1950) were used to obtain a measure of the ability to vary responses (originality) when describing what each figure represents. The Reitman figures are in very different poses, so that the more varied the depictions of their action, the higher the originality score, up to a maximum of 12 points. The community sample averaged 10.2 different responses and the study sample 9.4. This very significant statistical difference was revealed in the percentage of respondents in the two samples that gave nine or less different responses: only one out of four (27 percent) in the community sample, whereas almost half (44 percent) of the study sample on the waiting list. The following protocol, produced by a respondent in the community sample, illustrated the twelve different poses and received the maximum score of 12.

1. "Bending over."

2. "Bending way over—turning away from something."

3. "Bending over—crying."

4. "Oh, he's so happy! Tickled to death about something."

5. "Holding his back—he's got a pain."

6. "He's just exercising."

7. "He's running away from something."

8. "He's happy, singing."

9. "He's surprised at something."

10. "He's handing out something."

11. "He's printing."

12. "Kneeling, praying."

The following is a protocol scored 9 because the response to the second, fourth, and ninth stick figures are essentially the same as the responses to stick figures 10 and 11.

1. "Looks to me broken-hearted for something."

2. "Looks happy for something—he's excited."

3. "Got the blues."

4. "Happy guy."

5. "Looking for something."

6. "Happy-go-lucky."

7. "Dancing the kazatske *(Russian dance)*."

8. "Looks like he needs a partner to dance."

9. "Happy."

10. "Looking for a partner."

11. "Looking for somebody."

12. "Praying to God."

An extreme example of repetition of responses is shown in the following protocol that received an originality score of 5. Only the responses to figures 1, 4, 6, 10, and 12 were not repeated when describing the other figures.

1. "Looks like someone sad."

2. "He looks sad, too."

3. "He looks sad, too."

4. "He looks happy" *(same tone as above)*.

5. "I couldn't say *(?)* Don't know."

6. "He's just standing with his hands behind his back."

7. "He looks happy."

8. "Just standing there."

9. "He looks happy."

10. "I think he's thinking of something."

11. "He looks happy to me—like a comedian."

12. "Looks like he's crazy *(?)* he's standing on his head. Who does that?"

Signs of Cognitive Inadequacy. To obtain an overall index of cognitive dysfunctioning, a scale point was determined for each of the six tasks that clearly reflected cognitive dysfunction (see Appendix at end of this book). A score was then computed for each respondent by summing the number of tasks where performance was below this level. On this measure of cognitive inadequacy, the mean for the community sample was

.5, as opposed to 1.4 for the waiting-list sample, a difference that is highly statistically significant ($p = .02$). The average of 1.4 signs of dysfunction, as well as the typical level of cognitive functioning across the six tasks, both suggest that the waiting-list sample was not as much disorganized as they were cognitively constricted—that is, unable to fully use their comprehension of the environment in responding to the environment. Some disorganization, however, was apparent, particularly in copying Bender Gestalt designs.

Affective Responsiveness. Two measures were used to assess affective responsivity: range of affects and willingness to experience.

An affect range score was established by adding the number of different affects (up to a possible total of seven) that were introduced in stories told to the five Murray TAT cards. Each affect introduced was rated 1 point. The seven different affects were: hostility, sadness, dislike, job, affection, interest, and trying. (While both this measure and the perceptual accuracy measure are based on TAT stories, they are sufficiently independent [$r = .29$] to use as separate measures.)

The community sample averaged 5.8 different affects and the waiting-list sample 4.3, a difference that is very statistically significant ($p = .0001$). Two examples will illustrate this difference. The first protocol was scored seven because all seven affect categories were used. The second was scored four because an incomplete list of affects was generated. In the first example, hostility was expressed in stories to cards 2, 6BM, and 7BM; unhappiness in cards 1 and 2; dislike in 7BM; joy in 2; affection in 6BM and 7BM; interest in 2 and 17BM; and trying in 17BM. In the second example, hostility was expressed in card 6BM; unhappiness in 6BM; affection in 2 and 6BM; and interest in 2, 6BM, and 7BM. The affects of dislike, joy and trying were not included.

TAT COMMUNITY PROTOCOL (Range of Affect Score = 7; interviewer's comments in italics)

Card 1. "It's a boy—he's modeling something. He's thinking to do it. Looks like a violin. Looks like he's getting disappointed about it. *(How will it turn out?)* It don't look like he's happy. Way it shows—he'll think over and he'll play it."

Card 2. "Looks like a mother and her daughter. Mother is telling the daughter that she should go to school. Father standing by a horse. They look kind of mad—the mother and daughter. *(About what?)* Mad about—all look sore at the daughter. Why doesn't she go to school? She got her books in her hand. Daughter looks mad. Won't be successful. *(How does the mother feel?)* Mother feels bad about it—like every mother, she wants her daughter to be happy."

Card 6BM. "Mother and son—he's asking something of his mother and his mother doesn't care to listen to him. So both are mad and they don't talk to each other. *(How will it turn out?)* The son will change his mind. It will turn out good."

Card 7BM. "There is a father and a son. Are they talking very nicely about something? The father looks mad at the son like he *(son)* doesn't want to do it. They'll make up, I think, and the son will do it. *(Respondent hands me card.)* If I would know all this I wouldn't give you my name. It's too much." *(Needs encouragement to continue. This is the first of many stops).*

Card 17BM. "Well, there's a boy going on a rope. Very interested in that rope. He's going to jump down. He's going down. *(How will it turn out?)* He looks like he's going to succeed."

TAT WAITING-LIST PROTOCOL (Range of Affect Score = 4; interviewer's comments in italics)

Card 1. "He's very much interested in his violin. He's giving a great deal of thought as to whether he'll be a great artist. *(What else?)* If he becomes a musician it will require a great deal of practice. *(Will he be successful?)* Yes, if that's his aim.

Card 2. "Looks as if they were working in some kind of field. The girl has a faraway look and is probably thinking of what these men will make. The woman is the forewoman or overseer. Why is the girl holding a book? I think her thoughts are really on the field—what the outcome will be. *(What will it be?)* It's agriculture of some kind. Or maybe she's memorizing the lesson she's read in her book. Again, the overseer could be the man's wife and is watching him work. They hope so. They're laboring hard. I hope so."

Card 6BM. "There has been a grievance of some kind. The mother is awaiting news and he is implicated in whatever happened. In other words, he's guilty. *(Told respondent what a great storyteller she is.)* She's waiting to hear his side of the story. *(Story?)* He could have done away with someone over a love affair. Jealousy was probably the main thing. Just to look at his expression. He's hesitating and she's looking out the window, hoping that whoever it is will come back home."

Card 7BM. "Well, this guy needs advice of some kind and he doesn't seem to be taking it graciously at all. Whether he's going to venture into some new business, isn't familiar with it, and is trying to get advice *(Go through with it?)* He's hesitating—he's not quite sure what to do.

Card 17BM. "This looks like a fireman coming down from the firehouse. He looks half asleep, but his expression says, another fire—I'm ready—nothing new. He's certainly muscular, all right. As a rule, firemen are dressed, though. *(Respondent shrugged.)* Unless he's in a circus or something. Trapeze performer, maybe."

The Gendlin and Tomlinson (1967) measure of experiencing ability was used to measure willingness to introspect on one's personal feelings. Ratings of willingness to introspect were based on responses to the affect state of loneliness. High scores were assigned to self-reports that made reference to intense feelings, whereas low scores were assigned where feelings were

ignored or described impersonally. On this 7-point scale, the
mean for the community sample of 3.4 was quite different from
the waiting-list group mean of 2.1 (p = .0001).

The respondent was asked: "Can you tell me about the
times when you feel lonely?" If none was mentioned, the interviewer was encouraged to say: "We all get lonely—when do you
have these feelings? How often? How do you feel? What do you
do so as not to feel lonely?" and so forth.

The following are five protocols, the first two from the
community (scores of 7 and 4) and then three from the waiting
list (all scored 2).

1. "I very rarely am lonely. I suppose once in a while one
   does get that way but with me it's not very often. I just
   don't let myself feel that way long. I don't think it's
   healthy. I think a woman like myself who has no immediate family may be expected to get a feeling of loneliness once in a while. *(Can you give an example?)* When
   I was sick in the hospital and my roommate would have
   a great deal of family come and visit her, I would feel
   quite lonely. Of course my nieces and nephews were
   very good to me, but it isn't the same as having a very
   immediate family be attentive. I also feel lonely when I
   am invited to a friend's home for a holiday meal and
   they have all the family there too. It reminds me of the
   fact that I am not now a member of a large family. But
   on the whole, I don't give way to these thoughts of
   loneliness. It's a definitely infrequent feeling with me. I
   keep myself as busy as possible. Now I would say that
   loneliness is not a frequent enough experience with me
   to diminish my enjoyment with people and things in
   life."

2. "Loneliness. *(?)* At night I do. *(What makes you feel
   this way?)* Just knowing I'm alone in the world. *(Feel
   this way all the time?)* I try to call somebody or go out
   —I try to keep busy. *(Anybody in particular you want
   to be with at times like this?)* My daughter. *(How often
   does it happen?)* Not too often. *(Once a week?)* Yes.

(More?) I wouldn't say more—well, maybe twice a week. *(What if it's too late at night to call someone?)* I sew or watch TV."

3. "You just feel blue . . . lonesome. I don't know. I just feel as though I'm alone in the world. *(Can you give an example?)* Right now. No mail from California. As soon as mail or a call comes I'll feel better. Sometimes I'll just walk away. Other times I'll just tell you off. *(What do you do?)* I try to get interested in something around the house. *(What sort of things?)* If I hear that any of our family are sick, or good friends are in trouble. *(How often?)* Very easily. Very often. I just sit here crying."

4. "Loneliness: every evening. Look now it is bigger. The evening is like a bad day. I can't read. Louis fix the TV, but I can't look. I look for half an hour, then I'm dizzy. What I got to do? *(How do you get over being lonely?)* If I got someone to go to I go, but here everybody is sleeping or old. *(What do you do?)* Make a cup of tea. I don't got what to do. Should I scrub the floor? I got a day to scrub the floor. Or I start to think. Who I got to talk to? Maybe I feel better when I go in the home. *(Do you cry?)* No, I know where I am. I'm nowhere."

5. "Feeling. I don't feel that way too often but once in a while. I'm often happy just to be alone. But there comes a time when you'd like things to be just a little bit different. *(When, usually?)* No particular time. Just when I've had enough of being myself. *(Respondent laughs.)* It's a different life for me now. When I was north I was among my family but here, don't know too many people. Just my brother and his wife. And a few ladies I met on the patio this summer. But I don't make a habit of visiting with them. I don't like the gossip that goes around. In the summer I sit in the patio. It's beautiful there. But in the winter I stay up here in my room. Don't even visit in the lobby because it's too drafty there. *(When do you feel lonely?)* Go to sleep. Rest for an hour or so. It's so quiet here that I get tired of read-

ing and I take a little nap. I don't think that hurts anyone. *(What else?)* Nothing much. Sometimes I'll go to
the phone and call up someone and have a conversation
with them. That kind of eases up my loneliness a little."

Emotional States. Three dimensions were used to measure emotional state: feelings of well-being, hope, and the painful states of anxiety and depression. All three dimensions discriminated between the community and waiting-list samples.

An average score of 19.2 out of a possible 25 on the Life
Satisfaction Rating (Neugarten, Havighurst, and Tobin, 1961)
for the community sample reflected their relatively positive
feelings of well-being. The Life Satisfaction Rating (LSR) is
made up of five components: zest, resolution and fortitude,
congruence between desired and achieved goals, positive self-
concept, and morale. The mean of 15.8 for the waiting-list
group indicates a tendency toward apathy, condoning or passively accepting what life has brought, somewhat negative feelings about having accomplished what is regarded as important,
plus tendencies towards self-criticism, depression, bitterness, or
irritability. The difference in means was statistically significant
at the p = .0002 level.

As a variable of assessment, hope was defined as the "confident expectation of personally significant gratifying change in
that zone of experienced time which is the intermediate future"
(Haberland, 1972, p. 13). Defined in this way, hope is different
from and more inclusive than when conceptualized as the opposite of depression, which suggests a current emotion attached to
experience. A hope index was made up of seven components
considered to be critical to the concept: extension into the
future; past, present, or future time orientation; extent of
extension into the future; locus of control of one's own life;
current affective tone; expectation of gratifying change; and
purpose of life. These seven components of hope were tested
with a subsample of thirteen respondents on an intensive battery of instruments. A total hope score was then computed for
these thirteen respondents and scores from five measures (Srole
anomie scale, the interview time dimension, the Sentence Com-

pletion Test time dimension, willingness to experience, and self-esteem) in our standard interview were so weighted as to maximally correlate with the total hope score (e.g., the scores on the five tests were regressed against the criterion total hope score for the subsample of thirteen and the weights then used to derive a hope index composed of scores from five standard measures). On the hope index, the waiting-list sample struck a standardized mean of $-.09$, establishing the group as less hopeful than the community sample, which struck a mean of .7 ($p = .0002$).

States of anxiety and depression were assessed by the Gottschalk, Springer, and Gleser (1961) scoring system used for verbal responses but here applied to responses to the Sentence Completion Test. As with the measures of well-being and hope, the measures of anxiety and depression revealed important differences between the two samples. The waiting-list sample was decidedly more anxious and more depressed than the community sample ($p = .01$ and $.0001$, community means = 15.3 and 7.6, waiting-list means = 19.8 and 13.9, respectively).

Self-Perceptions. Two instruments were used to assess this area. The first was the Shanas Self-Care Inventory (Shanas, 1962) in which the respondent is asked how much difficulty he or she has in each of five daily activities: going out of doors, walking up and down stairs, getting about the house, washing and bathing, and dressing and putting on shoes. On this measure, a score of three is given to those activities the respondent feels he can manage only with difficulty. The range is 0 to 15. Both samples perceived little difficulty in their capacity for self-care (community mean = .8, waiting-list mean = 2.3).

The second instrument, the Self-Sort Task, was adapted from Leary (1957). It consists of 48 statements regarding relationships with others, from which respondents select those statements that they feel describe themselves. Usually about twenty were selected as self-descriptive. The respondent was then asked to give an example of each from his current everyday life.

For a self-esteem scale, each of the forty-eight items was weighted on a 5-point scale from +2 to -2 and the weights of the items selected by the respondent then summed up to give the self-esteem score. The mean score of 23.3 for the community sample reflected a rather high level of self-esteem (based on an average of twenty items selected and the possible weightings of each), whereas the mean score for the waiting list of 19.2, which was significantly lower than the mean for the community sample (p = .002), was interpreted to reflect a moderate level of self-esteem.

Another measure that employed data from the Self-Sort Task was adequacy of examples used to support the self-concept. Respondents were asked to illustrate how each item chosen as self-descriptive was characterized in present social interaction. Respondents varied in their ability or willingness to offer present examples. When examples were not stated in the present tense, they were either statements of conviction, examples from the past, statements of wish, or distortions of the present to fit the item. A weight was given to each of these five categories as to the appropriateness of the type of response for adequacy of present interaction to support the self-concept, and a summary score of adequacy was computed. Persons in the waiting-list sample, because they tended to use inappropriate or distorted examples to confirm a description of self, showed less adequacy than the examples offered by the community sample (p = .004). This difference suggests the relative inability of the aged persons on the waiting list to use present interaction as a means of self-definition.

The two major measures generated by the Self-Sort Task, however, are self-perceptions of dominance and affiliation in interactions with others. To tap these two self-perceptions, the forty-eight self-descriptive items were constructed in sets of six each to capture eight distinct styles of interacting (e.g., rebellious, aggressive, competitive, managerial, responsible, cooperative, self-effacing, and docile). In turn, from the number of items chosen for each of the eight different sets, two primary measures or dimensions were derived by arithmetic formulas: dominant-submissive and affiliative-hostile. Items reflecting dominance included: "I enjoy being in charge of things," "I am somewhat a dominating or bossy person," and "I frequently give advice to others." Items reflecting affiliation included: "I am a friendly person," "I am considerate of others," and "I am an affectionate and understanding person."

The aged persons in the community sample perceived themselves as more dominant in interaction than did the aged persons in the waiting-list sample (p = .05, community mean = .34, waiting-list mean = −.21). Stated another way, aged persons in the waiting-list sample perceived themselves as more submissive in interaction than their counterparts in the community sample. There was no difference, however, on the affiliative-hostile dimension (community mean = .08, waiting-list mean = .16).

Clearly the waiting-list and community samples were quite different in all four areas of psychological functioning: cognitive functioning, affective responsiveness, emotional state, and self-perception.

Contrast: Waiting-List and Institutionalized Samples. The institutionalized sample of 37 individuals was drawn from a pool of 141 aged who had lived in the institution from 1 to 3 years. Residents of less than 1 year were excluded to control for initial effects of institutionalization. Selecting residents who had lived in the institution at least 1 year biased the sample toward the more adequate old person; the less adequate residents would have died or become moribund. The upper limit of 3 years after institutionalization was chosen to increase the comparability of the age range with the other samples. All those who were included in the institutional sample were able to speak English and had not grossly deteriorated since admission.

The contrast between the waiting-list sample and this sample of 37 aged who had lived in the homes for 1 to 3 years was muted, as shown in tables 3 and 4. Differences that did occur generally support a view that the status of the institutionalized sample was better. The institutionalized sample showed less cognitive dysfunctioning, less constriction in emotional responsiveness, less anxiety, more use of current examples for self-definition, and greater feelings of dominance in self-other interaction. To what extent their better status reflected an ameliorative effect for those waiting-list people who would eventually

76   *Last Home for the Aged*

Table 4. A Comparison of the Waiting-List and Institutional Samples

Area of Psychological Functioning	Waiting-List Sample (N = 100)	Institutional Sample (N = 37)
Cognitive functioning	Constriction: minimal disorientation and disorganization[a]	Less constriction: slight disorientation and disorganization[a]
Affective responsiveness	Constriction in emotional responsiveness[b]	Less constriction in emotional responsiveness[b]
Emotional state	Moderate feelings of well-being	Moderate feelings of well-being
	Limited hopefulness	Limited hopefulness
	Anxiety[a] and depression	Less anxiety but equal depression[a]
Self-perception	Perception of adequacy in self-care	Perception of adequacy in self-care
	High self-esteem	High self-esteem
	Adequacy—much distortion and conviction used in maintenance of self-concept[a]	Greater adequacy—much distortion, but also the present used for maintenance of self-concept[a]
	Feelings of diminished dominance,[a] but not of affiliation	Feelings of more dominance and the same affiliation[a]

[a] $p \leqslant .05$
[b] $p \leqslant .01$

surmount the process of entering and living in the homes could not be measured. We will return to this issue in Chapter Four when we discuss changes for the study sample through the first year after admission.

The Two Contrasts. When the contrasts between the waiting-list sample and the other two samples—the community residents and the long-term institutionalized—were considered together, it became clear that the waiting-list sample was more like the institutionalized sample. These two samples—the waiting list and the institutionalized—were not only quite similar to each other but also very different from the community sample. Although the waiting-list sample was not yet an institutionalized group, and lived in environmental contexts similar to the community sample, the waiting-list sample was indeed decidedly different from the community sample. Stated another way, despite the similarity of environments, respondents on the waiting list differed markedly from respondents in the community sample and, to be explicit, *most of the psychological qualities attributed to the adverse effects of entering and living in an institution were already present in people on the waiting list.*

The aged residents-to-be were cognitively constricted, encompassing a slight disorientation in time and place revealed by errors on the Mental Status Questionnaire and a moderate degree of cognitive disorganization as reflected in deficiencies in organization when telling stories to the TAT cards and in copying the Bender Gestalt Test figures. The overall pattern was more suggestive of a constriction in response to the external environment than of a disorientation or disorganization in response.

There was also a constriction in affective responsiveness. In responding to the TAT, for example, respondents showed a blandness, a sparse expression of affect. Similarly, there was an unwillingness to introspect on inner feelings. The evidence is that there were intensely felt affects but that respondents emphasized containing the experience and expression of feelings.

Feelings of well-being lay only in the moderate range, with a tendency toward low feelings of life satisfaction. There were also limited feelings of hope and when expectations regarding the future were expressed they were narrowly focused on the impending event of entering and living in the home. Generally, respondents were anxious and depressed.

The perception of self-care capacities for elderly people on the waiting list was of minimal inadequacies such as difficulty in ambulation or taking a bath. In general, however, waiting-list aged people perceived themselves as rather adequate except for needing some prosthetic help, a cane or hand rail, whereas others felt they needed a helping person. Self-esteem, the perception of self as a meaningful and important person, was maintained at a reasonably high level. These findings suggested that those events that caused anxiety and guilt were not interpreted as deficiencies and inadequacies in oneself. In maintaining an integrity of self-definition, however, there was distortion of the current context, as reflected in the examples given to items selected as self-descriptive, where the waiting-list person often offered an example that did not at all support the sense of the item selected. Apparently, the interpersonal world of the waiting-list person was not perceived as containing interactions that were supportive of self-definition. Furthermore, the perceptions of self in relation to others were characterized by diminished feelings of potency and by feelings of affiliation or closeness to others.

Conclusion. If the waiting-list sample had not been available and a contrast had been made only between the community and institutional samples, then the many differences between these two samples would have been attributed to the deleterious effect of the institutional environment itself. The differences, however, between the sample awaiting admission and the community sample suggests that the decision to become a waiting-list person was associated with the negative effects usually attributed to entering and living in the institutional environment. Indeed, the psychological status during the anticipatory institutionalization phase resembled that of the aged already institutionalized. Possibly effects formerly attributed to responses to living in an institutional environment may more aptly be attributed to responses to situations that precede admission. The psychological status of the resident-to-be reflected the interaction between the meaning of past events and future events. The waiting-list aged person was indeed in a transitional phase, having applied to become an institutionalized aged person and awaiting admission to the institution.

From Predecision to the Anticipatory Phase: Three Case Studies

Three case studies will be used as a vehicle for understanding the psychology of the first phase of the institutionalization process—the transition from living independently in the community to being on the waiting list, awaiting admission to the institution. These three elderly women were interviewed twice as respondents in the community sample over a 6-month interval.

At the time of the 6-month follow-up interview, the three women were still living independently in the community and had not reached a decision to seek institutional care. All three applied for admission, however, after this second interview, one a few weeks later and the other two approximately 6 months later. Each was accepted for admission and placed on the waiting list.

These cases help explain several meanings that attach to becoming an institutionalized aged person, and are particularly appropriate for revealing issues of separation from family members and attitudes toward the home. For all three of these women, both issues were important. The interviews reveal not only the importance of these issues, but also how differently each woman dealt with them during the process.

The three cases appear to be typical of both the experimental and the community control samples. Each woman had experienced personal changes in functioning and had family members with whom they had frequent contact and who felt a responsibility for their well-being. All were aware of the likelihood of being accepted to the home if an application was made. They were familiar with the homes, usually because they had visited friends or relatives who had been residents. While the three women were typical in these and other ways of the larger sample of 85 that were followed from pre- to postadmission, as individuals, they were, of course, unique. Reconstructions of their past life have been included to highlight these individual differences.

Mrs. A.—"I'm a Busy Lady." When first interviewed in the community a year before she applied to a home, Mrs. A. was 77 years old. She was described as about 5 feet, 3 inches tall, somewhat heavy, with flabby arms and a protruberant abdomen. Of dark olive complexion, her face was somewhat pallid and sufficiently heavily lined to suggest that she was recovering from an illness. She spoke rather rapidly and with a slight accent. She spoke seriously, and she expressed her feelings strongly, but with good emotional control.

Her physical capacity and appearance was marked by the aftereffects of a right-hemisphere stroke 6 years earlier that left her left hand and foot minimally functional. Because she walked with a cane and with a slight turning of the left foot, which she dragged along the ground, her left shoe was scraped on both the toe and the inner side. While she had the capacity to grasp with her left hand, the grasp was weak and she had lost her capacity for fine finger movements. In addition to the stroke, she had had rectal surgery a year prior to the first interview. Her condition had worsened since the surgery, and her doctor had suggested further surgery. She questioned the advisability of such surgery because of her age: "Thank God I'm able to take care of myself." She watched her diet and took Orinase to abate a tendency toward diabetes. She also reported some trouble with her eyesight: "The doctor said I'm getting a cataract." Yet she felt her health was about the same as others: "It depends. A lot are sicker. Some better. Maybe I'm like most. The doctor says he gave me another 25 years, my heart is so strong." Six months later, still before application, when interviewed again, she was better able to walk with her cane, but often had to ask others to help her to cross busy streets.

Mrs. A. was described by the interviewer as extremely friendly, outgoing, warm, pleasant, and alert: "She has a real gift for gab and she loves to tell about her marvelous family, a trip she hopes to take, and so forth." She did show a great deal of depressive affect, however, when talking about her husband's death, which had occurred a year before. She felt that she needed to make a real effort to keep busy and active so that she did not become depressed. She expressed an admirable resoluteness and fortitude in confronting of present and past adversities. In the words of the interviewer, "She has a philosophical outlook toward life."

At the time of the first interview, she lived alone in an apartment hotel that was close to many facilities and was doing her own shopping. She had lived in this apartment for only a few months, having recently come from a western city where she had lived with her husband before his death. The apartment was furnished very tastefully and she filled it with many personal objects, valentines that she had received, and many pictures of her children and grandchildren. Before moving to the

Midwest, a niece had written to her about a convalescent home near the apartment. There had been debate among family members as to whether she should move into the convalescent home or a home for the aged, but when she stated her preference to set up her own apartment, her son and daughter-in-law located one and she moved. A sister, 5 years older, to whom she was very attached, lived nearby and visited her every weekend. They frequently got together to go to meetings. Neither, however, wanted to live with the other: "My love for her is great and I want it to remain that way." Mrs. A. was financially independent and able to maintain this independent living arrangement because she had made good investments.

Her daily schedule was to get up at about 8:00 in the morning, eat breakfast and do her daily chores of shopping, washing and ironing. Television watching was a prominent activity in her day, especially watching the news. In the afternoon, she often rested, but was quick to add: "I'm a busy lady; I belong to three clubs. Two have weekly meetings, one meets monthly." She commented that she always had something to do: telephoning her friends or they her; spending weekends with her sister; and visiting her son every Friday night. She received quite a bit of mail, which she enjoyed reading, and wrote many letters to assure the flow of correspondence.

Her relationship with all of her four children seemed very close. She displayed many pictures of her children, grandchildren, and great grandchildren and kept close tabs on what was happening in each of their lives, especially those relatives living near where she currently lived—one married daughter and a married son as well as eight grandchildren and two great-grandchildren. Her children were very attentive and she was very satisfied with how they had turned out and with her relationship with them. She said that she always consulted with her children. She indicated that she "lives to enjoy their marriages and graduations." Because these occasions were very important to her, she was making plans to attend family events in faraway states. In her own words: "The most important thing in my life is to see my children happy."

Memories of her early life were generally warm ones: "Our

family was an outstanding family in our town (a small village in Rumania). Everybody used to know us. We were well thought of." Her mother had eighteen children, eleven of whom died in various types of epidemics, and her mother had suffered because of these losses. Because Mrs. A. was very good at arithmetic in school, "They put me to work at 11 years as a cashier in my brother's wine and liquor store. I used to be in the store all the time. They knew they could depend on me. My brother was fond of me, but he took advantage of me and worked me 7 days a week. There were no high schools for girls in our town." Her resentment continued to gain expression when she discussed how her father could not afford to send her to a different town to go to high school and would not let her go to a music conservatory to study singing in another town, although family friends had suggested that they would sponsor her, because he was afraid something might happen to her. Busy in the store all the time, she did not have any friends as a teen-ager: "I didn't like my work, but you swallowed everything. In those days, you had to respect your elders."

Mrs. A. described her childhood home as a happy one. There were no quarrels between parents or between brothers and sisters; she described her father as a gentle man, religious but modern, with many friends; her mother as a plain, good woman, rather strict in her religion, always busy taking care of her children and her kitchen. After her mother's death, Mrs. A. emigrated to the United States and worked for a large retail clothing firm, sewing garments for $3.00 a week. Somewhat later, she worked in a costume jewelry factory for $5.00 a week. She lived with her sister and her sister's husband until she married her first husband, with whom she had two children. He became sick in the flu epidemic after World War I: "He had such a high fever, he didn't know what he was doing. Walked over to the window and he either jumped or fell." She then went back to live with her sister and her sister's family, but this did not work out. She later married a divorced man with a sickly daughter, but she did not marry for love and felt rather sad about it. Rather, she married him because he could be a father to her children, and he was a good father: "So we raised the children well, and they respected us. We never fought, nor did they." The family worked together in their own delicatessen, "all week, many hours." She characterized her life as a hard one, but felt that she had been able to withstand the difficulties that she encountered.

The interviewers saw Mrs. A. as a very admirable person who had taken the vicissitudes of life in stride and who felt that she had been successful. She felt that she had worked hard all her life, but had reaped the rewards of these efforts. The rewards, that she now took as given, were the warm and intimate relationships with her children, her grandchildren, and her sister. She had been able to make many new friends in the various social clubs in the neighborhood despite having moved there recently from another city.

Two events occurred that were to change this picture. Her sister, with whom she was very close, died. While only 5 years older than she, Mrs. A. thought of her sister as much like a mother: "Her death upsets me very much. She was like a mother to me. I always used to talk things over with her. She used to advise me." Although she said she felt that "nothing really matters," after the loss of her sister, she continued to have a warm and close relationship with her family. She had visited her daughter in a faraway state for a few months during the past year, and was planning to return there for her grandson's graduation the following year. Shortly after the death of her sister, she had undergone serious rectal surgery, which further increased her feelings of "nothing really matters." In spite of being in mourning for her beloved sister and close companion, the surgery went remarkably well and she recovered quite quickly.

Because she was depressed while recuperating from the surgery, the family suggested that she apply to an old-age home, and that in the interim she stay in a convalescent home. Nevertheless, she went back to her apartment and indicated that she was rather pleased with this decision. Finally, however, at the insistence of the children, she applied to the home and went to the convalescent home while awaiting admission. When interviewed at the convalescent home, she indicated that she now

stayed indoors most of the time, because with her "poor eyesight" she did not feel comfortable walking outside alone. She
would have liked to continue to attend meetings and to visit
friends, but these activities were not as available to her as before. Now she spent more time watching television, listening to
the radio, and trying to do some reading. Since her eyesight had
become worse, she said that she was unable to write letters and
that she did not get as many in return. While she used her visual
difficulty to explain her inability to move around and the need
to be in the home, it was clear that she was still reasonably
mobile and active. Her personal assessment: "Compared to
some, I'm a giant. I'm not in pain. It's just that I'm a little
weary, but that's my age. Just like a car wears out, people do."

What were the changes in Mrs. A.'s psychological functioning? Generally, her mood was marked by optimism. She looked
forward to going to the old-age home, both for the activities
and the people and "to be settled." Since her sister had died,
she had been very upset. She saw living in the convalescent
home as a transitional period before entering the old-age home.
There was a certain amount of realism in her expectations about
her future in the home. In the words of the interviewer, "She
knows what the score is."

On the other hand, adverse changes were -noted in three
areas from pre- to postapplication: cognition, affective responsiveness, and emotional life, particularly with respect to anxiety
and depression. While Mrs. A. remained lucid and oriented in
time and place she was beginning to have problems with her
memory for recent events. In the second interview she was less
able than in the first to remember at what ages she went to various places or to recapture the dates of her more recent trips. On
the Mental Status Questionnaire, the deficit was reflected in
errors in identifying the present month and in recalling the year
that she was born. While she continued to be warm, friendly,
and gregarious, she also seemed to be less responsive to her environment. Before application, she showed great sensitivity to her
own feelings and was quite willing to introspect about a range
of feelings, such as loneliness, sadness, and pride. But after
application, she was less willing to do so and exhibited obvious
preoccupation with the losses that she had incurred.

Her responses to many of the items in the Sentence Completion Test (SCT) changed markedly from the "predecision" to the anticipatory institutionalization phase. The shift was toward feelings of loneliness, loss of significant others, and wish for greater interpersonal intimacy. The shift toward feelings of loneliness is reflected quite poignantly in responses to two items. Before admission she completed the item "There are times when I . . ." with "feel a little depressed according to my present condition of losing my husband with whom I spent 44 years in harmony and peace" and after admission with "feel *very* lonesome!"; and the item "Time is . . .", before admission, with "the way you want to make it" but after admission with "sometimes very long when you are alone." The loss of others is found in the completions of the item "Brothers and sisters. . . .", which was completed before admission with "we always got along wonderful" and afterwards with "I haven't got any, they are all gone." In relation to intimacy, before admission she completed the item "If I had my way . . ." with "I would do volunteer work" and after admission with "I would see my children." Similarly before admission she completed the item "Each day . . ." with "I thank God for all my blessings" and afterwards with "I'm waiting for calls from my children which I do get."

These shifts in completions of so many of the 32 SCT items resulted in an increase both in SCT anxiety and SCT depression, apparently related to her feelings of abandonment. The shift is congruent with the impression that Mrs. A. suffered a protracted period of mourning that began with the loss of her husband 2 years prior to her application for institutionalization and was exacerbated by the death of her sister. In those 2 years she lost the two most important persons in her life, both of whom had helped sustain her independence through her eighth decade of life. Her children had not become replacements for her husband and sister, although she could depend on them for emotional support. With institutionalization impending, the form this support would take was now in doubt and she was apprehensive regarding what form her relationship with her children would take after she entered the home.

Mrs. B.—"They Call Me the Sunshine Lady." Mrs. B., a

79-year-old widow, was described as a short woman, about 5 feet, 1 inch in height, a little heavy through the middle, tense and hyperactive, with bright dark eyes and a very alert appearance. Her grey hair was short and fixed rather attractively. The skin of her face was unwrinkled, she dressed tastefully and wore costume jewelry and makeup. She appeared to the interviewer to be no more than 60 years old. Her voice was deep, vibrant, and commanding. She smiled easily and responded very well to encouragement.

Mrs. B. had had a heart attack about 7 years earlier and had been under a doctor's care ever since, living, as she said, "on the careful side." In spite of the heart attack, she was able to get out, though she had some difficulty with stairs. The year before, she had had a black-out, which she attributed to "eating something or taking too many pills," and was now taking phenobarbitol three times daily and sleeping pills at bedtime. Excitement had to be avoided so that she would not aggravate her "female problem": "The vagina feels like a revolving machine. It started eight years after my husband had passed away." He had died sixteen years earlier. "One in a million, and I happen to be the one." Although she wore bifocals, she had little difficulty in seeing. Her hearing was excellent. Absolutely refusing to compare her health to others, she obviously felt superior in many ways. On the other hand, she was very concerned about her body and emphasized not overdoing things. She was especially concerned about the sensations in her vagina, had a great deal of anxiety about becoming sick and dying, and mentioned that she "has had dreams of dying."

She was, to say the least, rather narcissistic: "I'm great. Other people say so. I want you to admire me too. I've given so much of myself." The interviewer said that "she gives affect easily"; and that she usually spoke as though dictating. She selected her words carefully and tried to make an impressive reply. Frequently, in a rather compulsive manner, she brushed off or picked up specks that to the interviewer appeared invisible. On one occasion, the interviewer commented: "She is a gracious and alert old woman who really has a pretty good defense system and is functioning well." At that time her defenses were indeed working, as reflected in the interviewer's assessment of her overt feelings of well-being, using the Life Satisfaction Rating System: "She is enthusiastic about many of her activities and about her interpersonal relationships; in general, she feels she has done a good job of directing her own life and influencing those close to her; she feels she had to sacrifice herself to some extent in the interest of her family, but feels that they have come through; and overtly she thinks she is pretty great and that other people think well of her."

Mrs. B. lived in an efficiency suite in an apartment hotel by herself, having lived alone, either there or elsewhere, since her husband's death. Other arrangements had not entered her mind: "I'll continue to do what I've been doing. I'm satisfied with my way of living and hope to continue this way for many years, since I'm not obligated to anyone and I'm not a burden to my family." Fortunately, she was financially secure because she had invested wisely and could maintain this autonomous, somewhat luxurious living.

Mrs. B. was indeed a very active lady: "Time doesn't mean anything to me. If I'm tired, I go to bed at 6:00 or 8:00. I get up at 8:00, bathe, have a little breakfast, and then sleep for a couple of more hours. On Monday, Tuesday, and Thursday, I attend the senior groups from 11:30 to 3:30. I rest after that, and I may go out to supper, then back to rest. I read the paper every day and listen to the news." She apparently played cards a great deal, and was out with her daughter on Fridays and often on Sundays. She wrote letters to her son regularly, and also to grandchildren, always remembering important occasions: "God blessed me with a wonderful family, so in case I should ever need help of any kind, every hand of my loving ones would be extended out to me."

She visited the daughter with whom she was very close, at least one day a week, and usually more often. She made sure to talk to the daughter on the phone every day, and she expected her two sons in other cities to celebrate her upcoming eightieth birthday with her. She wrote regularly to her sons or grandchildren: "I never forget their birthdays or anniversaries." Of her participation in the senior centers, where she holds two elected offices, she said: "It brings me in contact with all people. They call me the *sunshine lady*! I'm always filled with kindness. I enjoy my clubs immensely and I enjoy my friends immensely."

Mrs. B. was 1 year old when she came from Poland with her parents. Her father was in the jewelry business, and because he did fairly well they owned their own home. Her mother thought it was very important for a girl to learn to keep house and particularly to be a good housekeeper: "She taught me to be the way I am today. ' Mrs. B. was a good student, went to a local music college when she was 8 or 9 and "regrets that I did not keep up my piano playing," although she did teach piano later in her life. She describes a happy atmosphere in the family and was quite close to three older brothers: "My parents taught us right from wrong. The house was an open house to everybody. My parents had lots of friends and so did we children."

She described her childhood as a very healthy and happy one. She married when she was 16 and her husband 22, after her mother encouraged her to marry this attractive man whom she looked on more as a father than as a husband. When her father died in 1928, leaving three jewelry stores, her husband, who had been a tailor, went into the jewelry business and was successful until urban reconstruction removed the store. Afterwards, he returned to tailoring. Of her part in his work she said: "He didn't have time to visit with the customers. I met them all; they came to me with their troubles." She also managed the house and the children.

After Mrs. B.'s husband died, she went to live with her daughter and her daughter's husband. She said, however, that her daughter's husband "got nervous because I was always picking something up. He suggested I look for an apartment of my own. That was okay for a while, but then I had a heart attack." She had lived with her daughter and son-in-law for eight years before she moved into her own apartment where, 1 year later and 7 years prior to the first interview, she had a heart attack.

She had raised four children and described herself as a dedicated mother. This description was consistent with her descriptions of her adequacy, if not superiority, in every role area. Her descriptions of her husband were equally positive: "My husband was a wonderful person; intelligent, self-educated, read and read, very good in considering of others." Her children were also described in glowing praise. They were always wonderful to her, although obviously her son-in-law had not acted so and did ask her to leave their house and to live independently.

At this time, when asked her attitudes toward the home, she said that she had visited the home and that it was: "Beautiful! But not for me! Never! I like my way of living. I live by myself so as not to be obliged to children." In describing the activities of the senior group, she said: "Last week we went to the home and since then I've really counted my blessings."

One year after this interview, she was hospitalized because she "took too many pills for my female condition." She stayed with her daughter for a short time after her discharge from a psychiatric hospital but "I knew I was a burden to her, so I decided to come here [a local nursing home] because I needed constant supervision." When, 9 months after Mrs. B. had been hospitalized for taking too many pills, the interviewer asked her what room she was in, she said: "Oh, I don't have to tell you that. Just ask anybody around here. They all know me." Mrs. B. was still the sunshine lady.

When interviewed in the nursing home, she said: "I feel great changes have come over me since I'm not burdened with housekeeping. I feel much better and look much better." In general, there was a remarkable consistency in her activities while remaining in the nursing home awaiting admission to the home for the aged: "My activities here, and people here, are enough for me." She visited the day care center at the home for the aged once a week as she awaited admission. As before, she went out with her daughter on Sunday and Friday evenings. While she tended to continue her activity pattern, she placed greater emphasis on getting enough rest. She continued to correspond with the family, as earlier, but did not play cards as much as she used to: "I find more pleasure in the little things."

What had happened to change things in the life of Mrs. B.? She said: "I had taken too many pills for my female condition."

The record at the home revealed, however, that she had made a
suicidal gesture. This gesture was successful to the extent that
her daughter let her back into her house. But, again, there was a
rupture in the relationship with her daughter and son-in-law and
according to Mrs. B.: "I knew I was causing her lots of trouble.
She said it would be better for all of us if I went to the nursing
home, and I have made a speedy recovery. My female trouble
bothered me, so I took too much medicine to relieve it and I
just passed out. I couldn't eat and I couldn't sleep."

For this lady, who had hysterical conversion symptoms in
her vagina, there had been a decompensation. When first seen,
she was rather compensated, being able to maintain a sense of
being loved by all. Was there any specific precipitating event
leading to her greater feelings of anxiety regarding death and
dissolution? Was there a single critical incident? Or, on the
other hand, did she become overwhelmed as internal pressures
built up over time? If so, why, after 7 years, was there now a
rather sudden change and a need on her part for a further
rapprochement with the daughter? We do not know. More clear,
however, are the sequellae to the decompensation that had
brought her in a convalescent home waiting for admission to a
permanent home. From her interview data, it is clear that her
feelings of well-being declined; she was much less zestful; she
blamed herself for what has befallen her; and she had increased
anxiety and depression. While these decrements were related in
part to regrets about the past, they were more related to separation from her daughter. A year earlier, she had said that, for any
aged person, entering the home was a final separation from
community and family.

Her feelings of separation when on the waiting list are
expressed in the shift in her reports of her earliest memory.
When interviewed in the community, she said her earliest
memory was: "I remember as a child that my father was very
fond of cards, and that when the family would get together
they would spend their time playing, which I myself resented
very much even after I had been married. I resented my husband and his brothers playing cards. They would get together
and play cards. But an apple doesn't fall very far from the tree,

and I do now indulge, but not too often." When asked for her earliest memory when on the waiting list, her response had a rather different flavor: "I was a child of about twelve. I went to visit my mother's friend who had asked me to spend the night with her. I was miserable when I got there, really homesick for my mother, I couldn't sleep all night. My mother's friend had to take me home at about 5:00 in the morning. I guess I was pretty attached to my mother to be so homesick." This report-age captures her preoccupation with feelings of separation from a caretaking other, specifically her mother. There is a shift from a preapplication narcissistic preoccupation with the attention of men toward a regressive wish, when on the waiting list, to rein-state a lost attachment to mother.

This shift toward feelings of separation was also mani-fested when Mrs. B. was asked to name people who might act as resources in eleven different areas. Before application, Mrs. B. listed one or more persons for all eleven areas, but when on the waiting list she could not list a person in five of the eleven areas. She now felt she could depend on her friends to respond to her as they had formerly.

Another perspective on how she was coping with the feel-ings of separation and abandonment is apparent from her expectations regarding the home. Of the nursing home that she was in temporarily, she said: "I'm happy here and I hope to have the same results when I'm a resident at the home. I don't expect much there, only to give a little and take a little. I can-not live in a selfish world and be isolated from everyone else. If you are surrounded by people, then you have hope. You believe you will find someone you enjoy being with. I hope that will be the situation for me the rest of my life. I won't participate in all of the activities of the home. Not all, but some. Only when I'm able to." When asked why she had applied, she responded: "I'd mentioned to my daughter before I came here that I'd hoped that the home would be my home. I would want to go there in order not to be a burden to her. My daughter was pleased. She put in my application when I was so ill." She could not face her former feelings about how delighted she was that she would not have to give in to her feelings of illness and deterioration and could live independently in the community. The home was at that point perceived as a last resort. Now that there had been a change in relationship with the daughter and that there was no other alternative for her, she had to rationalize that it was really something that she was doing for her daughter.

Mrs. C.—"I Want People."   Mrs. C. was a 76-year-old, twice-widowed woman of large frame who carried herself well and appeared about 5 feet, 7 inches tall and 150 pounds. Her face had a rather long shape, with brown hair and hazel eyes. She dressed simply, without makeup or jewelry, but was well-groomed. Her English was poor but she understood most of what the interviewers discussed with her. There was a bluntness and directness in her communication, and her emotional control was excellent as she reported the incidents in her life. Her voice was crisp. She did not smile frequently, but tended to have a fixed and taciturn expression on her face. In general, she gave the impression that she was somewhat suspicious of others, especially of the stranger who had come to interview her.

Although her hands trembled slightly when she rested them on her lap, she had no serious complaints of any kind regarding her health, and prided herself on her good health. Her health was very important to her, and she prayed that she would keep well. She was able to get about, either walking or traveling by bus, was careful that "nothing should happen to me," and felt that her health was better than that of others.

She was a lucid and well-organized woman who was very straightforward in her responses, while often seeming stand-offish. She said of herself: "I don't think she actually likes people too much." Generally a passive woman, she said that she liked to be with people, but apparently has no close relationships. Her wish, it appeared, was to be *among* people rather than *with* people in intimate relationship.

Although passively accepting what life brought, she had felt a great sense of responsibility for her children after her husband died. She was unable to articulate clearly her expectations from life and now felt that if she could just hold her own, everything would be fine. Her opinion of herself seemed good, but she was preoccupied with what would become of her in the future. As judged by the interviewers, she had only a moderate feeling of well-being.

For the last 9 years she had lived with a widowed friend whom she has known for many years. When Mrs. C. had learned, a few years previously, that her friend was looking for someone to live with and to share expenses, she asked if she could move in with her. Mrs. C. had her own bedroom, her own cupboard in the kitchen for groceries, and also her own pots, pans, and dishes, although the furniture belonged to her friend. Of this arrangement she said: "I'm too old. I'm happy here. I got my own pots and dishes for myself." This response was very characteristic of the straightforward, factual answers that she gave to inquiries. The living arrangement was one permitted by her limited financial resources: she was on old-age assistance, had no income from investments, and received minimal financial help from her married daughter and married son. By the time of the second interview, she was experiencing problems with her roommate, who had recently been quite ill with arthritis. Of more importance was that the roommate's hearing, which was poor to begin with, had worsened and this change had placed quite a strain on Mrs. C. Because she was now less able to carry on a conversation with her roommate, she was becoming progressively more "nervous." She wanted to move, but felt that she could not do that to her friend.

Mrs. C. got up at 9:00 a.m. "Why hurry to get up?" she reasoned. She cooked breakfast, read, watched television, and walked a little. She cooked all her meals and she enjoyed shopping for groceries; did some visiting with the lady next door and, of course, spent much time with her apartment-mate. She went to a senior group meeting once a week and spent the day very leisurely, but because of limited funds could not afford to go to the summer camp for seniors. Only occasionally did she go with her family to a movie or to their house, if they came to pick her up, but generally relationships with her family were cordial. Two married sons lived in the metropolitan area, and a married daughter in a neighboring state. One son called every Saturday and the daughter called every Sunday. Occasionally she babysat with the son's child and was pleased to be included with the married children whenever they had special celebrations. Although face-to-face contact with her children was limited and rather sporadic, she felt that she was not alone: "I feel I got somebody."

She had very few social contacts, although she repeatedly stated that she liked to be with people. When she discussed visiting with friends, she was vehement in her disapproval of other people she knew who "visit others just to get something to eat." She was very concerned about being dependent or being looked on as someone who was manipulative. The general impression was of an elderly woman who wanted to maintain a distance from other people and who possibly did not establish intimate relationships. She did, however, show a continued allegiance to her roommate.

Mrs. C. was born in Russia and talked about how poor life had been for her family. She was 19 when she came to the United States with her mother, her father having died by then. Her mother's sister sent money for tickets. Because she had no education when she came here she worked in a factory sewing underwear. At 20, she married, and was only married 3 years when her husband died, leaving her with a 1-year-old daughter. Three years later she married again and remained married for 25 years until her second husband died. She lived with her mother after her first husband's death; her mother took care of the baby while Mrs. C. worked. She recalled how she took care of her mother in return when the mother was dying of cancer.

Of her married life, she said: "I had a good life with my second husband." She had two boys and considered her husband a good father. Later he became ill: "He became paralyzed and wouldn't let me out, even on the back porch. He was jealous, and thought I would find another man and leave him. He was a terrible sick man." After he had died, she lived with one son until he married.

Her view at this point toward the old-age home was somewhat positive. Her second husband had been in the home for about a year before he had passed on, and she used to visit him: "It is a nice home. They invited us [senior group] to visit. I had lunch there. They improved it. It is very nice." But then she added: "I'm happy here! I don't want a home *for me!*"

The significant change that had occurred was the further deterioration in the physical condition of her roommate, which made Mrs. C. "nervous": "She never talks and she can't hear. I want to be with people." An application was made to the home when it was necessary to make a change in living arrangements. Mrs. C. continued to live with her roommate while awaiting admission. There was no change in her relationship with her children, nor with the club, nor in her social round of activities. Physically, there had been no apparent change. She mentioned she had trouble with one of her legs and tended to sit down more, but she was still able to take public transportation and to walk around. She still felt that her health was very good. Another factor, beside the changes in her roommate, related to application to the home, was the financial security it offered. In making a new living arrangement she did not have the option of spending more money for rent, nor could she consider living alone. Her main reason for applying was to "be with people." She wanted to be with people of her own age in her remaining years. She had met several people from the home and from her perspective the home was a positive alternative: "I want to be with people so I won't be alone. I get along with everyone. People like me. I won't insult anyone."

Mrs. C. was a rather simple person who was concerned about financial security, about being alone if she were to deteriorate, and about relief of loneliness. Although before application she had said that the home was not where she would choose to go, when confronted with the need to make a change she saw no other alternative. Clearly, she had not had the type of relationship with her children in which she or they would expect them to take her into their homes. Clearly, she wanted to maintain their care and concern, but like most aged persons she did not want the closer contact that might bring her into conflict with them. Her life was one of avoidance of conflict, of being pleasant. Her hope was to meet one or more people to whom she could relate pleasantly.

There was great consistency in her psychological status from the community interviews to the waiting-list interview. One change was evident: that of a feeling of greater loneliness as her roommate progressively deteriorated. On the other hand, there was a slight lessening of the anxiety related to the need to change her living arrangements. For her, the home represented less a source of medical care and more a place where she could form one or more close attachments and feel financially secure.

Some Forces at Work

These three case histories are intended to dramatize how clearly the typical institutional portrait is in evidence before admission, that the effects of the actual impact of institutionalization may have been exaggerated in the literature, and that the significant transition in terms of "effects" may be from the community to the waiting list, from the time of application to acceptance for admission to an institution.

The histories reported in this chapter demonstrate factors that evoke changes present before the actual living in the institution. For each of these three elderly women, there had been a different precipitant to application to a home for the aged. For Mrs. A., it had been primarily the loss of the sister with whom she was very very close, with the additional event of surgery that necessitated a period of convalescence. Perhaps, because both events occurred about a year after her husband's death, she was left feeling depleted and, therefore, with the feeling that she was not able to manage in her independent living. For Mrs. A., there seemed to be an accumulation of events that overtaxed the strong residual capacity reflected in her quick recovery from surgery. Her family had played an active role in the transition to the home, having suggested it as a possibility when she first moved from California.

For Mrs. B., the precipitating event appears to be the suicide gesture, which may have been related to increased anxiety over her own aging. There was evidence of rather severe psychopathology, probably of a life-long nature, that had now taken the form of hysterical symptoms that were largely focused on vaginal sensations. Her suicidal gesture did not bring her the sought-for rapproachement with her daughter and the home then became the protective environment that she sought to resolve her intrapsychic conflicts.

For Mrs. C., deterioration in her roommate necessitated a change in her living arrangements. With lessened financial resources and a need to be with other people, the home appeared to be a suitable resolution. Her family played a more passive role than did the families of the other two women in this decision.

Attitude Changes. The case histories of these elderly women document the change in attitudes toward becoming a resident in a home for the aged during the transition from a predecision phase while living independently in the community through the waiting-list anticipatory phase.

Mrs. A., prior to the decision, resisted the urging of her family to enter an institution. After the decision, while on the waiting list, she began to look forward to the activities and people in the home. Although she now wanted to be settled in the home, she continued to have the appropriate apprehension. A realistic woman, she rarely denied the losses of freedom and privacy she would experience in entering the home. In the words of the interviewer, "She knows what the score is." Perceiving no other alternative, she had a resolute and realistic attitude, albeit a fatalistic one.

For Mrs. B., prior to the decision when she was living independently in the community, the home was, in the abstract, unrealistically beautiful, but personally she felt quite unattracted to it: "But not for me! Never! I like my way of living. I live by myself so as not to be obliged to children . . . . Last week we went to the home and I've really counted my blessings." When on the waiting list after the decision had been made, and living in a transitional convalescent home, she stated:

> *My activities here, and people here are enough for me . . . . I find more pleasure in the little things . . . . I'm happy here and I hope to have the same results when I'm a resident at the home. I don't expect much, only to give a little and take a little. I cannot live in a selfish world and be isolated from everyone else. If you are surrounded by people then you have hope. You believe you will find someone*

you enjoy being with. I hope that will be the situa-
tion with me for the rest of my life. I won't partici-
pate in all of the activities of the home. Not all, but
some. Only when I'm able to . . . . I mentioned to my
daughter that I'd hope that the home would be my
home. I would consent to go there in order not to be
a burden to her. My daughter was pleased. She put in
my application when I was so ill.

Mrs. B. had become the type of person that she had feared
becoming because she had lost her independence and needed
the home. Slightly disguised, but clearly conveyed in her re-
marks is her resentment of selfish others. She alludes to her
daughter who will not take her back, and implies a precon-
scious, frightening knowledge that others in the home, occupied
with their own problems, will not respond to her as the "sunshine lady." Her worst fears of becoming old and ill, of being
abandoned, have become a reality. She will enter the home with
a stiff upper lip, determination, and the ready and appropriate
rationalization for her abandonment that she "will not be a burden" to the daughter who is the covert object of her rage.

Mrs. C. is a rare applicant, in that, having had a husband
who was in the home, she had an unusually positive attitude
before application. "It is a nice home. They invite us [senior
group] to visit. I had lunch there. They improved it. It is very
nice." She had added, however: "I am happy here! I don't want
a home *for me*!" After application, when on the waiting list, she
said: "I want to be with people so I won't be alone. I get along
with everyone. People like me. I won't insult anyone." Mrs. C.'s
time had come. Like her husband who had died in the home, it
was her turn to enter the home for life. Her apprehension related to potential rebuffs, possibly not being admitted to her
haven. She anticipates that she will ask for little and will try to
be appropriate so that she can live her last years among people
and will not die alone.

While these three elderly women were indeed different one
from another, there appear to be some similarities in their transition from the predecision period to the anticipatory phase.

For each, for example, changes in the interaction between personal and social losses precipitated the decision to apply; for each, the home became a more welcomed solution after these losses occurred. The commonalities among these three women are typical of many older people who seek to become institutionalized.

To provide a more explicit understanding of the psychology of the anticipatory period as a reaction to the events that necessitated the decision and to the impending event of institutionalization, a series of separate analyses were undertaken of events particularly related to loss and abandonment. These analyses clearly show that the psychological status of waiting-list respondents was decidedly more negative than that of community aged persons.

Loss Meanings

What is the meaning of loss for waiting-list aged persons? Is there evidence to suggest that, in the transition from the pre-decision to the anticipatory period, there is a shift toward a particular loss meaning? Mrs. B. described a shift that revealed a change on this dimension. While living independently in the community, the major content in her earliest memory was: "I remember as a child that my father was very fond of cards, which I myself resented." Later, when on the waiting list, there was a change in her earliest memory: "I went to visit my mother's friend, who had asked me to spend the night. I was miserable when I got there, really homesick for my mother; I couldn't sleep all night." The content suggests a shift from narcissistic preoccupation with attention from father to a later, more primitive theme of separation from mother.

To determine if this shift toward the experience of separation could be supported by the types of themes introduced in the reconstruction of the earliest memory, the earliest memories of respondents in the community and waiting-list samples were compared. For this comparison, the themes were trichotomized into no loss, loneliness or separation, and personal injury (mutilation) or death. Assuming that this trichotomy also might form a scale from the least to the greatest expression of loss, each reconstruction was scored for the highest level of expressed loss. Thus, if both separation from mother and death of mother appeared in the reconstruction, the memory was judged revealing mutilation and death themes.

When the earliest memory was used to tap meanings of loss, the community sample was found not to focus on loss. As shown in Table 5, however, the study sample, while on the wait-

Table 5. Loss Expression in the Earliest Memory[a]

Sample	N^b	No Loss		Separation		Mutilation and Death	
		N	Percent	N	Percent	N	Percent
Community	28	17	61	3	11	8	28
Waiting-list	68	27	39	19	27	22	34
Institutionalized	30	11	37	5	16	14	47

[a]Contrast between community and waiting-list sample: $X^2 = 5.56, p < .05$; between waiting-list and institutionalized sample: $X^2 = 2.04$, n.s.
[b]These Ns are lower than in other analyses because many respondents were unable to report an earliest memory.

ing list, introduced losses of separation, as well as mutilation and death. The waiting-list sample differed most from the community sample in the percentage of "no-loss" themes. The majority of respondents in the community sample had no-loss themes (61 percent), whereas the majority in the waiting-list sample had loss themes (a similar 61 percent). The difference in the percentage of no-loss themes is 22 percent; a difference that is accounted for primarily by the difference on themes of separation (a 16 percent difference) rather than by the difference on themes of mutilation and death (a 6 percent difference). While the dominant themes among the sample of waiting-list aged persons were of the no-loss nature, the large difference between the two samples in the introduction of loss relates to the introduction of themes of separation.

Themes of separation are an important indicator of differences between the waiting-list and community samples and account for a significant difference between these samples (X^2

= 5.56, $p < .05$). The most likely interpretation of these differences is that a significant proportion of aged persons who became waiting-list respondents shifted to introducing themes of separation in reconstructing their earliest memory. If this shift is interpreted as a consequence of the transition from the predecision to the anticipatory period, the meaning of the transition process would appear to be that of separation.

In turn, the difference between the waiting-list sample and the institutionalized sample, although not statistically significant, suggests a difference in themes of mutilation and death. If this difference is not an artifact, then a change from separation to mutilation and death themes can be expected for the study sample when followed from before to after admission.

The Precipitants

In what way does the study of the events that precipitate application shed light on the experience of separation? Regardless of the types of precipitating events or crises, after a decision has been made to apply to the home and the application accepted, the resident-to-be must begin to relinquish a former lifestyle and prepare for life in the institution. If, however, the dissolution of a previously stable social support system is critical in the decision to apply for admission, then it would be expected that feelings of separation would be heightened. Similarly, if deterioration in the physical status of the aged person in the predecision phase was met by the family's reluctance to continue to support independent community living, the heightened feelings of separation could not help but be mixed with feelings of rage at rejection and abandonment. The precipitating events that led to application were explored by reconstructing the experimental pathway to the home by the aged persons who were on the waiting list. Data gathered on the community sample regarding changes in the past few years permitted a contrast between the waiting-list and community samples on recent crises.

The three elderly women who were followed from the time when they were community residents not considering a long-term care facility, underwent different precipitating events that led to application: for one, the critical precipitating events were physical illness and loss of a sister; for the second, a worsening of her mental status; and, for the third, difficulties with the woman with whom she shared an apartment. As the types of precipitating events were studied, it appeared that the events were not unique to those who applied for admission, as shown in Table 6. Many of the aged in the community control sample had been through similar events in the past few years.

Table 6. Comparison of Adverse Changes between the Waiting-List and Community Samples (in Percentages)

Adverse Changes	Community (N = 40)		Waiting List (N = 100)		Difference (Waiting list > community)	
Physical illness	62		77		15	
Economic	8		19		11	
Social	50		73		23	
Move of other		0		13		13
Death of other		40		38		−2
Relationship change		18		47		29
Living arrangement	42		80		38	
Homemaking		10		33		23
Neighborhood		0		13		13
Move by respondent		32		54		22

Either the accumulation of events rather than a single type of crucial event, or events in interaction with personality differences, might account for the differences between aged living independently in the community and those on the waiting list.

When the waiting-list sample was compared to the community sample, there were differences in the accumulation of events. As shown in Table 7, the distributions on this variable were quite different for the two samples ($p < .001$, Kolmogoroff-Smirnoff Test). Note that five of forty (or 12 percent) of the community sample *did not change* in any of the four areas as compared to only 2 percent in the waiting-list sample. Moreover, whereas one of every two respondents (50 percent) in the community sample showed changes in two to four areas, the large majority (about nine of ten, or 89 percent) of the respon-

Table 7. Accumulation of Events Across the Four Areas
(Kolmogoroff-Smirnoff Test for Difference in Distribution, $p < .001$)

Number of Areas	Community Sample (N = 40)			Waiting-List Sample (N = 100)		
	N	Percent	Accumulated Percent	N	Percent	Accumulated Percent
0	5	12	12	2	2	2
1	15	38	50	9	9	11
2	11	28	78	33	33	44
3	8	20	98	48	48	92
4	1	2	100	8	8	100
Total	40	100		100	100	

dents in the waiting-list sample showed changes in at least two areas.

While the samples do indeed differ on the accumulation of adverse changes, it is also true that one of two of the aged in the community sample (50 percent) reported changes in two or more areas, suggesting that some aged persons who remain in the community weather changes of the same nature or intensity that cause others their age to decide to give up independent living. If only the data regarding the waiting-list sample were available, one might speculate that the severity or number of adverse changes for those awaiting admission was the salient variable in explaining the decision to be institutionalized. One might be impressed, for example, with the fact that only 2 percent of the waiting-list sample reported stability in the previous 3 years, that 98 percent reported at least one area of adverse change, and that 89 percent reported at least two areas of adverse change. When the data regarding adverse change for the community sample are considered, however, the accumulated percentage of adverse changes for the waiting-list sample seems less impressive.

Why might more of the aged in the community sample who had endured many adverse changes not apply for admission? Does the explanation relate to a specific type of critical event that happens to the waiting-list sample and not to the community sample? Are there one or, possibly, a few events that most differentiate the two samples?

To explore the possibility that a particular type of event is more characteristic of the waiting-list sample than of the community sample, the two samples were compared with respect to the frequencies for each of the four areas and for each of the eight possible adverse changes. The single largest difference between the two samples was an adverse change in the relationship with a significant other (29 percent difference), as shown in Table 7. Large differences were also found in the area of increased difficulty in homemaking (23 percent difference). The 22 percent difference in moves by respondents relates to the 17 waiting-list aged persons who temporarily moved to a nursing home while awaiting admission. These comparisons suggest the importance of changes in the social system, as well as in the interaction between personal difficulties in homemaking and social supports. Of special importance is the smaller difference in loss through increased physical separation from others because of either their relocation (13 percent difference) or death (2 percent difference), a finding that suggests strongly that it is not events themselves that cause some older people to seek institutional care, *but the perceived response to these events, especially the response of responsible family members.* In any event, these findings raise some interesting questions. For example: Had there been changes in the nature of relationships with significant others prior to the decision to seek institutional care? Might not the encouragement by significant others to seek institutional care change the relationship of those others to the older person during and after the decision-making process?

The Social Network

To explore further the relationship with responsible others, responses were analyzed to an eleven-item questionnaire that was developed to measure the perception of other people as personal resources. For each item, the respondent was asked to mention one or more people. The items included:

1. Whom do you like to be with when you feel happy?

2. Whom would you ask when you need someone to go shopping for you?

3. Whom would you call for help when sick?

4. Whom would you like to see when feeling down-in-the-dumps?

5. Whom would you ask for a charitable contribution?

6. Whom would you go with if you won a trip for two to Florida?

7. Whom would you like to see if you felt lonely?

8. Whom would you ask if you were short of money and needed to borrow $5 for two days?

9. Whom would you ask if you wanted company on a walk?

10. Whom would you ask if you needed help in filling out income tax?

11. Whom would you see if you felt like having company of the opposite sex?

Scores were computed for the number of different people mentioned by name and the number of items for which no one was named. On both measures the waiting-list sample was significantly different from the community sample ($p < .05$): the community sample had a mean of five different people mentioned, while the waiting-list sample had a mean of 4.1; the community sample mentioned no one for only one item, while the waiting-list sample mentioned no one for two items. Although the two samples are different on this variable of people as resources, the waiting-list respondents do appear to be interacting with meaningful others. For example, *all* the waiting-list respondents were able to identify *at least one other* person in response to the task, and only 3 identified *just one other* person (while 24 just two and 14 identified three others). The majority of respondents (59), that is, identified four or more specific others. Every respondent was able to identify one or more specific others in response to at least three items. Indeed, 84 respondents identified one or more others for seven or more items. These data show that the waiting-list aged persons characteristically had others, or others that were perceived as available to them as person resources.

The responses were further analyzed for whom the respondent would turn to when sick, sad, or lonely. For these three items, ninety respondents mentioned one or more family members. Three others mentioned friends. Thus more than nine out of ten respondents had an intimate or confidential relationship with another person who could be turned to at least for solace and comfort, and who invariably was a family member. The elderly on the waiting list, then, did not appear to be isolated individuals.

In another approach to the social system of the waiting-list aged persons, the presence of family members was measured. While there was no difference in the number of living siblings among the two samples, there was a difference in the number of living children. A greater percentage of the waiting-list aged than community aged had no living children (30 percent as compared to 18 percent). Of these 30 percent (or thirty) waiting-list aged persons with no living children, however, only ten were living alone and had neither children, siblings or child surrogates; the other twenty had either siblings, roommates or child surrogates. Of these twenty, eight were living with one or more siblings who were themselves 70 years old or older; six others had living siblings but had not lived with them, but either were close to these siblings or had nephews and nieces who were child surrogates; and another six, who did not have any siblings, had child surrogates. In all, ten of the twenty aged who did not have living children did have a relationship with one or more meaningful child surrogates who felt a personal responsibility for the welfare of the aged person.

Having siblings or child surrogates, or even both, probably provides a less stable social system than having children, especially a responsible daughter, but is probably a more stable system than having none of these supports. If the presence of a responsible child is the criterion of a viable social system, then more of the aged persons on the waiting list were living in a precarious social system than were those in the community sample. Only 12 percent more of those on the waiting list had at least one living child, however, while 28 percent more had undergone adverse changes in social relationships. As noted earlier, this difference of 28 percent does not include the actual separation from significant others by death or relocation.

To explore further the role of social relationships in influencing the decision to become an applicant to the home, the 17 aged persons on the waiting list who were in nursing homes as a transitional living arrangement before admission to the home were compared to the 83 applicants who were living in the community. Those who were living in nursing homes were more apt to emphasize increased physical incapacity (90 percent compared to 75 percent), while the applicants who were living in the community while awaiting admission were more apt to emphasize adverse change in the area of social relations (75 percent compared to 60 percent). Aged persons who lived in a nursing home during the transitional phase, therefore, tended more to emphasize adverse changes in their physical condition while applicants who were living in the community tended more to emphasize changes in the social system.

Whether these differences were a function of actual changes or were rationalizations for seeking of institutional care is a question beyond the power of the available data to answer. For both groups, however, the change in relationship with significant others was very prominent: 41 percent of the waiting-list aged persons who lived transitionally in nursing homes and 48 percent of those aged who had not entered nursing homes reported substantive negative changes with significant others. We have already noted that only 17 percent of the community sample had perceived similar adverse changes in social relationships. Do these figures suggest that the most salient characteristic is the perception of change in the support system? If so, when the pathway to institutionalized status is interpreted in relation to community aged who do not apply, it would appear that although many community aged had undergone adverse

changes similar to those experienced by the applicants during
the 3 years prior to the first interview, the two groups differed
significantly on the perceived or actual availability or willingness of others to support an effort for independent community
living.

In summary, the significant difference between the waiting-list and community samples on the accumulation of adverse
events during the 3 years before the former entered homes can
best be accounted for by the difference in the relationship with
significant others. Aged persons on the waiting list experienced
a greater frequency in the deterioration of relationships with
significant others, but not in actual social losses through death
or moving away of others. For some aged on the waiting list,
the social system appeared more precarious than for many aged
persons in the community before the decision to apply for institutional care; and, for others, no more precarious than for many
aged in the community who did not apply for admission. The
reasons for application, then, often became highly idiosyncratic
and appeared to be an interaction among factors such as the
personality of the older person, rate of decline in physical functioning, more subtle interaction between parent and child, and
seeking help from social services. Although some older people
had greater resistance than others to institutionalization as a
solution to adverse changes, some occurrences more than others
—say a sudden decline in homemaking ability—led to a greater
need for reorganizing living patterns. Attempting to protect the
relationship with a child, the older person may have initiated
the decision-making process or, on the other hand, a child or
child-surrogate may have initiated the decision-making process,
fearing that in the future their own personal life circumstances
would limit their availability to the older person. In either pathway, once help is sought from the family service agency, the
caseworker may further have induced or facilitated the decision
for institutionalization, particularly when the worker perceived
the burden on children or child-surrogates to be overwhelming
and the older parent as unable to maintain any type of viable
independent community living.

The Psychological Experience: Abandonment

The decision to seek institutional care is usually a family decision. Because the family is intimately involved, the loss meaning associated with the decision is that of separation. The theme of separation is evidenced in the respondent's discussions of current adverse relationship changes and in the reconstruction of their earliest memories. Indeed, of the 47 respondents who discussed a relationship change of any sort, 26 introduced the issue of rejection. The configuration of separation, rejection, and the dread of the finality of entering the institution suggests a perception of abandonment. The sense of being abandoned implies a more painful feeling than separation. It means being separated from another person because the other person has purposefully chosen to leave one to his own devices at a time of great personal need. If the perception is indeed that of being abandoned, then how did the respondents cope with it?

Coping with the Sense of Being Abandoned

For those who seek custodial care, the institution represents a solution to the problems of maintenance of physical capacity and a mechanism for the replacement of a lost social world. Because the most frequent adverse change among those in the waiting-list sample was an increase in physical illness during the previous 3 years (77 percent of the waiting-list sample), it is not surprising that most of these respondents (58 percent) gave the need for physical care as the primary reason for entering the home. Only 21 of these 58 residents, however, emphasized medical care *in particular*, whereas 37 focused more on the "need to be cared for." This somewhat subtle distinction between the desire for medical care and more generalized care by sympathetic others in an environment that offers total protection and security for the remainder of one's life is congruent with the rather large number (34) who gave relief of loneliness or adverse changes in social relationships as the primary reason for application. Taken together, these data mean that 71 of the

100 waiting-list aged perceived the home, in one way or another, as a social system that could offer a replacement for a lost, or nonviable, natural support system.

Because the reasons for application may be several for any individual, the waiting-list respondents as related to application were systematically analyzed. Responses to the following questions in the questionnaire focused on environmental orientation were used for this analysis.

1. It is often a difficult decision to apply to a home. What made you decide to apply to (name of) home?

   When did you first begin to think about going into the home?

   Did relatives or friends play any part in the decision? (Probe decision making process. Try to get specific influences on respondent in the decision-making process. If not covered, ask: What did children or relatives think about the decision?)

2. How long have you been living here? (Inquire about shifts in last five years and reasons for changes.)

   What other plans did you consider or try out before applying to the (name of) home?

   (If appropriate, ask:) Have you lived or considered living with relatives? (If respondent lived with relatives, ask how that was.)

3. Do you know anyone in (name of) home? If yes, how is he or she getting along there? (Find out respondent's impression of the person and how he or she feels the person is doing in the home.)

4. Everything in life means giving up some things to gain other things. I'm sure that going to (name of) home means this to you. What do you feel you're giving up? (Probe for answers related to independence, physical belongings, and so forth.)

   What do you feel you're getting? (Possible gains: medical care, companions.)

What sort of things that you do now won't you be able to do in the home?

What new things will you be able to do in the home that you can't do here? (Probe present living arrangements.)

Do you think there are things you'll have to learn (understand, find out about) in order to adjust to the home? Tell me about them.

(Past associations with institutionalization.) What events, things, and so forth does going to the home remind you of? (For some respondents, you may wish to preface the question, "This may be a difficult question, but could you tell me . . . .")

The responses to these questions revealed five issues of importance to the respondents (Pincus, 1968). The first three issues can be considered positive aspects of orientation to the future environment: care and security, people or companionship, and activities. The next two are negative aspects: loss of freedom and loss of privacy. These five issues or environmental orientations were rated for the extent to which an aspect of the respondent's current or future institutional environment was raised as an issue in discussing reasons for applying to a home, as well as concerns about entering one.

Each orientation was rated on a 4-point scale ranging from no mention, to some concern, an important issue, a central concern. For 83 percent of the respondents, care was of at least some concern; for 60 percent, people; for 66 percent, activity; for 43 percent, privacy; and for 30 percent, freedom. The analysis supports the view of care as a central issue, as well as of the importance of the gains of people and activities. Losses appear less important when considering the impending event.

Focusing on the care that one needs and that can be offered by the institution would appear to be an appropriate maneuver. If nothing else, the home offers residents a custodial and medical environment. The introduction of people and activity as orientations is understandably second to the conscious concern with care. That, however, only approximately 60 percent had at least some concern with these two issues, related to care, appears surprising. It would appear that while on the waiting list the major preoccupations of respondents were with separation, with the lack of support from the family, and with the need to survive the relocation. If these were the prominent preoccupations, then the restitutive potential of the home for people and activity would, understandably, not be emphasized. People and activity can help fill time but cannot replace independence or intimacy with significant others. It is as if people and activity, as aspects of the future environment, were recognized as important gains but were currently secondary to the need to cope with abandonment, the experience of separation, and the dread of the impending move.

When confronted with imminent admission to the home, the typical resident-to-be appeared to focus on the positive aspects of the institution. The losses of privacy, as noted previously, were not mentioned by 57 percent of the waiting respondents, and, similarly, the loss of freedom was not mentioned by 71 percent. In stressing the positive and underplaying the negative, was the respondent using the mechanism of denial? Denial, as defined by Eidelberg (1968) in the *Encyclopedia of Psychoanalysis* is "a defense mechanism which is aimed at the elimination of traumatic sense organ perception" (p. 101). In this manner, the offensive perceptions and those effects mobilized by it are kept from consciousness. Denial is a purposeful avoidance of the perception of those characteristics of the environment that are anxiety-producing. Was the aged person on the waiting list, who has been through a lengthy process of application that has included actually visiting the institution, able to deny the meaning of the impending event to himself?

Two manifestations of denial, which each relate to a different process of consciously thinking about the event, were examined. The first manifestation relates to the avoidance of mentioning the event when discussing a range of topics, such as relationships with family and the future use of time. In all, twelve open-ended items that were free of references to the home or the impending move were selected as appropriate for this measure. Of the twelve items, two were from the Self-Sort instrument and two from the Sentence Completion Test; the other eight were obtained from various sections of the focused interview. The items were:

1. Tell me about your health.

2. Are there any particular events in the future that you're anticipating?

3. What do you hope will happen to you as you grow older?

4. Are there times now that you like privacy, to be alone?

5. Have there been any recent changes in how you get along with children?

6. Have there been any recent changes in how you get along with your friends?

7. (In Self-Sort example for Item K2) I prefer to let other people make decisions for me.

8. (In Self-Sort example for Item 61) I am a cooperative person.

9. (Sentence Completion Test item) "If I had my way . . . ."

10. (Sentence Completion Test item) "I look forward to . . . ."

11. What would you like to be doing a year from now?

12. What does the future mean to you?

Although each resident had these twelve opportunities to introduce the home, only 30 percent did, in fact, introduce the home more than one time. The majority, or 70 percent, did not introduce the home in response to any of these items, or did so only once. Indeed, 34 percent did not mention the home even once.

The second measure of denial was that of avoidance of the latent meanings of the event. The source of data for this measure was a special series of TAT-type cards. These Institutional TAT cards were developed by Lieberman and Lakin (1963) for a study of the attitudes of aged individuals concerning institutionalization. As described by Lieberman and Lakin (pp. 478, 479), the series of drawings depicted:

> . . . a range of situations considered character-istic of the transition to institutional living. Where the institution was involved, the details were closely pat-terned after its actual physical plant [one of the insti-tutions used for the present investigation]. Figures were drawn to suggest ambiguous attitudes, although age differentiations were made clear. The original drawings were in charcoal. They were photographed and enlarged to 11 × 14 (inches) cards. The series was constructed to provide alternate forms for male and female subjects.

Four cards, selected from a total of seven, were used to assess avoidance of the latent meaning of institutionalization among waiting-list respondents. The situations depicted, hypothesized stimulus demand, and three levels of denial follow.

Card 1. An aged person packing a suitcase as several people depicting younger adults and children stand in the foreground and background. (Separation and/or rejection.) No denial, old person leaving; some denial, someone else is leaving; high denial, no one is leaving.

Card 2. An elderly person walking down a path into a building clearly signified as an old-age institution. (Person entry into the institution.) No denial, the elderly person is entering an old-age home; some denial, the elderly person is entering an old-age home but for a visit; high denial, avoidance of labeling the old-age home.

Card 3. Two aged people of the same sex sitting in a bedroom drawn to represent a typical room in the institution. (Being a resident with other elderly.) No denial, figures are roommates in an old-age home; some denial, figures are residents; high denial, figures are other than residents.

Card 4. An aged person about to enter a room clearly marked as the office of an institutional director, who is drawn as a middle-aged man. (Authority and dependency.) No denial, figure is director of old age home; some denial, figure is some other kind of director; high denial, avoidance of any identification as a relative or physician.

A total denial score was generated for each respondent by scoring no denial as 1, some denial as 2, and high denial as 3, then summing the scores for all four cards. The range of scores, therefore, is from 4 to 12, where a score of 4 reflects the absence of denial and a score of 12 complete denial of the meaning of the impending institutionalization.

Extreme to complete denial was present in over half the sample (56 percent). Scores of 8, 9, and 10 were used to reflect extreme denial (42 percent were in this range) and scores of 11 and 12 were used to reflect almost complete or complete denial (14 percent were in this range). Only 8 percent manifested no denial in stories told to the four cards.

Both manifestations of denial (e.g., avoidance of introducing the event and avoidance of dealing with the latent meaning of the event) were quite prevalent in the waiting-list sample. Although some respondents manifested denial in one way and some in another (the correlation between the two types of avoidance was only a modest $r = .30$), it was rare if a respondent did not manifest some form of denial. The unavoidable implication of these analyses was that denial was central to coping with the impending event.

Stories told to these Institutional TAT cards by the women whose care histories were introduced earlier illustrate one prevalent type of denial. (Mrs. A. did not respond to the Institutional TAT cards because of an administrative error.)

Mrs. B., "The Sunshine lady," told the following stories to the first two cards when on the waiting list:

> Card 1. "Well, whether the woman's ready to depart or has just arrived I don't know. It's either one or the other. From the expression on her face I imagine she must have just arrived. *(Pause.)* In the back here it's like they are in conference. She evidently—it must be a widowed mother surrounded by her children. This is her grandson. What their attitude towards her will be later on she will have to find out for herself. Whether she's a parent or a grandparent I don't know. Whether she's packing or unpacking it's hard to say. From the expression it looks like she's just arrived. That's all I can say."

> Card 2. "That's the home. *(Smile.)* She's entering the home with a great anticipation. Yes, she is entering with great anticipation. She's hoping to find the home *(pause)* will hold everything that will make her comfortable and happy for the rest of her life. That applies to me too. The last picture before this must be that she is preparing to go to the home. Now you're giving me something right up my alley."

In these two stories, Mrs. B. was responding to the latent meanings depicted, and both were scored as low on denial.

In her first story, while responding to the issue of separation, Mrs. B. vacillated between departing and arriving. The issue of separation was confronted but could not be resolved. Mrs. B. would have preferred to have been accepted by her children rather than to be awaiting admission to the institution. The thought of not returning to her daughter's house was a painful one and she did not want to contemplate the alternative that she was now facing. She could not, however, deny the reality of the event of institutionalization. Rather, she responded to the latent meaning of the second card with a euphoric denial of the reality. Only after reestablishing her hysteric defenses of sunshine and hope, could she recognize that the first card could be interpreted as packing for the home. Her defenses were working and, as was characteristic of her, she veiled her depression with a mask of joy.

Her stories to the next two cards again reflected her willingness to respond to the latent meaning of the cards, but again she attempted to romanticize the future event:

> Card 3. "Here she has made friends with her roommate and they evidently are talking things over in a companionable way, which I hope to find too. The lady to the left is listening to the lady on the right. I suppose asking questions of a different nature. Perhaps these questions are applying to the home. Perhaps the other lady is giving us some insight what to expect. And I suppose that like myself her life there shall be a happy one. I don't think people who are residents at the home—I'm talking for myself now—expect it to be like your own home but next to your own home I think—and I hope—it'll be a happy one. Of course, speaking for myself I'm looking forward to becoming a resident there."

> Card 4. "The woman is asking questions, applying—now this applies to me—when I get to the home I hope that I will not have any unpleasantness to encounter. If and when I arrive there and have to share a room with somebody that will have a little understanding what human kindness means and not to expect too much because in this world we are not living alone. *(This lengthy sentence was said slowly, with hesitation and while Mrs. B. had her eyes closed.)* We have to share and share alike. So I am share and pray that everything we plan for will prove to our satisfaction. It will be a little different in the beginning but with a little patience we hope to become friends to each other. I am not of a demanding nature, but I do try to analyze a situation and hope for good results. That's the only way one can live. You can't expect anything and not give something in return. You have to share everything if you're going to get along. It applies here the same thing.

(Mrs. B. had obviously become fixated on the previous card.) (Anything else on this card?) No, I've told you all I see there."

Mrs. B., in other words, did not deny the latent meaning in the four cards but rather used the cards to work through her fears regarding separation: being abandoned to an institutional world. Her statement, for example, "I'm looking forward to becoming a resident there," is an attempt to convince herself that her fears are unfounded, when in reality she is very fearful of antagonizing her daughter or the staff in the home.

Mrs. C. ("I want people") handled the four cards differently. She told the following stories to the first two cards:

Card 1. "She has a satchel; also's looking in satchel, what does she have to take out. Man with little boy, maybe it's his bag—I don't know. Maybe in a house. Looks like his mother, otherwise there wouldn't be no relation. *(Happy?)* No, unhappy, the mother is crying. Mother looking at something. Food maybe. *(End?)* Well, I think that will be good. *(How?)* That's his mother and maybe she will go with him."

Card 2. "Lady looks like she's going in car or something. Maybe going in car. Maybe going over there like me—not a young woman *(pleasant tone)*. She's walking to that old-age home. Her face looks sad, maybe she don't want to go. I don't mind *(shaking head)*. Lived with my daughter *(Mrs. C. muttered—shook head). (How does she feel?)* She feels all right—like me. *(How will it end?)* She'll be happy over there—it's very nice."

The response to the first story is sparse but clearly one of separation; but it is the son that is leaving and the mother who is saddened at the separation. There is moderate denial; someone is leaving, but not her. The separation is resolved, however, by the mother joining her son. This theme of potential separation and reunion with a son or daughter is not at all congruent with Mrs. C.'s real expectations of her future. Nowhere in the extensive interview data did Mrs. C. discuss a reunion with children. Rather, she repeatedly discussed her voluntary decision to enter the institution and to replace the loss of her roommate with others in the institution.

After recognizing that it depicted an old-age home, Mrs. C.'s first response to the second card was that it showed a sad woman who did not want to go. Mrs. C. then said that she was different, that she did not mind the move. She then mulled over the alternative of living with her daughter and appeared to be reconciling herself to her only available option.

She then continued:

Card 3. "That's like two older ladies. She listening to her tell a story. *(What kind?)* How to get along with the whole life. You know sometimes they tell each other their whole lives. I live my own life. Looks like they're talking a happy story. I like happy story—nothing sad. *(How will it end?)* One happy, one upset. *(Then?)* Everything went good."

Card 4. "He's working in that office and that lady's coming looking for a job. *(Then?)* She's ready to come in office. He looks like he's holding a cane. She looks like she's afraid to come in. *(Why?)* She looks afraid. *(Then?)* She's waiting he call her in the office. *(End?)* Maybe he will be ready now."

Mrs. C. recognized that the roommate card might have personal relevance to her living in the home. Concerned with the intrusion of others, she was determined to live her own life in the home and not be upset by others. This expectation was a more realistic one than Mrs. B.'s, who would like "human kindness," to be loved and admired.

The story to the fourth, or "director" card, revealed Mrs. C.'s difficulties. In her first three stories, she recognized her personal future: when a younger man and an older woman were depicted, her response changed to exhibit greater denial. The older woman is asking the executive for a job. Given the age and physical condition of the woman depicted on the card, the story is unrealistic. The distortion is, however, consistent with Mrs. C.'s firm resolution to be independent: she was not going to be a burden, nor would she go to her children pleading for solace. Mrs. C. could not perceive the woman as needing help from the younger executive. The only relationship with him that she could permit herself to acknowledge was as a woman who is prepared to carry her share, to put in a day's work for a day's pay. This mutual, functional, and independent relationship characterized Mrs. C.'s expressed preferences and also clarifies why, in responding to the first card, she said that "maybe she will go with him." She could only accept an independent relationship with her children, which would allow her to ward off any feelings of abandonment.

Conclusion

The reason why some aged persons applied to live in institutions and others did not was not readily apparent in the data. Goldfarb (1969) hypothesized that it is a dependent type of person that seeks institutional care. Yet the three case studies certainly do not reveal a common personality type that can be labeled as *dependent*. Nor do our measures of personality suggest that any one type of person seeks institutional care. There is little reason to doubt that a wide array of types of people apply to and become residents of homes for the aged.

Lowenthal and Haven (1968) have offered another explanation for who becomes institutionalized. They found the lack of a confidante to be a critical variable in the admission of elderly patients to the state mental hospital. A lack of a confidante, however, is not characteristic of the present sample. Indeed, all but a few maintained relationships to but two or more significant other people.

We must rely on a more complex explanation that encompasses the interaction among three variables: personal deteriorative changes in the older person, the inability or unwillingness of responsible others to offer the care that they or the respondent perceive to be required, and the inability of the current system of services to assure independent living. All three factors appear to be prevalent in the sample.

Respondents in the present sample, along with most elderly Americans, are aware that institutional care might indeed be necessary if personal deterioration and disruptive changes were to occur in the familial support system. Seeking and obtaining institutional care is one alternative, but it is a dreaded one. For those without another alternative, and for whom institutional care symbolizes survival, it becomes possible to focus on gains of care, people, and activity that can be afforded by the institution. By so doing, the underlying feelings of abandonment are superficially contained. Yet the psychological portrait before entering and living in the institutional environment sufficiently resembles that of older people already institutionalized to justify the conclusion that these feelings are potent.

There may be little further deteriorative change after entering and living in the institution. Indeed, the contrast with the institutionalized sample—although this sample is composed of more hearty individuals, who have survived the institutionalization process relatively intact—suggests some amelioration in psychological status after admission. If so, environmental discontinuity, institutional life, or selection biases do not explain the debilitated status of institutionalized elderly as parsimoniously as the postulation of the effects from the experience of loss, especially abandonment, that attend the process of seeking, finding and anticipating institutional care. The extent to which entering and living in the institution explain what have typically been labeled as "institutional effects" is the focus of the next chapter.

3

Initial Adjustment

The impact of institutionalization is generally felt most acutely during the first few months following admission. The severe stress of institutionalization occurs in its most extreme form just after entering the home, when the old person first has to sleep in a bed foreign to him, adjust to the idiosyncrasies of a roommate, live in a congregate environment, and learn the positive and negative sanctions of a new social world. The manifest consequences of this acute experience have often been labeled "the first-month syndrome." The manifestation of the first-month syndrome for some residents takes the form of almost total disorientation in time and place; for others, affective disturbances such as deep depression; and for others, rather bizarre behavioral symptoms. The first month is a period of continual ups-and-downs for some residents, whereas for others there is immediate disorganization followed by an upswing and then a stabilization at a level of functioning that is somewhat worse than their preadmission level. Whatever the pattern, most residents achieve some degree of stability at some point within their first 2 months in the home. The variation in the acute response to impact makes it extremely difficult to assess initial adjustment until 2 months after admission.

Stress-Producing Factors

To understand the factors that contribute to the discontinuity of institutionalization, it helps to make a distinction between what has been left behind and what is being confronted. Family members who have been collaborators in the decision to enter the institution have been left behind. Often the new resident has focused a great deal of anger and resentment on these relatives while working through the feelings of abandonment that the decision for institutionalization has aroused. The elderly person may anticipate relief of these feelings as he enters the institution. Still, the new resident cannot envision minute-to-minute life in the institution. It is only when he is actually living in the home—for life—that he feels the full impact of the institution.

At the actual moment of entering the institution, the leaving behind of those prized possessions that have represented stability and continuity over a lifetime is crucial. Although small personal possessions may be brought to the homes such as the ones entered by the respondents in the present study, the new resident cannot bring in the bed in which he or she may have slept for over 40 to 50 years. Having left behind the people and possessions that are symbols of attachmenf to one's past, the new admission is initiated into becoming a resident by being introduced to his roommate or roommates. While the homes studied attempt to match the new resident's needs with those of the roommates, even the best efforts at matching tend to be fraught with difficulty because most residents are ill and old. The confrontation between roommates over whether to open or lower a window an extra inch or two can become a vigorous conflict for even the best of friends. For the very aged, who have developed their personal style of life over a period of 80 years or so, it is indeed often these small comforts that reassure them of their own security. The small room becomes the focus of the world to the resident who has just entered the home. To be sure, the new resident is assured that the room is his space, to make of it what he will. He may soon learn, however, that there is an invisible line down the middle of the room dividing his own space from that of the roommate. The closet space appears extremely limited to the person who has had to give up a spacious apartment. Indeed, everything centering around the use of space is very confusing to the new resident who has had his own fixed places for putting glasses, false teeth, and other personal objects. Just the decision about where to place personal possessions can become very taxing.

Now the resident has to confront a new and totally foreign experience. The roommate, in inducting the resident, may point out that it is necessary to lock up certain valuables or bring them to the office, and to be sure to mark everything for the laundry or suffer the consequences of loss. Because of space limitation, a choice has to be made over which pictures of children and grandchildren should be on the dresser and which put away. The messages that come to the resident are like a rapid-fire list of instructions about heretofore inexperienced adjustments. On the very first day, therefore, the pressure is felt to reorient oneself to living in surroundings where one's private space is rather limited.

In moving out to the more public space, the sense of institutionalization can be overwhelming to the new resident. To the outsider, the many aids that facilitate the older person's walking and safety appear extremely helpful, but the new resident often perceives them as a nuisance that gives the "home" a further institutional flavor. The non-skid floors are more suggestive of the kitchen floor at home than of a living room. The bathrooms throughout the institution are not homelike, but are specially constructed for the ill aged. If the older person has not been aware of personal frailty up to this point, there is now no escape; the very aids that facilitate care of the ill aged force the newcomer to become aware of the prevalence of infirmity among his cohorts. The press for redefinition of self is again emphasized in the congregate dining hall and other meeting places. Although residents may choose where and with whom to sit, and though there are also alternative menus at various times, eating occurs in a large room that is not at all like either a home or restaurant atmosphere. There are, of course, set hours for meals. Even though the new resident may feel that the food is rather tasty, he frequently hears other residents complain that they have had that meal recently, and it is exactly the food that they have disliked all their lives.

In the public world of the institution, it is apparent that the newcomer is a low-status person in the interpersonal system. The old-timers are eager to induct a new resident into the institution and exert their own authority and savvy. The more independent the newcomer, the more angry and resentful he may be of this intrusion and of his own personal inadequacies in coping with the strange and foreign environment. When venturing into the public space, it is not uncommon for new residents to get lost on the first day or two. The floors and rooms have a certain sameness and it is a relief to have one's roommate show one through the maze.

As the new resident explores the community of the home, the list of rules and regulations becomes incredibly long. Becoming acquainted with the medical facilities of the home is alone complex. Learning where to go, and how to get medication and other medical services, becomes something of a task; the aged resident becomes a consumer among many other persons of similar age and incapacity. Adjusting also means learning who is in control. The nurse becomes an extremely important person because she appears to be the gatekeeper for medical services. Implicit rules are learned that help to obtain the necessary services from a network of staff that includes many people throughout the service areas in the institution. Simultaneously, the new resident begins to relate to medical staff, paramedical personnel, housekeepers, aides, and so forth. Some of these staff people appear as intruders, such as the maid who comes in and cleans daily. Prior to entering the home, when living in the community, the old person could hire whomever he wished, if he could afford it, to come in and clean up, but now it is an aide whom they have not met and who feels more comfortable cleaning up the room than the new resident does living in it. Suddenly the world seems to be populated not only by other old, sick people, but also by a great many staff having various functions that one slowly begins to differentiate. Overall, the problems in the early days in the home usually center around the relationship to roommate or roommates, and it is the fortunate resident who does not have roommate troubles.

It is no wonder that previous investigators have interpreted their cross-sectional findings to mean that the new resident reacts to institutionalization by becoming cognitively disorganized, less functionally adequate, less emotionally responsive, less happy, and so on. Each possible negative change may be related to varied components of the adaptive task. Cognitive disorganization may result from the perceptual discontinuity associated with the unfamiliarity of the new environment. If in adapting to the environment the aged person accepts the role of resident, a redefinition of capacity for self-care may develop that incorporates the medical orientation of the setting. Using the aids to care that are offered, and, in turn, redefining one's capacity in terms of these aids, encourages a self-perception of less functional adequacy than was present before admission. Cognitive constriction may find a parallel in a lessening of affective responsiveness because of active withdrawal from coping with the dissonant environment. The net effect on emotional life may include lowered feelings of well-being, increased hopelessness, anxiety, and depression.

Psychological Changes from Preadmission to Postadmission

The assumption of pervasive adverse psychological changes taking place after the transition from the waiting list into the institution was not borne out in testing 2 months after admission. As shown in tables 8 and 9, most measures did not reveal additional adverse change; generally, there was a persistence of the status found before admission: cognitive constriction, a constriction in affective responsiveness, moderate feelings of well-being, anxiety and depression, moderate self-esteem, moderate adequacy in using the present environment for self-definition, and moderate feelings of dominance in interpersonal relations. There was no evidence of the destructiveness of the institution on these aged persons. Only scattered adverse changes in hopefulness, perception of capacity for self-care, and affiliation in interpersonal relationships were found among the four psychological areas.

Table 8. Psychological Changes from the Anticipatory Phase
to the Initial Adjustment Phase ($N = 78$)

Area of Psychological Functioning	Anticipatory Phase	Initial Adjustment Phase
Cognitive functioning	Cognitive constriction	Cognitive constriction persists
Affective responsiveness	Constriction	Constriction persists
Emotional states	Moderate feelings of well-being	Moderate feelings of well-being
	Limited hopefulness[a]	Less hopefulness[a]
	Anxiety and depression (low body preoccupation)[c]	Anxiety and depression persists (high body preoccupation)[c]
Self-perception	Perception of capacity for self-care[b]	Perception of less capacity for self-care[a]
	Moderate self-esteem	Moderate self-esteem persists
	Moderate adequacy and high distortion	Moderate adequacy and high distortion persists
	Moderate dominance and moderate affiliation[a]	Moderate dominance with a lessening of affiliation, more hostility and distance[a]

[a] $p < .01$
[b] $p < .05$
[c] $p < .001$

Cognitive Functioning. Only one of the six measures of cognition yielded a statistically significant decline: the number of errors on the Mental Status Questionnaire (MSQ) increased from an average of 1.3 to 2.2 errors. In analyzing this change in performance on the MSQ, it became apparent that mistakes were made generally on two items: not knowing exactly where the home was located within the city, and not knowing "today's" date. Many residents were generally aware of what section of the city the home was located in, but could not specify the street name. With respect to time orientation, many residents were correct only about the year, but had difficulty specifying month and day. Where there is the need to develop a daily and weekly schedule, as when living in the community, the aged person is more apt to be aware of calendar time. In the institution, where the planning of activities tends to be scheduled by

Table 9. Change in Psychological Status: Anticipatory Phase
to the Initial Adjustment Phase ($N = 78$)

Dimension, Variable, and Measure	Means		t	p
	Waiting List	Initial Adjustment		
Functional adequacy				
Cognitive functioning	1.4	1.2	.21	–
Orientation (MSQ)	1.3	2.2	5.00	.001
Time estimate (60 seconds)	21.7	23.6	.93	–
Retention (Paired Word Learning)	11.5	10.8	.53	–
Organization (BGT)[a]	36.2	32.4	2.80	.01
Perceptual accuracy (TAT)	21.7	21.9	.29	–
Originality (Reitman)	9.7	10.5	1.67	–
Affective responsiveness				
Affective expression	4.5	4.3	.68	–
Introspection	2.1	1.9	1.61	–
Emotional state				
Well-being (LSR)	15.9	16.3	1.01	–
Hope	.0	–.2	2.41	.02
SCT				
Anxiety	19.7	18.3	1.59	–
Depression	13.5	13.5	.16	–
(Body preoccupation)	3.8	5.0	3.64	.002
Self-perception				
Self-care	2.5	3.7	2.80	.01
Self-esteem	20.3	19.7	.79	–
Adequacy	–.86	–.74	.18	–
Self-in-interaction				
Dominance	–.04	–.18	1.00	–
Affiliation	.27	.02	2.41	.02

[a]The statistically significant improvement is not greater than that shown by the control groups and is attributed, therefore, to a test practice effect rather than to entering the institution.

others, it may not be as necessary to know the date. For the other eight questions that comprise the MSQ, such as one's own age and name of the current President of the United States, there was rarely an increase in errors above those made while on the waiting list.

There was no systematic change on the other five tests. For the group undergoing institutionalization, improvement on the Bender Gestalt test was no greater than that manifested by aged in the control groups, suggesting that positive changes can be attributed to a test practice effect. The means were quite alike both before and after admission for estimation of one minute, for the learning and retention of word pairs, for perceptual accuracy on the TAT, and for originality in response to the Reitman Stick Figures.

The lack of impact on cognitive functioning is most likely a function of the disorganization found initially while on the waiting list. Entering the institution did not increase the preadmission level of cognitive dysfunction; rather, the level of functioning remained at a somewhat disorganized state from preadmission to postadmission. This is an important finding: actually, living in the institution does not increase the amount of cognitive disorganization suffered as a result of anticipating institutionalization!

Affective Responsiveness.   As with cognition, there appeared to be little, if any, decline in emotional responsiveness. Given the findings reported for many of the cross-sectional studies that compared community and institutionalized aged, this again is an important finding. Actually living in the institution caused neither a deterioration in cognitive functioning nor a lessening in emotional responsiveness. There was a constriction in responsiveness before admission that did not appear to be increased by living in the institutional environment.

Emotional States.   There was no systematic changes in feelings of well-being or of anxiety and depression, but there was a lessening in hopefulness. How can we explain a lessening in hopefulness in the absence of negative changes in other emotional states? Hopefulness, or its opposite hopelessness, is not simply an affect state such as mood or depression. Hope involves a temporal dimension—the pleasurable anticipation that things will change for the better and that, at least in part, the application of personal effort is likely to make a difference. Haberland (1972) has defined hope as "the confident expectation of personally significant gratifying change in that zone of experienced time which is the intermediate future" (p. 13). According to Frankl (1963), hope is also the expectation that the future will offer a sense of "purpose in life" that can be realized in the face of tragedy, suffering, and death. Actually living in a total institution appears to diminish such expectations of the future.

Support for this distinction between hope and the affective states of anxiety was found in a more detailed analysis of response patterns to the Sentence Completion Test (SCT): the data used to generate anxiety and depression scores by use of the Gottschalk system. The responses to the SCT were divided into six categories suggested by Gottschalk, Springer, and Gleser (1961) for the analysis of verbal behavior: despair, mutilation, abandonment, symptoms of anxiety, unhappiness regarding self, and unhappiness regarding others. Of these six categories, there were increases only in two: in despair and mutilation. The increase in SCT responses that contained themes related to despair is congruent with the decrease in hopefulness: there was a diminished expectation that the institutional environment would be a personally gratifying one. The concurrent increase in themes of mutilation help to clarify the changes noted in feeling hope. The increase in themes of mutilation perhaps reflects the new resident's response to the highly medical environment of the institution, an environment that has meanings related to one's own vulnerability.

Self-Perception. The significant change in the perception of capacity for self-care reflects the adoption of the perception of oneself as a patient in the institution. A perception of a lessened adequacy for self-care relates, in part, to the presence of custodial staff whose job is to give care. The structure of the environment also induces a lowered perception of capacity for self-care, as, for example, having elevators that reduce the need to walk up or down stairs. These two factors, as well as several others, encourage an excessive sense of disability (Kahn, 1971). Obviously, when there is less need to prove to oneself that one is not old, much of the health-maintaining, counterphobic behavior of independently living aged evaporates. It is not atypical for an elderly lady in the community to negotiate three flights of stairs a few times daily. In the home, counterphobic maneuvers to deny illness and aging do not serve their former function. The lessened sense of capacity for self-care reflects acceptance of the status of being an ill, aged resident of a nursing home.

Consistent with the perception of less incapacity for self-care is an increase in body preoccupation. The body preoccupation score was generated by counting the references to one's whole body or a bodily part when completing twenty of the Sentence Completion Test items that did not contain a reference to the body, such as "I wish I . . . ." "People think of me as . . . ." and "My only trouble is . . . ." The increase in body preoccupation appears related not only to the custodial aspects of a highly medical environment, but also to living with sick aged as peers in a closed institution. The coin of the realm in social interchange among residents, as well as between residents and staff, is health and illness. The new resident learns quickly that to use the home according to the wishes of staff is to participate actively in the use of "healthful" resources. Most telling is the need to live congregately with other elderly ill in an age segregated institution. The new resident is now not a significant member of an extended family, but only another resident who needs care and protection.

Among the other measures in this area of self-perception, only affiliation changed. There was a lessening of affiliation and a more hostile presentation of self in interaction with others. The general issue of stability and change in the self-system will be considered after a discussion of change in loss meanings.

Significance of Systematic Changes.   Entering and living in the institutional environment was not associated with changes that would support belief in the "destructiveness of institutions." The changes that were found did not suggest institutional effects of destructiveness; changes such as a lessening of hopefulness, in the absence of an increase in depression, or the adoption of the patient role. Apparently the institution forces the adoption of the patient role, including increasing the preoccupation with bodily concerns and personal vulnerability, which, in turn, reduces the elderly resident's expectations for future gratifying experiences that can give purpose to life.

Loss Meanings

Is there a particular meaning to the losses associated with becoming a resident? To assess change over time in the meaning of loss for the sample undergoing institutionalization, the changes in earliest memories for the study sample from pre-admission to 2 months postadmission were compared to changes in four groups of memories: earliest memories 1 year apart from aged persons living independently in the community, earliest memories also gathered 1 year apart from long-term institutionalized aged persons, earliest memories gathered at a 6-month interval while on the waiting list, and earliest memories gathered 6 weeks and then again 1 year after admission. For all five groups, the two earliest memories were compared.

In the repetition of earliest memories, the earliest memories from preadmission to postadmission did indeed manifest significantly more shifts toward the increased introduction of loss than was the case for the other four groups of repeated earliest memories. As reported in detail by Tobin and Etigson (1968), 51 percent (or 23 of 45) of the repeat memories of those becoming institutionalized manifested such shifts in introduced loss as contrasted to only 20 percent (or 14 of 70) of all the other repeat earliest memories. These figures represent a significant mean difference of 31.1 percent (t = 4.8, $p <$ .001). Moreover the 51 percent shift in introduction of higher levels of loss for the group undergoing institutionalization was appreciably greater than the shift in each of the four groups. The corresponding percentage for the community group was 22 percent (6 of 27); for the long-term institutionalized group, 18 percent (3 of 17); for the waiting list group, 0 percent (0 of 7); and for the short-term institutionalized group, 26 percent (5 of 19).

A further analysis was performed to determine if the overall negative shift on the 5-point scale reflected a shift from "no-loss" (levels 1 and 2) to "loss" (levels 3 and 4), as well as from "no-loss and minimal loss" (levels 1, 2, and 3) to "extreme loss" (levels 4 and 5). Statistically significant differences were also found in these comparisons of the memories of the aged who were becoming institutionalized and the memories gathered from those in more stable environments. These findings suggest, therefore, that the impact of becoming institutionalized is reflected in the changed reports of earliest memories, as manifested by an increase in the introduction of loss in the repeat reconstruction, particularly the losses relating to mutilation and death.

Memory changes sometimes occurred where the same incident was reported at both times. For example, in the following earliest memories there was a reconstruction of the same incident, but from Time 1 to Time 2 there was also a shift to a higher level of introduced loss.

> Time 1. "I remember my mother. She had hair like braids, open and falling upon her shoulder. She was sitting up in her bed and near her on her table was a bottle of honey and I remember asking her for honey. That's all I remember—nothing before and nothing behind. I still can see her sitting in bed. I must have been 2 years, 2 or 3. Closer to 2, I guess. But that's a picture I have. *(What did you feel?)* I just didn't know she was ill or nothing. It's just a picture. I just remember I wanted that honey. *(Did you get it?)* No, I don't remember. I can see the spoon and the bottle." *(Level 3.)*

> Time 2. "I remember my mother's death. I remember at least one moment of it. She had honey on her bed and I wanted some of that honey. I didn't really understand that she was dying. I was almost 3 years old. That's all I remember. I can see her face clearly even now. She had two braids hanging down. This picture is all I remember of her." *(Level 5.)*

The contrast between the two memories suggests that a breakthrough of repression had occurred in which previously withheld, archaic material was now being expressed. It would appear that in the first report the pain of mother's death is defended against, but breaks through in the second telling of the same incident. In the reconstruction of the same incident at both times, there is a central theme of oral deprivation (e.g., wanting, but not getting, the honey), as well as the personally meaningful symbolism of mother's braids.

However, more often the increase in loss in becoming institutionalized was associated with a shift in the incident, as in the following three examples of the repeat earliest memory.

Time 1. "I remember when I was a little girl my father used to wake me up in the morning to go milk the cow. We used to go for a swim in the lake." *(Level 1.)*

Time 2. "Remember my brother died of very bad sickness when I was about 8 years. He lived 1 week and that's all. Doctors did not know what to do for him. I suppose I felt bad but I don't remember so far back. He was 4 years older than me." *(Level 5.)*

A second example:

Time 1. "When I was 6 years old, I remember playing in the street. We were shaking trees to make the apples come down *(respondent laughs)*. That's what the boys were doing. I remember falling down once but nothing happened . . . 6 or 7 years, about." *(Level 3.)*

Time 2. "I was born next to the world-famous Black Forest. The first things I remember were all tragic things. The early death of my father. *(How old were you?)* Eight years. Three months after my father passed away, my mother had her sixth child. I have 4 sisters. All of us had to work a little. It was a small town and I used to sell Chanukah candles and do other light work. We were poor." *(Level 5.)*

A third, and final, example:

Time 1. "I liked to go swimming and mother wouldn't let me. Once I stood on the pier and fell in. I remember how they took me out and took me to my mother. That's all I remember. I wasn't sick." *(Level 3.)*

Time 2. "Didn't have coffins in the old country like they do here. My father died. I remember my sister was still a

breast baby. My mother was going to him and crying. It
was in the fall of the year. My father had gone over to the
Succoth (a Jewish holiday) booth. It was a cold day. My
mother said, "Don't go." But he was a stubborn man and
so he got pneumonia and died. He was very young. My
mother was left with five children. *(What was your age?)* I
was maybe 7 or 8 years old. I remember my father laying
on the floor. It wasn't like here in America with a coffin.
My mother carried on so much and my younger sister and
I held her by her skirt. The two of us were very scared."
(Level 5.)

These three examples suggest that these aged respondents
had a repertoire of meaningful early events that could be selected as the earliest memory. In turn, the selection of a particular meaningful early memory to be the reconstructed earliest
memory was influenced by the fact of institutionalization.

The Meaning of the Shift. When describing an early
memory, many respondents emphasized different themes from
one time to the next. Measured after entry into the homes, the
amount of change in respect to the introduction of themes of
loss was greater for those undergoing institutionalization (51
percent) than for the control samples (20 percent). The difference in percentage suggests that the one in three aged persons
who shifted toward expressing more loss would not have done
so had they not entered the homes. The increase in themes
related to mutilation and death suggests a shift toward an increased underlying experience of being vulnerable, a greater
consciousness of personal physical frailty and mortality. This
change is specifically related to entering and living in the institution, to the actual relocation from the waiting-list environment
to the institutional environment, and to living in a total institution with other sick elderly in a home that is to be the last one.

It is surprising that with such a significant shift toward
greater loss, and especially to the loss meanings of mutilation
and death, that so little change was observed in psychological
status. Although there was indeed a shift in the meaning of loss
—from abandonment to an increased personal vulnerability—

becoming a resident in these total institutions brought few manifest changes in behavior. The relatively small change in self-perception, which has been so often claimed to be sensitive to the effects of institutional life, is particularly surprising.

The View of Self

Goffman has been an early and convincing proponent of the position that profound and pervasive modification in the self-concept results from living in a total institution. The modification is postulated to occur in both self-esteem and the stability of the self—to be a "de-selfing" process that lowers self-esteem while injuring the ability to maintain a consistency in self-definition. To emphasize the destructive consequences of the stripping of personal identity by the total institution, Goffman (1961) has developed the concept of mortification of the self. His characteristic logic is expressed in the following quote (p. 23):

> *Whatever the form or the source of these various indignities, the individual has to engage in activity whose symbolic implications are incompatible with his conception of self. A more diffuse example of this kind of mortification occurs when the individual is required to undertake a daily round of life that he considers alien to him—to take on a disidentifying role.*

Most studies of the effect of institutionalization on the aged, however, have focused on the lowering of self-esteem rather than on the dimensions of the self that change. These several studies of self-esteem and institutionalization, which have typically used a cross-sectional design, were reviewed in an earlier chapter (see, for example, Laverty, 1950; Mason, 1954; Pollack and others, 1962; Webb, 1959). The present investigation was more concerned with the dimensions on which a person perceives himself; and, in turn, with whether there is a shift on the dimensions associated with becoming institutionalized. If the aged person who enters an institution is able to maintain the same self-image he had before admission, this ability would be evidence for stability of the self. In the present approach, it was assumed that a highly stable sense of self in the face of varying ecological demands would reflect an active process of coping, with a goal of maintaining a unified sense of self (Hilgard, 1949; Lecky, 1951, 1956; Rogers, 1951; Snygg and Combs, 1949). A stable self-image is thus conceptualized as the product of an active process aimed at assuring continuity when the integrity of the person is threatened.

As stated by Lecky (1956, pp. 89-90):

All of an individual's values are organized into a single system, the preservation of whose integrity is essential. The nucleus of the system, around which the rest of the system revolves, is the individual's evaluation of himself. The individual sees the world from his own viewpoint, with himself as the center. Any value entering the system which is inconsistent with the individual's valuation of himself cannot be assimilated. It meets with resistance and is likely, unless a reorganization is made, to be rejected. This resistance is a natural phenomenon; it is essential for the maintenance of individuality. The changing situations present continuous problems of adjustment, but the organization can make a unified movement in only one direction at a time, which explains why a single tendency can be dominant at one time. The striving for unity and organization or integrity is constant. The individual's organization of values makes itself evident in the regularity of his behavior. This organization not only defines his role in life, but furnishes him with his standards, which he feels obliged to maintain.

The interpersonal framework developed by Leary (1957) was used to construct an instrument that permitted three aspects of self-perception to be measured: self-esteem, self-image, and adequacy of examples to support the self-image. As explained in more detail in the appendix at the end of this book, Leary's framework permits a specification of sixteen areas of interpersonal behavior that are systematically related to each other. These sixteen interpersonal areas can be grouped, in turn, into eight octants and then into two global dimensions: dominance-submission and affiliation-hostility. For each of the sixteen areas, three items were developed and, from this pool of forty-eight self-descriptive items, the respondent could select those he felt particularly relevant to himself. After he selected those statements that he felt described his own interaction with others, the respondent was asked to give an example for each of the items from his current relationships. Weighting items for self-esteem permitted the computation of a self-esteem score. Similarly, a weighting of examples, positively for examples from the present or past and negatively for examples that supported the selected self-descriptive items through invalid or distorted evidence, generated an adequacy score. The instrument also permitted an assessment of the content of the social self. From the percentage of items selected from each of the sixteen interpersonal areas or eight octants, the two interpersonal dimensions of dominance-submission, and affiliation-hostility could be assessed.

To explore stability in the self-concept, three indices were developed by Rosner (1968) to contrast stability for the study sample from preadmission to initial adjustment with the institutionalized and community control samples over a 1-year interval. For this analysis, three carefully matched subsamples were selected (twenty, twenty-two, and sixteen in the respective samples). The first index was the percentage of initial items that were selected at the second administration. The stability of item selection was found to be very high and comparable for the three groups: in each sample, four of five items selected the second time had also been selected initially. The second index was also the percentage of items selected the second time that had been selected initially but now with those items eliminated that were selected by 75 percent or more of the respondents. The stability of these less generally chosen items was also high and comparable for the three groups: in each sample, close to three of four items chosen after admission had been chosen before admission. On this index of the more idiosyncratic items, there was also no effect on the consistency of the self-view as a result of entering and living in the homes. For the third index, shifts in the proportion of items chosen within each octant were computed. Respondents showed very little shift in the proportion of items selected within octants: the actual shifts were about one item per octant. Again, all groups tended to be comparable, and, for all groups, stability was very high.

Further evidence of stability was obtained through an analysis of a group of sixteen respondents who were tested on the Self-Sort Interview Task weekly for the first 6 weeks after their entrance into the homes. Stability of item selection from week to week remained as high for these sixteen respondents as for any other group studied, despite the immediacy of the disruptive life change.

The stability of self-perception was also compared to the stability evidenced within the other dimensions by correlating Time 1 and Time 2 scores. Measures related to the self-system showed the highest stability coefficients (generally in the .50s). Coefficients for emotional state measures were also high (in the .40s) with the measure of well-being, the Life Satisfaction Rating, having the highest stability coefficients (.70 for the study sample, .81 for the community sample, and .76 for the institutionalized sample). For measures in the other two areas, cognitive functioning and affective responsiveness, there was lower stability, reflecting changes of respondents over time in relation to other respondents in the sample.

These several findings suggest strongly that the actual entering and living in the institution are not very disruptive to the self-system. Overall, the amount of change found in self-view, as assessed by the Self-Sort Interview technique, was rather minimal. The evidence, therefore, does not support the view that there is a stripping of the self on entering and living in the institution.

To further clarify the stability of the self-concept, the adequacy of examples used to validate self-descriptions was examined. Possibly, after entering the home and living there for 2 months, the older person is able to develop ways of interacting with peers and staff that reinforce the self-concept. As described earlier, five types of evidence, or categories, were generated that reflected a range of self-maintenance mechanisms or self-validating techniques used by the aged to support the consciously expressed self-concept. The categories allowed examples to be classified as from the present, from the past, statements of conviction, statements of a "wish to be," and distortions of evidence. An overall score was generated by summing scores for each of the five categories for adequacy of response. On this overall score there were no differences from one time to the next for any sample. Nor did the percentage of responses within any of the five categories change from one time to the next. Yet there was a great deal of change for individuals. For example, at both times—before and after admission—47 percent of examples were from the present. Yet the average change of examples related to the present was 22 percent, reflecting the fact that some individuals increased their percentage of present examples to this extent while others decreased their percent of present examples to a similar large extent. When change in examples was analyzed for each octant, similar shift in the nature of evidence was found. The large variability in type of evidence to support the content of the self appears to be more of a phenomenon of aging than of the impact of institutionalization. Young adults that were studied used only current evidence whereas the elderly resorted to a variety of sources, past as well as current, for evidence to validate their self-concept.

There was generally, therefore, a rather high stability in the dimensions of the self-concept before and after institutionalization. Indeed, the high stability among aged undergoing institutionalization was comparable to the high stability of the control sample. Thus there was no apparent massive disorganization of the self-system, as the literature would suggest occurs when aged people enter and live in a total institution. An explanation for this stability may relate to the use of defensive maneuvers to maintain the sense of self. The inability to maintain a rather high stability may be the ultimate sign of complete disorganization. The maintenance of a high degree of stability may be of greater importance for aged persons because of their need to cope with external crisis and internal degenerative change. Living until the late 70s or 80s may necessitate an ability to maintain the sense of self in the face of environmental and personal upheavals.

The only shift that did occur was on the affiliation-hostility dimension, which has been shown not to reflect any pervasive change in the content of the self-concept. The shift in affiliation does, however, suggest a perception of less friendliness and more hostility toward others. Using Leary's description, it is a shift from perceiving oneself as helpful, sympathetic, affectionate, and cooperative to perceiving oneself as aggressive, critical, rebellious, and skeptical in relation to others.

Interpersonal Relations

Does this diminution in affiliation toward others suggest a decline in interaction with others? It has also been shown that there was no lessening in affective responsiveness, which would suggest that in portraying oneself as less affiliative and more hostile there was no corresponding affective withdrawal from others and the social situation. Because institutional environments such as homes for the aged encourage engagement with others, possibly there is increased interaction with others—but apparently it is a type of interaction that, at least at first, stimulates hostile rather than affiliative responses, which residents then incorporate into their self-image. One reason for seeking institutional care is to be with other people, and the resident may indeed gain increased opportunities for interaction with other people, but the interaction may be of a type that creates an actual or perceived change in interpersonal posture.

One instrument used to assess interpersonal relations was the Personal Resources Questionnaire, an eleven-item scale that requires the respondent to mention the names of one or more specific others who can, for example, be turned to when lonely, for help or when happy. After admission the task was expanded to include the inquiry of "who here in the home?" as well as who, in general. This additional inquiry encouraged an increase in the number of others who were mentioned and also demonstrated whether the resident could identify specific staff members, roommates, and other residents by name.

Typical of the increase in the number of others mentioned after admission are Mrs. F. and Mrs. S. Before admission Mrs. F., an elderly widow, introduced five specific others: grandchildren (scored as two), two daughters, and a friend across the street—a lawyer (too vague to be scored). After admission, ten specific others were introduced, three of whom were in the home: a friend, the social worker and her roommate. At preadmission Mrs. S. introduced six specific others: a cousin, this cousin's husband and a sister-in-law, the janitor and his wife, and a lady across the street. After admission she introduced nine specific others: four were from the original six (the janitor and the lady across the street were eliminated); the additional five were a male and female friend in the home, two of her three roommates, and the director of the home. Both of these women exhibited a rather typical pattern after admission of introducing some of the significant others who were available when they on the waiting list as well as others who were in the home. These others usually were roommates or friends who lived in another part of the home and staff—usually the director, assistant director, or social worker.

While new people from the home were introduced, it was also typical to continue to mention family members. Are the same number of family members introduced as personal resources at both times? A subsample of 29 residents was assessed on several dimensions related to interpersonal orientation, in addition to the number of family members mentioned in response to the Personal Resource Questionnaire (Kuypers, 1969). On this questionnaire there was a significant decline in the number (from 4.7 to 3.6, $p < .05$). Clarification was provided by the responses to six direct questions regarding family relations. The questions were: (1) "Have there been any changes in how you get along with your children?" (2) "We all find faults with our children. What do you see as faults in your children?" (3) "What do you see as the best thing in your son (daughter)?" (4) "Is he (she) a different kind of person than when he (she) was a child?" (5) "What kind of things does he (she) do for you?" and (6) "What kind of things do you do for him (her)?" Responses to four of these questions (1, 2, 3, and 5) did not provide evidence of change, but responses to the other two questions did yield significant shifts. As expected, the parent's role changed after entering the home. In response to the sixth question, one in two (53 percent) reported that they had performed instrumental functions for children, such as babysitting, before admission but only one of thirteen (or 7 per- cent) reported such functions after admission. A more subtle change is revealed in responses to the fourth question. Before admission, only one of five (or 21 percent) reported that one or more of their children had changed for the better as they ma- tured, whereas after admission more than one of two (or 56 per- cent) reported positive change.

Why was there now a change toward perceiving children as more favorable, when only a few months before the children were seen as abandoning the respondent? Possibly there was an amelioration in the feelings of abandonment that were so perva- sive earlier when the respondent was on the waiting list. Al- though children tend to recede into the background with the increasing engagement with peers and staff in the home, there is apparently greater psychological involvement with intimate others as reflected in stories told to the TAT cards. For this measure, Kuypers (1969) assessed involvement in stories told to the TAT cards on a 3-point scale, from solitary noninter- personal activity, to minimal interaction with others, to active interpersonal exchange. On this measure, there was a significant increase of involvement (at the .05 level). One speculation that takes into account the more favorable perception of children, the lessened interaction with them, and the apparent greater psychological involvement relates not so much to a lessening of feelings of abandonment as to the task confronting the now institutionalized older person. This speculation is described as follows.

As the end of life approaches, the older person has the task of perceiving his life as a meaningful one (see, for example,

Erikson, 1959; Butler, 1963). Children can be used to fulfill this task because they are the carriers of cherished values and traditions. To the extent that children can be transformed into mythic figures who carry on values and traditions, the task can be successfully accomplished. Once living in the institution is a *fait accompli* and once the rage at being abandoned subsides, the older person can then return to transforming offspring and future generations into mythic figures that assure generational continuity and the meaningfulness of one's life. The "mythicizing" of children is reinforced in the institutional world of the old. The coin of the realm is famous offspring who are attentive and caring. Family attention provides leverage for personal prestige.

At the level of everyday life in the home, the expected activity with peers and the relief of loneliness may become secondary to roommate problems and to persistent feelings of loneliness. The gains of care, people, and activity are forthcoming, but these gains are not "packaged" differently as was anticipated. Staff members who were expected to provide for all one's needs do not have the time to dispense "tender loving care," and any fantasy of reunion with good mothering is soon to be severely taxed. The staff members have specific jobs to do and are rewarded for their efficient performance. In an institution, the lower staff personnel may exert powers that are unfamiliar to the new resident and that soon enough become evident if the new resident demands attention rather than approaching staff with the appropriate etiquette. On the other hand, care may have an intrusive quality, when the premium is on being alert, staying active, and being healthy. The staff may be successful in promoting interaction but the interaction with peers may be quite full of conflict. Losses of freedom and privacy may become secondary to perceiving oneself as more aggressive and hostile in establishing one's place in the interactional environment.

As a way of synthesizing the findings on interpersonal relations with other findings—including psychological status, the meaning of loss associated with entering and living in the homes, and the stability of the self-system—we shall return to one of three elderly women who were followed from the community before a decision was made to seek institutional care to the period of anticipatory institutionalization and, as now will be presented, through entering and living in the institution.

Case Study: Preadmission to Postadmission

The postadmission histories of the three women whose cases were presented earlier illustrate changes that typically occurred during the 2 months following admission. Because Mrs. A. ("I'm a Busy Lady") followed a more typical process than either Mrs. B. ("They Call me the Sunshine Lady"), whose son died a few days after she entered the home, or Mrs. C. ("I want People"), who was given a room in a small annex, across the street from the large main building, the changes for Mrs. A. will be discussed.

Mrs. A. before Admission. As described in the Chapter Two, Mrs. A. was first interviewed as part of the community sample before her decision to apply for admission to the home. She had recently moved from a faraway city, following her husband's death, in order to be closer to her beloved older sister, her daughter, and other family members. Mrs. A.'s daughter had helped her find a small apartment close to her sister where Mrs. A. could live by herself. Although 6 years earlier she had suffered a stroke, Mrs. A. was able to care for her homemaking needs and participate in a wide range of activities. She was described by the interviewer as an "admirable woman" who dealt with life's vicissitudes in a realistic, competent, and resolute manner. The interviewer was especially impressed by the warm feelings Mrs. A. expressed about her family.

A year after that interview, Mrs. A. applied for admission to the home. Her sister had died a few months before while Mrs. A. was still mourning the loss of her husband. The chief precipitant of the decision to apply to the home was her slow recovery from an operation. Depressed and lonely, Mrs. A. agreed with her daughter that she should not live alone and applied to the home, thinking it a reasonable alternative to her present arrangement. She went to live in a convalescent home until her admission to the home.

Marked psychological changes had occurred during the interim between the first interview, held before Mrs. A.'s decision to apply, and the second interview, held while she awaited admission to the home. Assessment on the standard battery of tests revealed negative changes in cognitive functioning, emotional responsiveness, and emotional states. Responses to the Sentence Completion Test showed a shift toward loneliness, depression, feelings of distance from children, and a wish for more intimacy with others. Her attitude toward the impending relocation was described by the interviewer as "very realistic," in light of her awareness that the home could not replace meaningful lost others, but did instead offer security and the opportunity to be active. She felt that she could avoid interpersonal conflicts with other residents by going her own way and expected that daily phone contact and weekly visits with her daughter would make life in the home more tolerable.

Postadmission Impressions. After her admission to the home, the interviewer noted no apparent change in Mrs. A. As before, she was neatly dressed, wearing jewelry, and carefully made up. Warm and friendly, she talked eagerly about her family and showed the interviewer pictures, cards and valentines from her children and grandchildren. Again, the interviewer praised Mrs. A.: "I enjoyed her very much. She's pleasant, has a cute sense of humor, is interested in others, and outside affairs. She asked me to stop and see her whenever possible, and I will do this, as I enjoyed talking to her." What impressed the interviewer most was "Mrs. A.'s ability to adjust to a difficult situation. She still maintained a philosophical outlook toward life. She has great fortitude." Significantly, however, the interviewer detected a receptive attitude toward death that was apparent in Mrs. A.'s answer "Why doesn't He take me, I've lived long enough," in response to the question: "What are the worst features about life?"

The interviewer indicated that Mrs. A. had apparently made a good adjustment and appeared to enjoy various activities of the home and the company of others. She described Mrs. A. as somewhat selective in her choice of friends and activities. Yet she noted that Mrs. A. got along well with others and seemed to be liked by them. Continuing to maintain a close

relationship with her family, Mrs. A. went out each weekend
with her son. Of her overall adjustment, the interviewer said,
"The transition was probably not too difficult. She had a pretty
good idea of what to expect and, being the warm, friendly
person she is, seemed to fit into things quite well. She did not
describe any difficulties."

The impression Mrs. A. made on the assistant director and
the floor nurse corroborated the interviewer's opinion. "Mrs.
A.," the assistant director said, "seems to have come home. She
is doing well. She gets along with others, though she hasn't
made it as far as the 400 (the elite group of patients, in the eyes
of the staff). She takes advantage of most of the recreational
activities; she is very philosophical about her adjustment. Her
family takes her out frequently." The nurse observed: "She's
friendly with the others and they seem to like her. She's a sweet
lady."

These impressions suggest that Mrs. A. had indeed made
the transition to institutionalized life in a very admirable fashion. The only hint of maladaptation to becoming institutionalized appears in the implication that she would welcome death.
Mrs. A.'s response to open-ended questions in the interview, in
general, however, did not reveal a preoccupation with morbid
concerns.

Mrs. A.'s Comments after Admission.   Mrs. A. had only
good things to say about the institution.

> *It has been fine, I'm not the kicking kind. Peo-
> ple are nice. I get along fine. It's an excellent home.
> We had a seventy-fifth anniversary of the home last
> night. It was a big affair. So many people came from
> all over . . . . It was a very nice affair. Very interest-
> ing. I've been doing a lot of things; going down to OT*
> (occupational therapy). *I do what I can; weaving a
> potholder, and now I'm making a doll. Going back to
> my young age* (she said in an amused way). *With me
> things go pretty well all over.*
>
> *I make up my mind to come. I had trouble with
> my eyes and couldn't cook for myself. . . . I signed*

up for a class here. Got my nose into everything (laugh). *May even try a little painting. After all, Grandma Moses did it at 90, and I'm 80. I felt very good when I got in because I knew this home from some friends who had been here awhile. Family all near here. My niece, son, daughter . . . I just got my clothes and came. Glad that they assigned me to this lady who's not much of a talker, but we get along. Only thing is, she's immaculate, I'm not a housekeeper, I was always in business or something and never had time . . . . that [assigning the roommate to her] was very nice and they [the staff] helped [her to settle in]. It was very sweet, couldn't be better.*

I don't remember when I first arrived. The time —I think I just came before lunch. They assigned me to a table with two ladies. They just sat there and threw daggers at each other. But I never paid attention to them . . . . I felt at home. You see, sometimes the parents live with the children. They bring them here. I came of my own accord. I had an apartment by myself. When I couldn't take care of myself, I couldn't cook or do shopping, I came here to make this my home and I'm very satisfied. I just adapted myself just as if it was my own home. You get used to the rules and regulations. My niece visits, my son comes every Friday and takes me to his house for dinner. His son is very religious. My daughter-in-law respects this and changed the house all around . . . . I think they have a good manager around here.

First thing they give you is a nice room—try to match you up with a nice roommate. I don't know how others are. Some have difficulties but that's not the management's fault. They're bitter within themselves. I'll never be unhappy here. Everything's good. The meals are not like at home, but what can you expect when you cook for 200. If I don't like something, I just don't eat it . . . . I get along with my roommate because she minds her business and I mind mine. She hollers at me sometimes for not making the bed, but I don't mind it. She always goes down and sits by the reception desk . . . she thinks she's a big shot. The social worker says she said she might be able to teach me to type. So I could help out in the office.

Friendly with just some of the others, just a couple that I knew before and I met some new people. I sit and talk. Mr. D., a resident, asked me to write something for the brochure he's doing. . . . I don't know what they, the other residents, think, but I can fit in with anybody. I'm sure they say that I get along fine. I think I've been accepted. Maybe, I find everyone congenial. . . . I sit in the lobby and like to see people coming and going. I liked to be with people all my life. I see the people who come to visit . . . my son comes, my daughter comes, my niece; I call them up and they call me up, not as often as before, but we talk. I got several Christmas and Chanukah cards.

Describing her daily routine, Mrs. A. said:

First when I get up in the morning I have breakfast, about a quarter to 7:00, then I come up here and rest a little, and then go to OT. So far, I'm making potholders. Some sew, some paint; I always sew, then I go for lunch. In the afternoon, usually there's some sort of activity. Last week I finished up in the newcomer's club, even got a diploma for attending all the sessions. (She got up to show it to the interviewer.) *I'm sorry that the sessions ended; they were very interesting. I went to the current events and that was very interesting. Signed up for that and also signed up for the scribblers [the residents who write for the home's monthly newsletter], but we haven't met yet. I wrote an article for Mr. D. for the brochure. Sometimes movies and other things. They*

*were going to a Chinese restaurant for lunch. I don't
really like Chinese food but I want to go for the ride.
I lay down a little and take a rest. I saw movies of
Canada. In the evening after supper they always have
something. If they don't, I go in the television room
or come in and watch my own TV. I go to bed after
the news. The days have about the same routine.
Some days they have a lecture or show slides I
used to go to meetings and belonged to a social club.
The change is that I don't go anyplace, except when
my son comes and takes me to his club.*

Her review and evaluation of her life was very much as that
expressed earlier. She discussed in realistic fashion its ups and
downs. She felt, however, that she was very successful. She said,
"I put nine thousand dollars into the home when I came. I
think I made out pretty good because I provided for myself and
prepared for the future." When asked about the future, she said,
"I just fear I shouldn't get more incapacitated than I am, so I
couldn't take care of myself." She continued: "The most
satisfying was that I accomplished with my children what I
wanted and that they are all happy. I think that's the most important thing, the welfare of my children."

In regard to various affects, she tended to respond as she
did before admission. She began by denying feelings of depression, loneliness, and anger, but then went on to elaborate on
these very internal states. When asked whether she had feelings
of depression she answered: "No! I'm sure there were times that
were depressing to me. Life is not a bowl of cherries. . . . I start
to think of all the others who are worse off than I." To the
question "How do you feel when you are depressed?" she
responded:

*You start to think of your past what you was
and did before. Only thing that I do is to start to
read. Reading helps me to forget everything. I don't
feel lonelier here. When I was alone, I was more
lonely. Here, I always find someone to talk to and*

*I'm a good listener. I don't feel lonely too often. But
sometimes when I think about my past, I pinch myself to see if I'm alive.*

To a query about whether she had experienced loneliness, she
answered: "Since my sister is gone, those 2 days on the weekends are very lonely for me. Otherwise, the other days, I try to
fill them up with the different activities in the home." When
asked how she overcame depression she said: "just think it over
and try to make the best of it."

In describing her feelings of anger she said:

*I remember when I remained alone with the chil-
dren when my first husband passed away. I was depressed. I came to this city to stay with my sister. She
took care of my children and I went to work. Nineteen sixty-five was a bad year for me. I was sick and
had to give up my apartment. I gave up my independence, but I made up my mind to make the best
of it. I cannot think of anything, but I am a human
being. Even when I heard that my roommate had told
someone I was a big fool, I didn't get angry.*

Obviously, Mrs. A. has feelings of depression, loneliness,
and anger which she can articulate only hesitantly. She is especially concerned with controlling her anger toward her roommate, with suppressing the anger rather than creating a confrontation.

When asked to discuss her present interpersonal relationships, Mrs. A. became very talkative. She discussed her daughters in faraway states and the daughter and son that visited her,
as well as her son with whose family she ate dinner once a
week:

*He comes and picks me up. I am in touch with
my daughter and son everyday. They come as often
as they can, either every week or every two
weeks . . . . They think I am tops. I'm important to*

*my family. I worked hard to provide them with an
education. Now they want to do for me . . . they have
no faults. They're doing all they can to make me
happy. My daughter is always very good to me. I
pulled her out of a sickness that no one else would
have had the patience to do. She always appreciated
that.*

At the end of the interview session, she again reviewed life
in the home and the pathway to the home. She said, "I had
several people here that I knew. So I knew it was a good place. I
felt I couldn't keep up my apartment, couldn't go out because
of my eyesights, couldn't cook, if I got sick. Here they have
medical care." She continued to talk of the various activities in
which she had been involved including occupational therapy,
current events, scribblers, and so forth.

*When I felt I could not take care of myself, I
wanted to have someone come and stay with me for
board and room and salary. But I couldn't find anyone. The family, to tell you the truth, always left the
decision to me. I always had to make my own decisions. As long as I could take care of myself, it was all
right. It was the saddest day when I turned in my
keys to the apartment. I felt I had lost my independence . . . I haven't given up too much. When I
was living there I went to my meetings, I hope to go
to them again.*

Coming into the home was associated with the loss of independence for Mrs. A. She had always felt able to master the
world and had always prided herself on not being dependent.
The decision to come to the home had to be her own, perhaps
in order to balance the loss of independence it symbolized.

Assessment: Preadmission to Postadmission. Mrs. A.
made an overall improvement in cognitive functioning from before until after admission to the home. She showed only one
sign of inadequacy at both times, because of two errors on each

administration of the Mental Status Questionnaire. On the first
testing, she was unable to recall the present date and her date of
birth; on the second, she could not remember the location of
the home and the current President of the United States. On the
other five assessment procedures, Mrs. A. scored above the
deficit level and improved her performance on three of the six
(retention of paired word associates, organization as reflected in
copying the Bender Gestalt Designs, and perceptual accuracy as
reflected in stories told to the TAT cards).

On the dimension of affective responsiveness, Mrs. A. also
showed improvement. She showed an increased affective range
while maintaining a high level of willingness to introspect. Mrs.
A.'s preadmission and postadmission TAT protocols illustrated
this improvement in affective range. (Note that the TAT was
also used to assess preceptual accuracy within the dimension of
cognitive adequacy.) Mrs. A.'s stories after admission were more
fully structured and richer in feeling than before:

Card 1—Boy with Violin.

> a. *Preadmission story*. "It seems to me that this kid is
> talking by the telephone . . . telling somebody what
> gift to buy him. Is that right? What can I tell you
> now? *(What was the outcome?)* Well I suppose he
> didn't get what he wanted; he looks kind of sad."

> b. *Postadmission story*. "Is it a child or a woman? Dif-
> ferent kind of story if it's a child or if it's a woman.
> *(Respondent paused, studied picture some more.)* I
> think it's a boy and he's looking at this. Maybe some
> kind of ammunition. Think maybe he'll grow up and
> have to go in Army. Trying to think what to study,
> trying to make up his mind, tho' I don't know from
> where—maybe his parents. Very much interested and
> kind of worried, too, about it. Looks like a smart
> child. Just think how to start. Will need some assist-
> ance on that—from folks or friends. *(What will hap-
> pen?)* May work out his own way—you ask a lot of
> people and then you do what *you* want."

Card 2—Farm Scene.

   a. *Preadmission story.* "I don't see very well. To my idea, this party wanted to take this girl for a ride and the mother is not consenting. She looks too stern. The girl is not so happy about it.

   b. *Postadmission story.* "That looks to be the mother and that's the father and that's the daughter and the mother is asking question whether they should go horseback riding or not. Father seems to look over horse to see if it's fit for daughter. Daughter can't make up her mind whether to go horseback riding or go to school. I think she would rather go to school than go horseback riding. She looks to be very intelligent girl who is more interested in her studies than her pleasures—and I hope that she accomplishes what she is starting out to do. The mother looks to be one of those mothers who likes to dominate. The father looks like he is more concerned about the child, whether she should go horseback riding or not."

Card 6BM—Mother and Son.

   a. *Preadmission story.* "It seems to be that fellow is asking—that must be the mother of the girl—something, and she is not consenting about it, and she feels very sad."

   b. *Postadmission story.* "Son is coming to ask the mother about some girl he likes. He looks very sad because he doesn't know if mother will like the girl. Mother trying very hard to do the right thing. Maybe he wants to marry a Shiksi *(respondent laughed)*. You can never tell. The mother is very much concerned about him—and she looks up and prays to God that things will work out the right way—that's my story."

Card 7BM—Father and Son.

   a. *Preadmission story.* "The son has asked him something, and the father is meditating. He doesn't know whether to say yes or no. *(Respondent puts card down.)* That's what I think. Whatever it is, I don't know."

Card 17BM—Boy on Rope.

a. *Preadmission story.* "He is climbing up to look for something. It seems that he has noticed something. He looks so interested. He seems to be kind of pleased with what he sees up there."

b. *Postadmission story.* "Oh baby—what is he trying to go up? He's looking up and trying to see how far he can go. Doesn't want to fall and hurt himself too much. Maybe he wants to go up to moon—but not on rope. *(Respondent laughed.)* Never make it on rope. This really portrays life, too—if somebody think too high, don't know if he'll achieve it, what he's going to be. But he just keeps on trying."

The attitude of passivity implicit in the structure and content of the stories rendered at the first administration was replaced by a more active orientation by the respondent to the same cards at the second administration. At both times, the issue of mutual help was raised. It was resolved, however, in the constructing stories at the second administration. In the second story told to Card 1, for example, Mrs. A. urged, "you do what you want"; in the second story to Card 6BM, she decided that the father was going to consent to his son's wishes; and in the second story to Card 17BM, she says, of the boy on the rope, that he just keeps on trying. The recurrent outcome theme after admission was that of resolution of interpersonal conflict.

There was a change in her emotional states. Although she maintained a high level of feelings of well-being, she also sustained rather high levels of anxiety and depression. She became less hopeful, as reflected on the Srole Anomie Scale. On four of the five statements—which require the respondent to state their agreement or disagreement on a 5-point continuum—a shift occurred toward a more negative appraisal of the world. These four statements were: "It's hardly fair to bring children into the world with the way things look for the future" (*disagree* to *undecided*); "Nowadays a person has to live pretty much for today and let tomorrow take care of itself" (*agree* to *strongly agree*); "These days a person doesn't really know on whom he can count" (*strongly disagree* to *strongly agree*); and "There's little use in writing to public officials because often they aren't really interested in the problems of the average man" (*undecided* to *strongly agree*). On the fifth item, "In spite of what some people say, the lot of the average man is getting worse," however, she become more positive (*undecided* to *disagree*). Yet the overall impression is to a more negative outlook. Apparently, Mrs. A.'s attitude toward the world after admission reflects a disparagement of institutional life and, perhaps, the inability of family members to make her life in the home a more enriching experience. The clearest example of the general change appeared in the shift from strong disagreement to strong agreement with the statement: "These days a person doesn't really know who he can count on." Why did such an extreme shift occur? Possibly her family, as in the past, could be counted on to visit and offer some emotional support but could not diminish her conflict with a roommate or feelings of loneliness on Saturday and Sunday.

Mrs. A.'s response to the last item on the interviewer's Time Dimension Question also revealed this shift toward hopelessness. To the inquiry "In general, do you find yourself thinking about the past or the future"? she responded, before admission: "I think about the past. If I think of the past I know what I am thinking about. But who can tell about the future? No one can!" After admission, she said: "If people knew what the future might bring, many people might commit suicide." What future is she talking about? The future that brought her to the home, or the prospect of life in the home that once only existed in the future, but now is a reality? Possibly both. Mrs. A.'s message might have been interpreted as: "If I had only known what it really would be like to live in a home for aged, I would have considered suicide," or possibly "If I were to change, to deteriorate as other old people do before my eyes, it would be better for me to die." Despite these dramatic shifts in her emotions and point of view toward the future, Mrs. A.'s feeling of well-being remained consistently high during the period of becoming a resident. This high level of well-being is apparent from Mrs. A.'s scores on the Life Satisfaction Ratings presented below. The rationale for the interviewer's ratings was the same at both administrations.

1. *Zest versus apathy.* Mrs. A. was rated five on this scale because she showed an active interest in people and events.

2. *Resolution and fortitude.* Rated four because she appeared to have maintained a philosophic attitude while coping with many difficult situations.

3. *Goodness of fit between desired and achieved goals.* Rated five. Having provided a good education for her children who she felt loved her, Mrs. A. evinced feelings of pride that reflected the successful accomplishment of her goals.

4. *Self-concept.* Rated four. Mrs. A.'s good self-image was manifested in her sense of her importance to her family, who, according to her, "think I'm tops." Pride in her appearance, and her ability to take care of herself, as well as to get along with others, indicate a good self-image.

5. *Mood.* Rated four. The interviewer noted a balance between Mrs. A.'s differing moods. Thus, although she spoke of occasional depression, she also described her attempt to master it and to count her blessings. Similarly, her statement that she would like to die was accompanied by indications that she enjoyed life, family, and activities in the home and usually experienced positive feelings.

A change in body preoccupation was reflected in the introduction of themes related to bodily function in Mrs. A.'s responses to the Sentence Completion Test. Before admission, among her responses to the thirty-two stems, Mrs. A. made three unsolicited allusions to bodily functions, whereas after admission six unsolicited allusions to bodily functions appeared in her responses. Before admission: "(I can't understand what makes me) weak"; "(To me death is) a big relief to people who are suffering or have incurable sickness. It's a blessing to them"; and "(My only trouble is) my eyes at the present." After admission: "(I can't understand what makes me) be *so* weak"; "(My only trouble is) that I'm not strong enough to do the things as I would like to"; "(I wish I) be a little stronger than I am, so I could do something"; "(I would like to be) well, of course—which I never will, but I would like to"; "(If only) I would be well. I would like to do all I could to help others"; and "(The thing I like about myself [shook her head]) what can I say about myself. I don't know. Only thing I like about myself is I thank God he didn't paralyze my brain." Besides this general shift in bodily preoccupation, some other shifts appeared. For example, in response to the stem "To me, hope means . . . ," Mrs. A. first added "to achieve something you have wished for" and later, "*everything*,"—a change that perhaps reflected her feelings of hopelessness. One stem evoked two answers with a consistent theme. As noted above, to "*To me death is* . . . ," Mrs. A.'s first addition was "a big relief," and after admission, "the best thing that can happen to anybody." Before coming to the home, Mrs. A. indicated that she would welcome death if it were to avert physical pain and suffering. In the second interview, however, after she was in the home, but *with no evidence of a deterioration in physical status,* she expressed that she had no qualifications regarding the benefits of death.

What was there in living in the home for the aged that made Mrs. A. feel no difference between herself and those who were "suffering" or stricken with an "incurable sickness." It may be that her experience among the home's sick inmates led Mrs. A. to believe that her only possible future was to become progressively more deteriorated. If so, she had indeed become incurable at that point. To paraphrase Ben Franklin, before admission she was long-lived, but now she was irreversibly and incurably old.

In the dimension of the self-system, a change occurred only in perception of capacity for self-care. Before admission, Mrs. A. said that she had difficulty walking up and down stairs. While this difficulty persisted, she had no need to climb stairs in the home. After admission to the home, she claimed difficulty in getting out of doors "because of my eyes," and in washing and bathing. Before admission she did not complain of difficulties in these two areas. Apparently, living in the home had made her conscious of these difficulties. The home's medical milieu probably created an expectation of managing with difficulty. To some extent, this effect of life in a home for the aged is unavoidable, because caretakers in the home wish to protect older persons such as Mrs. A., who might stumble in an unfamiliar outdoor area as a result of poor eyesight. Thus, one can understand why anxiety over falling and a fearful self-consciousness absent in the past became manifest in Mrs. A.'s behavior after she moved into the home. Washing and bathing oneself is made a more difficult task in the home because the tubs are designed for bathing the most deteriorated residents. Fixtures such as swinging metal seats used to ease the weak into the tub make it easier, if not necessary, for the ablest of people to ask for help in washing and bathing. Residents such as Mrs. A. are thus continually made aware, in a very personal sense, of actual or potential deficits in their capacity for the caring of themselves.

The other aspects of self were assessed by the Self-Sort Interview Task. This task was not administered to Mrs. A. while she was on the waiting list, because it was one of the last tasks on the battery and Mrs. A. was admitted to the home before the last session. Mrs. A. had completed the task, however, while a member of the community sample. Comparing her responses at this predecision period to her responses after admission, Mrs. A.'s self-esteem did not change; she used fewer examples to support her self-image and tended to draw them from the present. She greatly lessened, however, her sense of her own dominance in interaction with others. Other data suggest that more of the shift occurred in becoming an applicant than in entering the home. Unlike others tested on this task, there was not a decline in affiliation. But the stability of item selection was like others tested. In all, Mrs. A. chose a total of 38 different items at both interviews, choosing the same 27 twice, and because 34 items were selected after admission these 27 represent 84 percent of the items chosen before admission.

The examples that Mrs. A. offered, however, differed at the administrations. She tended to show the typical shift in most residents toward greater preoccupation with physical competence, active engagement with other residents, and distrust of other residents. Although most residents, however, typically shifted toward lessened affiliation, or toward greater hostility in interaction with others, Mrs. A. did not. The examples do, however, suggest a distrustful engagement with others beside her roommate. For the item, *I find fault with myself,* which was selected at both times, she was unable to offer concrete examples but after admission she chided herself for "trusting somebody that I shouldn't." Similarly, she selected the item *I am a trusting person* both times, saying after admission that "I do trust a little too much." Distrust may indeed be necessary in the interpersonal world of the home, where feelings can easily be bruised. Basically an open and trusting woman, Mrs. A. was aware of potential conflicts with other aged peers in the home. She had buttressed herself against hostile interaction before entering the home, however, and had determined to be an active participant in the life of the home. This she accomplished, even though it meant tolerating a caustic roommate. Mrs. A. had directed her energies to transcending bickering and abrasiveness in social interaction by walking away and turning to more pleasant people and activities. As she said to the item *Give in without a fuss,* "If somebody says something I don't feel too comfortable about I just don't talk back." Overall, Mrs. A. displayed less retaliatory hostile tendencies than most residents in the examples she gave in the testing after admission.

The More Latent Shift. Most respondents showed a marked shift in the focal concern as reflected in the earliest memory. While on the waiting list, Mrs. A. reported her earliest memory as follows:

> *When I was very little, 2 years old, I went out to*
> *the yard. A little chicken had just been hatched and I*
> *didn't know. I picked him up and the mother hen*
> *flew on my head. My mother told me she was still*
> *nursing me because she didn't want to get pregnant*
> *again. After all, I was the eighteenth child."*

Here an issue of birth is spelled out both in relationship to a chicken and to her mother.

Her initial description of the same memory, a year before application was as follows:

> *I remember one thing that happened when I was*
> *only about 2 years old. My mother nursed me until I*
> *was that age. She was afraid to have another baby. I*
> *guess eighteen was enough for her. I remember I was*
> *walking. There were some chicks in our yard. I put*
> *my hand out to them. A chicken flew on my head. I*
> *was very scared. I ran to my mother. Who else does a*
> *child run to? Later my mother told me that I was*
> *only 2 at the time.*

Here, too, concern is expressed with being one of many children and with the issues of birth, being nursed, and the possibility of personal injury. There was no introduction of death now or later when Mrs. A. was on the waiting list.

After admission, another issue emerged. Two months after admission, she described her earliest memory as follows:

> *One thing I remember very distinctly. My*
> *mother said I was 2 years old and still nursing. I re-*
> *member I saw a chicken was hatching an egg. I went*
> *out and squeezed the egg. The chicken flew out of*
> *my hand. My mother said I was 2. I was still nursing.*
> *You know why I was still nursing? Because my*
> *mother said if she were nursing, she wouldn't get*
> *pregnant. I was the eighteenth child. Of course, they*
> *didn't all live. They had epidemics in those days. No*
> *medicine like today.*

While the third version describes the same incident, it contains a reference to epidemics and death.

Mrs. A. described her earliest memory before she applied very much as she did while on the waiting list. Thus, the shift in content and the addition of the death theme cannot be explained simply by the passage of time. The increased concern with death and bodily functioning that Mrs. A. evidenced in the third description supports a belief that an inner experience of increased personal vulnerability results from living in the institutional environment among debilitated elderly.

Manifest and Latent Levels. Mrs. A. can be characterized as having shown minimal change at the manifest level, but marked change at the latent level. There were no manifest indications of an adverse reaction to becoming institutionalized. Indeed, her cognitive functioning and sensitivity to her own problems and the environment improved and her sense of well-being remained remarkably high. At the manifest behavioral level, the indication is of amelioration in functioning and emotional expression and of an overall self-consistency. Only minimal deteriorative changes occurred within the four areas of psychological functioning following entering and living in the institution. The three changes that did occur within the four areas, however, should not be minimized. These were: (1) less hopefulness; (2) an increased concern with bodily functioning and a perception of less capacity for self-care; and (3) more distrustfulness, if not anger and hostility, in interaction with peers in the home. That these changes occurred to Mrs. A. is of special importance because she was considered to be making an admirable, if not superb, adjustment. The importance of these three adverse changes is supported when considered together with the shift in the reconstruction of the earliest memory—the introduction of the theme of death after admission. The underlying shift is toward increased narcissistic loss.

Summary

The home is a world of very old people who are frail and in need of protective care. There is no escaping from this world. The future is foreshortened and hopefulness regarding an extensive, gratifying, and controllable future cannot be maintained. It is also impossible to escape from an identification with aging and deteriorating peers, which impinges on the new resident every moment of the day. Reminders of physical deterioration come not only from peers but also from the constant attention of the staff to nursing and medical care. To be sure, vigorous efforts are made to create a social and even homelike environment, but the needs of the resident population dictates that the home be, above all, a sound medical facility.

Beyond the unavoidable identification with peers are the problems of actually relating to them. Such relating indeed is often abrasive. Mrs. A., who was more self-sufficient than most, could usually avoid conflict with others. She made a shaky truce with her roommate while smoldering and infuriated inside at the roommate's efforts to control her. Having to cope with fear-laden identifications with peers, as well as having constantly to be vigilant in personal contacts with other residents, leads to a preoccupation with one's own metamorphosis—to becoming irreversibly old. The most optimistic future then becomes to die without suffering, in isolation from beloved family and friends. Peer identification, as an explanation of effects, is a major component in environmental discontinuity; peers in the home symbolize the anticipated fears of abandonment generated during the waiting-list period and reinforce the fears of narcissistic losses that increase with age.

Mrs. A. was not typical, however, insofar as she was able to cope with this fearful identification without becoming cognitively disorganized, withdrawn into an unresponsive existence, and immobilized by anxiety and depression. Yet, the meaning of the identifications were of being mutilated and closer to death—in short, of being much more personally vulnerable. Why did these underlying malignant feelings not cause Mrs. A. to be more manifestly unhappy, anxious and depressed? More cognitively disorganized? More paralyzed and unresponsive to the world about her?

For answers to these apparent incongruities between latent and manifest symbols of adaptation, it may be most parsimonious to look to the psychology of aging. A central task of aging is to transcend bodily decline and the imminence of death. The task may take on a different complexion in a home for the aged, but it remains the same task. Explanations for the capacity of the very elderly to cope successfully with transcending deterioration and imminent death range from Erikson's (1959) explanation of how secondary narcissism (the investment in those who will survive oneself when resolving that one's life has been a meaningful one) to the more psychodynamic explanations of the use of denial and counterphobic mechanisms to defend against a very human anxiety that can never really be resolved.

Apparently, very aged people who live in homes for the aged can continue to maintain a sense of selfness, as the present data suggest, and can continue to perceive themselves as meaningful, unique persons. The home does offer an opportunity for a reaffirmation of self. Because relationships with others are conflictful, energy must be expended to avoid these interactions. Yet, at the same time, mechanisms such as denial have their place in the psychic economy of the resident. Mrs. A, for example, attempted to dissociate herself from her peers by offering to help with the office typing.

The model that has been presented to explain the affects of the institutionalized older person begins with the fact that the new resident is embedded in an interpersonal world of elderly who need institutional care. Interaction with roommates, other residents, and staff who treat one as a frail elderly person all force the resident toward a fearful identification. Issues related to bodily functioning and deterioration and suspiciousness in interaction are reflections of the environment as not reassuring. The appraisal of oneself as an actor in the situation, a fearful appraisal that may quickly lead to its own suppression, is that one's future holds only further deterioration and death. The meaning of the new environment has been established. The more articulate resident can verbalize feelings such as a welcoming of death as preferable to future suffering. These feelings do not appear to overwhelm the new resident. Perhaps the ability to verbalize the malignant feelings reflects a capacity to deal with them without becoming overwhelmed by anxiety or depression. The underlying feelings are coped with in several ways. Residents reassure themselves that they are the same people they have always been, which is accomplished by using activities and people in the environment for self-definition, even if distortion of interaction must occur to insure self-consistency over time. Efforts are made to identify with staff and select groups of residents in order to deny being like the frail elderly who are on the brink of deterioration and death. A daily routine is established that patterns the day and the week, filling time and offering opportunity to play out those idiosyncratic psychodynamics of one's own that offer reassurance of self-sameness, importance, and vitality. Within the constricted world of the institution, daily happenings become important and selected events become anchoring points to be anticipated with regularity, if not satisfaction. The world becomes intelligible and manageable, but the feeling persists of having become that which one has feared to become.

Institutional life itself can thus explain the changes found. Yet environmental discontinuity as an explanation for effects can not be completely discounted. This explanation will be considered in the next chapter when we discuss the changes throughout the first year, including the prediction of intact survivorship.

❧ 4 ❧

Through
the First Year

The findings reported in the previous chapter suggest that, 2 months after admission to an old-age home, old people function at a level remarkably similar to the level of functioning maintained prior to admission. Although there were shifts in the inner life, these shifts were not manifested in behavior to any significant degree. It was thought that 2 months after entering and living in the institution might be too soon to assess institutional effects—that, say, a year after admission, behavioral effects might be manifested that would more truly reflect inability to cope adequately with institutional life. The advisability of following new residents for as long as 1 year is suggested by the many reports of high mortality rates among elderly people following institutionalization (Blenkner, Bloom, and Nielsen, 1971; Camargo and Preston, 1945; Costello and Tanaka, 1961; Goldfarb, Shahinian, and Turner, 1966; Josephy, 1949; Kay, Norris, and Post, 1956; Killian, 1970; Lieberman, 1961; Roth, 1955; Triers, 1968; Whittier and Williams, 1956). Although high mortality rates are a reality, the reason for the high rates is unclear. (These studies only suggest that mortality rates are particularly high among men, the very old, and those with focal lesions of the central nervous system; and, also, that the rates were higher for state mental hospitals than for homes for the aged.)

The difficulties in identifying causal factors for mortality rates are the same as the difficulties in identifying factors that cause psychological and physical deterioration. These difficulties include sample selection (those institutionalized may already be closer to death than control samples); process effects preceding admission; environmental discontinuity; and institutional life. Statistics can be presented, in other words, on global outcomes —such as enhanced functioning, no essential change, some negative change, extreme deterioration, or death. But the excess mortality rate associated with becoming institutionalized cannot be determined, largely because it is inappropriate to use procedures whereby clients would be randomly placed in institutions or helped to remain in the community. The several studies cited, however, make clear that it is sensible to assume that some of those who deteriorated or died by the end of 1 year after admission would have deteriorated less or would not have died had they not been relocated to institutions. Thus the group who did manifest extreme deterioration or who died during the year may be presumed to include some residents whose deterioration or death was hastened and other residents who would have deteriorated or died in the same period had they not become institutionalized. Although the residents studied would include the debilitated or dead of both these groups, comparisons between those who suffered harmful effects and the intact survivors can, nevertheless, be instructive in several ways.

We may ask, for example, whether there are psychological attributes evidenced before admission that discriminate between these two outcome groups as they appeared 1 year after admission. The attributes that discriminate would suggest reasons for consequent deterioration or death. Explanations could be generated that might help differentiate between noninstitutional causal factors and factors within the institutional environment. Such explanations might indicate which types of institutional factors are most critical to consequent deterioration or death.

Indeed, a wide assortment of psychological components, ranging from personality traits to cognitive functioning, expectations, hope, and so forth, were examined to assess their predictive power. For each psychological characteristic, however, it is important to show that the characteristic is not simply a reflection of underlying deterioration (e.g., associated with survival) but actually sensitizes the individual to the impact of entering and living in the institution and in that sense "predicts" heightened vulnerability to morbidity or mortality. Stated another way, characteristics that are not associated with survival, but that are predictors of vulnerability to stress, can be assumed to decrease the person's resistance to the destructive potential associated with entering and living in the institution. In turn, the reasons for destructive effects can be inferred from the person's pattern of sensitizing characteristics.

A second type of question relates to the relationship between short-term psychological effects (2 months after admission) and long-term global outcomes (1 year after admission). Although for the entire sample of eighty-five there were minimal short-term effects, possibly those who showed the most adverse short-term effects were more likely to subsequently deteriorate or die.

A third question regards the systematic behavioral changes through the first year. Although the sample did not remain complete through the first year (sustaining some losses from death, other losses because some respondents were now too deteriorated to respond, and still other losses from those who refused to be interviewed for now a third, or even a fourth time), those who survived intact after admission and then again through 1 year after admission—the least vulnerable, to be sure —permits us to ask questions germane to understanding the unavoidable ubiquitous effects of institutional life itself. The adverse changes among this select sample from 2 months post-admission through the first year after admission can surely be interpreted as being, to a great extent, produced by the intervening 10 months of institutional life.

These three issues will be sequentially addressed in this chapter; first, psychological predictors of outcomes; second, short-term effects and outcomes; and, third, systematic changes in the surviving remainder of the sample, as observable a year after admission.

Psychological Differences Between Outcome Groups

As a first step in exploring psychological differences between (or covariates or predictors of) outcome groups, a classification system was developed to assess changes from preadmission through the first year after admission. Five levels of change were identified, the first four referring to physical, mental, or behavioral functioning, or, more typically, some combination of all three. The five levels, with the number and percentage of the 85 residents in each, were:

1. Enhanced functioning (5, or 6 percent).

2. No essential change (14, or 16 percent).

3. Some negative change (25, or 30 percent).

4. Extreme deterioration (28, or 33 percent).

5. Died (13, or 15 percent).

Thus about 1 of every 2 (41, or 48 percent) either deteriorated markedly or died. Stated the other way, only 1 of 2 were intact survivors 1 year after admission.

With the exception of the respondents who died, placement in a particular outcome category was not made on the basis of absolute status after 1 year, because respondents varied in their capacities before admission. Instead, relative change from preadmission to 1 year postadmission was the basis of placement, because it was necessary to separate the effects of preinstitutional level of functioning from the effects of change during institutionalization. For example, a respondent who was noted after 1 year of institutionalization to have difficulty walking and to require a walker might well have less functional capacity than most other respondents and, on that basis, might be assumed to show marked decline in performance. If, however, he had entered the institution with this difficulty in walking, then obviously it was not institutionalization that led to decline in performance; indeed, there was no change in performance.

On the other hand, assessing outcome on the basis of relative change from preadmission to 1 year after admission presented measurement problems. Assessing and equating magnitude of change across respondents is difficult because respondents vary in initial level and changes are qualitatively different across respondents. It was necessary, therefore, to develop a classification system that took into account very different levels of baseline functioning and also equated the magnitude of qualitatively different changes.

Of the 85 aged persons who comprised the initial sample, complete follow-up data after 1 year were obtained for 61 (or 72 percent) of the original sample. Respondents who died in the interim (13 in all) are included in this number. Only partial data were obtained for the remaining 28 percent. For these 24 respondents, incomplete data usually reflects inability to obtain full interview material because of extreme deterioration. There were, however, 14 respondents who remained intact and able to be interviewed but refused to respond to all or most of the 12- to 15-hour interview for what was now the third or fourth time. Partial information was gathered on very deteriorated and resistant respondents through the administration of a short-form interview as well as by asking informants about the respondents. Data used in assessing level of adaptation 1 year after institutionalization included all available data, which consisted of eighteen structured instruments and nine focused interview sections. Of course, these data were available only for survivors, since those who had died had done so before 1 year elapsed.

The initial effort in the development of the five-level measure of outcome consisted of an analysis of change in status from before admission to 1 year after admission for a sample of cases selected to include respondents interviewed by each of the interviewers. This analysis suggested guidelines related to (1) areas of assessment for change, (2) data useful for assessment, and (3) the process of classifying respondents into one of the four levels of outcome. Only after these guidelines were established were all respondents then classified by two members of the interview staff.

Areas of Change.   Three areas of change were identified: physical, mental, and behavioral functioning. Changes in physical functioning included shifts in perception of functional self-care capacity, as well as verified changes in physical status. Change in mental functioning was focused on orientation in time and space, and perceptual adequacy. Changes in behavioral functioning included shifts in both mood and behaviors, including psychiatric symptoms.

Data related to physical change included: (1) changes in self-reported ability to care for self; (2) changes in self-reported physical symptoms and diseases; (3) changes reflected in comments about physical capacity that were interspersed throughout the interview; and (4) changes in physical appearance, self-care capacity, and ambulation as reported by the interviewer and also by staff of the home. Although some respondents obviously had considerable physical dysfunction and distress before admission, no respondent was considered terminally ill, because intake procedures precluded acceptance of terminally ill applicants. It should be noted that physiological measures of function were not used in assessing the magnitude of physical change. The rationale for this omission was that many diseases are present in a very aged population and for people of very advanced age, functional capacity or actual disability in many ways is more important than the pathology that a medical examination might reveal.

Data involving mental changes included: (1) changes on the Mental Status Questionnaire, which assesses orientation in time and place; (2) changes on several tasks that measured ability to organize information and respond to complex interview and test material; and (3) interviewers' assessments of change in mental status and functioning a year after admission.

Data involving behavioral changes included: (1) interview material; (2) interviewer's ratings; and (3) staff assessments.

For each of the three functional areas, a rating of change was made on a 7-point scale ranging from death at the negative extreme to improvement at the positive extreme. These scales were then used in forming a global judgment as to marked decline, some decline, no change, and improvement. Placement in the fourth group, death, of course, did not require weighing evidence.

Because of the high interrelation of change among the three areas of functioning (correlations above .9), placement for most respondents was rather easy. For those few respondents who did not manifest negative change in all three areas, the highest level of negative change was used in making the global judgment. For example, three of the twenty-five in the waiting-list sample classified as "marked negative changers" had become confused but did not show a marked change in physical functioning. It is important to note that those classified as marked negative changers tended to function so poorly after 1 year of institutionalization that if they were now applying for admission to the homes they would be considered too incapacitated to be admitted. Thus, the group showing marked decline was composed of respondents who had all shown adverse changes after 1 year of institutionalization to a functional status that tended to be below admission standards.

These procedures allowed a reliable classification to be made for each case. For example, when classifications were completed for all respondents, the two judges each selected three of her "hard-to-judge" cases for the other judge to rate. Exact agreement was obtained for all six cases in placement into the marked decline, some decline, or no change groups.

Although it was possible to develop a high degree of inter-judge reliability, the process of judging individual cases raised some thorny problems. Placing a respondent in the dead group, for example, obviously indicated a change that did not permit a disagreement in judgments. Nevertheless, respondents who died appeared to vary in the "distance" traveled from the baseline evaluation point while on the waiting list until actual death. One respondent who died was categorized as in rather poor physical health at baseline because when first seen he was in a nursing home and was suffering acutely from Parkinson's disease and had a marked tremor and impaired speech. He was further weakened by having had four operations (for bowel and prostate obstructions) during an 8-week period about 5 months earlier. Because he needed help in washing, bathing, and dressing, he was placed in the "urgent" category on the waiting list. By contrast, another respondent who died was living in a walk-up apartment and was cooking, shopping, and cleaning for herself and her husband at the baseline interview. Just before this interview she had been to two family parties, and complained only of some fatigue; she had been placed by the home on the "not urgent" waiting list. Clearly, at an observable level of functioning, she was not deteriorated to the same extent as the first respondent at baseline; yet she had suffered the same outcome by the point of long-term evaluation. Similarly, the "distance" traveled for some residents who died within the first year after relocation appeared to be less than the "distance" traveled for other respondents who showed extreme deterioration but who had not yet died.

Similar diversity existed in the group showing marked decline. The variability in "distance" for the respondents who died is similar to the variability in the respondents who showed a marked decline. One man who was judged to show "extreme" change was living by himself in a furnished apartment at the time of the initial interview. Although he had some difficulty in walking and some trembling because of Parkinson's disease, he walked around the neighborhood, visited friends, and dined in restaurants. He took care of himself, was very well oriented in time and place, and was of a pleasant, cheerful disposition. One year after institutionalization, however, he was confined to a wheelchair, required care for all his physical needs, was very disoriented, spoke in a whisper, and often could not make any intelligible sounds. He was, furthermore, deeply depressed and would not cooperate in any therapy efforts. By contrast, a woman who seemed more deteriorated at the initial interview also showed a marked decline 1 year after admission, but the distance she had traveled from baseline appeared less than that traveled by the man just described. This woman, who was suffering from hypertension that made it difficult for her to walk and to see, initially needed considerable physical care and felt depressed and hopeless. One year after admission, she had been hospitalized several times for severe hypertension. She felt weak and did not participate in any of the home's activities. She felt persecuted, was constantly complaining, quite depressed, and described herself as "the most unhappy person who ever lived." While she had deteriorated markedly, she did not show the same degree of change as the man with Parkinson's disease. While recognizing this variability in the group that showed a marked deterioration, it is also true that each respondent in this group shared a rather striking degree of deterioration.

Comparisons with Control Sample. How does the distribution of outcomes for the study sample compare to the distributions for the two control samples? The distribution for the sample who already had been institutionalized from 1 to 3 years is almost the same as for the study sample. One half of the institutionalized sample (18 of 37, or 47 percent) had markedly deteriorated or died. The community sample, however, had far less negative outcome. Less than one fifth of the community sample showed the extreme outcomes of marked deterioration or death (6 of the 35, or 18 percent; 2 refused to be interviewed). These findings are difficult to interpret. It can be argued, for example, that the difference between the entire study sample and the community sample reflects the excess deterioration and death associated with institutionalization. This argument would be valid if the samples were "randomly assigned" either to community living or institutional life. If so, then 1 of 3 (that is, the difference between the 48 percent rate of deterioration and death for the study sample and the 18 percent rate for the community sample) of those older people who deteriorated or died after becoming institutionalized could be said to have done so because they entered and lived in homes for the aged. On the other hand, the similarity in percentages for the sample undergoing institutionalization to percentages for respondents who had been institutionalized for 1 to 3 years suggests that no *excess* morbidity and mortality was associated with the process of becoming institutionalized. We shall return to this issue after entering some further differences between outcome groups, specifically between the deteriorated or dead and the intact survivors.

Differences Between the Deteriorated or Dead and the Intact Survivors. Did those who severely deteriorated or died (the "not-intact") differ from the elderly who survived with little or no deterioration (the intact) by the end of 1 year after admission? The two groups did not differ systematically in age or sex: the average age of the intact survivors was 77.8 years old and of the not-intact, 79 years old; of the 44 intact, 12 (or 27 percent) were males, and of the 41 not-intact, 13 (or 31 percent) were males. There was a difference, however, in the living arrangements prior to admission. Of the 85 respondents, 17 had lived in nursing homes while on the waiting list and 65 had lived alone or with others in community dwellings. Of the 17 admitted from nursing homes, 13 (77 percent) were in the not-intact group—had deteriorated or died by the end of the year— as opposed to only 4, or 23 percent of the intact group (X^2 = 17.70, $p < .001$). Relocation from a nursing home to a home for the aged is obviously associated with more negative outcome than relocation into the home from independent community living.

This finding was somewhat surprising, because residents who were admitted from nursing homes were similar on most measures to those admitted from community dwellings. Living in a nursing home, for example, was not associated with less functional adequacy nor with the severity or number of events leading to the decision to seek institutional care. Possibly the difference between the groups before admission to the homes was a combination of deteriorative processes not isolated by standardized measures and the nature of the family decision-making process. This process included, for some respondents, but not for most, residing in a nursing home while awaiting admission to the home for the aged. Although respondents admitted from nursing homes may indeed have been more deteriorated, none of the eighty-five was considered terminal at admission. If the residents who were admitted from nursing homes were more deteriorated than those admitted from community dwellings, it is also possible that their deterioration partially resulted from the earlier relocation. They had to adapt to the stress of two relocations in a rather brief time interval. This double relocation may explain the few differences that were found between those elderly who lived transitionally in a nursing home and those who did not. The elderly admitted from nursing homes tended to be more passive, to use denial more, and to have a lowered sense of futurity, characteristics that in many ways reflect an institutional profile. Their lower anxiety and greater comfort in relating to the interviews may have related to their assurance of care while in the nursing home and to their being further along in their resolution of the issues of loss and abandonment than the respondents who were admitted directly from the community.

Yet the health status of those admitted from nursing homes cannot be discounted as an important selection factor related to outcome. An investigation of physical status as revealed in the medical records, however, did not appear useful because of the incompleteness of these records. Disease states and therapeutic regimes were carefully recorded, but precise physiological indices were not available. Furthermore, while physiological indices have been associated with longevity in general, the types of deficits that have been predictive were not found in the study sample because the admission procedure eliminated terminal and psychotic applicants. Those who were admitted who were incontinent or severely confused were screened out by the study sample criteria. It is these types of disease states that have been found to predict against longevity. After reviewing a compilation of studies, Palmore and Jeffers (1971), for example, state that "physiological predictors are especially important among the very old, the institutionalized or the otherwise physically impaired" (p. 286). The study lending most credence to this conclusion is that of Goldfarb (1971), who found that incontinence, marked physical disability, and extreme confusion are the strongest predictors of mortality among the elderly who become institutionalized. Although the aged with these symptoms were eliminated from the study sample, it still may be possible that some psychological measures reflected or prodromatized declines in health that preceded death.

Respondents from nursing homes were pooled with those admitted directly from the community for two reasons. Pre-admission living arrangements were used as a covariate in the analysis of variance as a way of correcting for the effect of liv-ing arrangements on the psychological measures. A first reason for pooling was because of the similarity between those ad-mitted from nursing homes and those admitted directly from the community. The *only* differences found were that those admitted from nursing homes were less willing to discuss the impending event of moving to the home, were more passive, and had less current role activity. The degree of similarity suggested that these two groups were drawn from the same rather homo-geneous population. A second reason was that the same pre-admission measures differentiated the intact survivors from the not-intact within the two groups. Although the distribution of outcomes was decidedly different among the elderly admitted from nursing homes and among those admitted from the com-munity, the same psychological attributes at preadmission were associated with global outcomes 1 year after admission.

Psychological Predictors. What were the psychological predictors of morbidity and mortality? To identify predictors, the intact and not-intact respondents were contrasted on mea-sures assessed before admission. For this analysis, variables were grouped into nine realms, arranged somewhat differently than for the study of effects. The rationale for the inclusion of each realm is briefly presented here. Measures used in the prediction study that were not used in the study of effects will be clarified.

The literature (see Lazarus, 1966, for a detailed review) suggests a linear relationship between the capacity to adapt and successful adaptation to severely stressful events such as reloca-tion. Better functioning before entering the institution, in other words, is expected to be associated with positive outcomes afterwards, whereas poor functioning before becoming institu-tionalized would be expected to be associated with negative outcomes because of lacking those resources necessary to recuperate from the taxing disequilibrium. To assess this realm of functional capacity, five variables that reflect different aspects of functioning were measured: cognitive adequacy (cognitive sign), functional health capacity (self-care), expressive vigor as taped by word counts, feelings of well-being (LSR), and mental health. To assess mental health, a Q-sort technique was used. Block (1961) developed 100 behavioral descriptions that are sorted into nine categories from "most like" to "least like" the respondent. The actual mental health score is the correlation between the scores from one to nine for the 100 descriptions for each respondent and the scores of these 100 items for the optimally adjusted person as judged by experts. While these five indices of functional capacity were suggested by different studies, all appear sufficiently in evidence to be relevant for predicting vulnerability to relocation for the present sample of very elderly persons.

Emotional states such as feelings of lessened well-being, depression, or continuous high anxiety all have been found to be associated with negative consequences and, specifically, to increased susceptibility to diseases or slow recovery from illness. (See, for example, Le Shan's [1961] work with cancer patients and Greenfield's [1959] work with patients with infectious diseases.) The typical explanation of this relationship is that negative emotional states are, on the one hand, the precursors of further maladaptive responses, especially to severe stressful events, because they reflect the incapacity to use inner resources and, generally, to cope adequately. In the present study, it was thought that negative emotional states while respondents were on the waiting list might reflect the inability to cope with the issues of loss and abandonment that were associated with the transition to the waiting list—the transition immediately preceding relocation. If so, these emotional states would probably be associated with a negative response to the actual relocation. Feelings of well-being, anxiety, and depression were assessed, as well as willingness to introspect about feelings.

Hope was considered a type of emotional state that merited special attention. As a predictor of negative outcome, hopelessness is suggested both by the general rationale used for determining relevant emotional states (Le Shan, for example, attempts to relate hope to recovery from cancer), and by the rationale used to explain how expectations relate to vulnerability. If, before entering the institution, the older person did not anticipate gratification, a set of expectations would be created that could lead to severe consequences. The less the future was perceived as potentially rewarding, the more the future life—in this case, in the postrelocation institutional environment— would be likely to be severely harmful and stressful. Hopelessness before relocation creates a wish-fulfilling prophecy of harmful personal consequences after relocation. An underlying assumption in exploring the predictive power of hope was that the relocation to the new environment was not equally stressful for all, in part because the less hopeful would expect dire effects of the event and thereby experience it as more stressful than those with more hope. This assumption differs from the assumption underlying the selection of the first two realms— that the relocation is about equally stressful for all and that it is the strength of prerelocation ego and affective resources that facilitate or impede ability to cope with the stressful event. As noted earlier, hope was assessed by an index that combined five measures, each weighted by their association to a criterion measure developed in a special study of a small number of cases. A second approach to the assessment of hope was anomie (Srole, 1956). The third was that of extension of self into a personally gratifying future, which was measured by rating the responses to a series of seven open-ended items.

Adaptive capacity was also approached through the portrayal of self in everyday life. Two measures generated by the Self-Sort Task—self-esteem and adequacy of examples to support the self—were included in this realm.

Personality traits also proved to be predictors. Some types of people may do better than others when confronted with a stressful situation. The term "type of people" is meant to suggest those aspects of personality structure that are both pervasive and persist through time—as contrasted with the more discrete qualities and the greater fluctuations that are assumed generally to characterize the variables assessed within the first four realms. Rather than create typologies, which themselves are based on relationships among individual traits, a trait approach was taken (see Turner, Tobin, and Lieberman, 1972; Turner, 1969). In this approach, it was assumed that traits can be identified that capture qualities, or persistent styles, that reflect better or poorer ego functioning. Poorer ego functioning would, in turn, be expected to be related to adverse consequences. To assess these traits, two systems were initially used. One system consisted of assessing the traits of dominance-submission and affiliation-hostility, using the Self-Sort Task. The second system used the Cattell (1962) sixteen-personality-factor (16PF) system to measure the global factor of introversion-extroversion. A third system was also used, based on a very different assumption: that possession of an attribute that is congruent with the particular adaptive demands of the relocation environment would reduce the amount of taxation caused by the stressful event of relocation. (See, for example, Gunderson, 1964, on the isolated individual and adjustment to arctic isolation; Jackson, 1966, for criminal careers and adjustment to prison life; and Wolf and Ripley, 1947, who suggest that a psychopathological ruthlessness facilitates adaptation to concentration camps, as evidenced by former criminals who became inmates.) These two assumptions could lead to contradictory findings if a trait that was congruent with adaptive demands typically reflected poorer functioning in everyday situations. An environment that rewards hostility, for example, may be a facilitating one for the hostile, and even paranoid, person. Thus, for the third system of assessing traits, we first rated nine specific attributes that appeared congruent with the adaptive demands of the relocation environment and then, by a factor-analysis technique, generated four congruence traits: authoritarianism, passivity, introspection, and friendliness.

Another approach to the measurement of adequate coping involved assessing seven reminiscence qualities. These qualities were: life evaluation, life review, affect, amount of reminiscence activity, amount of satisfaction portrayed, amount of deprivation portrayed, and emphasis on childhood. For each of these measures, a rationale could be developed relating the quality being assessed and adequate coping. A positive evaluation of one's past life, for example, may reflect a capacity to deal with and make sense of one's life.

Coping with the impending event of imminent institution-alization represents yet another approach to the assessment of functional adequacy. Avoidance or denial of the event was assumed to capture a current maladaptive coping style that was expected also to be maladaptive for dealing with actual events when living in the new environment. To assess the degree that aged persons in the sample denied, or avoided coping with the impending event, three measures were used: avoidance of think-ing about the event, unwillingness to discuss gains and losses inherent in the relocation, and avoidance of dealing with the latent meaning of the event.

In the realm of interpersonal relations, several questions were considered that primarily tapped issues related to the age of the respondents and to the particular relocation situation. For example, we asked whether those who were engaged in more activities were apt to do better. Total role activity was measured by summing activity across seven roles such as parent, friend, and neighbor. Another question was related to the per-ception of others as available resources: Did the availability of others help when a person relocated to an institution? A Per-sonal Resource Questionnaire was developed that consisted of eleven items that require the respondent to specify others he would turn to for help, when lonely, when happy, and so forth. The score was the number of specific others mentioned. Still another question related to the quality of interaction. Thus, in addition to assessing total role activity and the perception of the availability of others as resources, we used the quality of the relationship with the interviewer as an index of the capacity to interact with others. Here the question was whether those who related with more warmth, depth, cooperation, spontaneity, and motivation were more likely to adapt better to a new environ-ment. The fourth type of question concerned the degree to which there was avoidance in relating to significant others in conflictful situations. To assess interpersonal avoidance or denial, an Interpersonal Role-Playing Task was developed, con-sisting of nine conflictful or potentially conflictual situations with children, peers, and authority figures, for which the score was the number of situations where denial occurred.

The final realm, accumulated stress, consisted of the amount of adverse change that had occurred prior to admission. We felt that those with more accumulated stress might find the move to the institution to be the proverbial straw that broke the camel's back. One more extreme disruption would have been added to an already taxing load.

Findings. Of the nine realms, seven contained measures that differentiated between the two outcome groups, as shown in Table 10. To determine whether these measures were general predictors of morbidity and mortality, independent of institutionalization, similar analyses were made on measures of the intact and not-intact institutionalized control sample. Measures differentiating the two outcome groups within both samples were taken to be associated with survival, whereas measures predicting only for the study sample were considered sensitizers to the effects of the institutionalization process.

Most measures, as is also shown in Table 10, that predicted for the study sample also predicted for the institutionalized control sample and, thus, are associated with survival. Entered on the table are measures that showed the intact to be functioning better initially than the debilitated (using a probability level of .05 for one-tailed tests). (The actual means for the intact and the debilitated in the study sample and the institutionalized control sample, as well as probability levels for the t-tests can be found in Lieberman, 1971.) Thus functional capacities, hope, self, and interpersonal denial are predictive variables, independent of institutional effects. Affects, curiously, predicted for the control sample but not for the study sample. Our working assumption was that any characteristic that was associated with survival would be associated with outcome for the study sample. Yet respondents with more negative affects in the study sample were no more likely than those with more positive affects to survive intact, whereas in the control sample those with more negative affects were less likely to survive intact. The only explanation we can offer for this discrepancy is that the anticipatory period in causing a general reduction in positive

Table 10. Measures that Differentiate Between the Intact and the Not-Intact

	Predictor Measures		
Realm	Study Sample	Institutionalized Sample	Interpretation
Functional capacities	Cognitive malfunctioning Self-care inability (No significant differences between the intact and the non-intact)	Cognitive malfunctioning Self-care inability	Associated with survival
Affects		SCT–Anxiety SCT–Despair SCT–Body preoccupation Introspection	Associated with survival but not a sensitizer for the study sample
Hope	Time extensionality	Time extensionality Srole–anomie Futurity	Associated with survival
Self	Futurity Self-esteem Self-consistency mechanism	Self-consistency mechanisms	Associated with survival
Personality traits	Self-sort–dominance Self-sort–affiliation Passivity	(No significant differences between the intact and the not-intact)	Sensitizer
Reminiscence	Reminiscence activity Amount of deprivation	(Not measured; not applicable)	(Cannot determine)
Coping with the impending event	Denial Working Anticipatory loss	(Not measured; not applicable)	(Because denial, as assessed by IP Task–denial, as shown in the row below, predicts for both samples, this realm is most likely also associated with survival)
Interpersonal		Relationship quality IP Task–denial	Associated with survival
Accumulated stress	IP Task–denial (No significant differences between the intact and the not-intact)	(Not measured; not applicable)	Not a sensitizer

affects tends to make the study sample too homogeneous—with relatively uniform negative affects—to obtain an association between affects and outcome for the group undergoing stress. What is clear is that personality traits were the only sensitizers that were *not* associated with survival. Coping with the future event and, though less so, reminiscence, may have been sensitizers, but because the measures were not assessed for the control sample this possibility could not be determined. In other words, older people with poor functional capacity, specifically cognitive malfunctioning and self-care incapacity, were more likely to deteriorate or die than those with better functioning, regardless of whether they became institutionalized. Similarly, respondents who had less hope, who used present evidence to support their self-concept, and who used denial in resolving interpersonal conflicts, were more likely to deteriorate severely or die soon after admission. To the extent that the effects of the preadmission process reduced functional capacity, increased hopelessness, decreased the use of present examples to support the self-concept, and increased denial, serious adverse sequelae were associated with becoming institutionalized. A similar logic may obtain for personality traits, but here the effect of weeding out those with the trait of passivity must be considered, because, by the end of a year, few intact survivors would have possessed this personality type.

The Self-Sort personality traits of dominance and affiliation acted quite differently for the two samples. The two traits differentiated between the intact and the not-intact within the study sample but not within the control sample. The trait that most significantly differentiated the outcome groups within the study sample, but not within the control sample, was passivity. The difference between mean scores on passivity for the intact and the not-intact within the study sample was significant beyond the .01 level, whereas within the institutionalized control sample the means for the two outcome groups were virtually identical. Extreme passivity was rarely found in the institutionalized control sample, suggesting that people who are more passive when they enter do not tend to survive through the first year of admission. To what extent passivity, as measured here, is a persistent, lifelong trait is impossible to determine. In either case, whether the person had always been passive or whether the person increasingly became passive (as appears to be the case for those respondents who lived transitionally in nursing homes), a passive orientation is associated with morbidity and mortality following entrance into a home for the aged.

How does passivity operate to cause severe consequences? Or, asked another way: What does passivity as a sensitizer indicate about the demands of institutional life? To be sure, the move is one of environmental discontinuity, which taxes adaptive capacities. Yet passivity apparently operates relatively independently of functional capacities. Indeed a series of step-down analyses of variance (the actual F and p levels are reported by Lieberman, 1971) revealed that the measure of passivity was the strongest predictor among the major six predictor measures. Passivity may reflect a particular kind of adaptive incapacity—the inability to mobilize resources when confronted with a taxing situation. Assertiveness or aggressiveness, that is, is necessary to cope adequately with adaptive demands. If not mobilized to cope adequately, the person has less possibility of managing biological deficits. Being very old means having many underlying physiological deficits. The more a very old person functions at a level appropriate to the deficits, the more likely he is to deteriorate rapidly.

The particular demands of the institutional environment interact with passivity as an indicator of the inability or unwillingness to mobilize psychic resources to cope with stress. The homes studied reward assertiveness. The passive resident is most incongruent with these interpersonal adaptive demands imposed by the institutions. The greater the incongruity, the more likely that the facts of institutional life will increase the stress experienced by the resident. The grouchy older person apparently is best prepared to deal with the stress of institutional life; he is the one most likely to be congruent and therefore most likely to be rewarded by staff.

Initial Effects and Later Outcomes

Are the later outcomes reflected in earlier changes? For the two outcome groups, changes from preadmission through the initial adjustment phase were compared. Few changes were found. Essentially, both groups had become institutionalized older people: Both groups, for example, showed about an equally increased concern with mutilation and death (a 47 percent increased loss expression for the intact survivors and a 57 percent increase for the not-intact). Both groups showed a similar slight increase in disorientation, a slight constriction in affective responsiveness, a marked increase in body preoccupation, a moderate increase in the perception of capacity for self-care capacity, and a marked increase in describing the self as hostile in interpersonal relationships.

There were, however, significant differences in the area of emotional states, suggesting some therapeutic benefit for the intact survivors. For them, life satisfaction had improved and anxiety lessened, whereas for the not-intact, life satisfaction had declined and anxiety increased. Similarly, hopelessness among the not-intact had markedly increased, whereas for the intact hopelessness had increased only slightly. Thus, the direction for the intact was also toward greater hopelessness. The improvements in the emotional states of anxiety, depression, and life satisfaction among the intact reflected therapeutic benefits. But these benefits were accompanied by shifts toward hopelessness, more body preoccupation, a perception of less capacity for self-care, a sense of self as less affiliative in interaction, and a focal concern with mutilation and death. In these latter shifts, the intact showed adverse changes similar to those shown by the not-intact. Yet they did have feelings of greater well-being, which, because of the initially low level of feelings of well-being, suggests an alleviation of diminished feelings of well-being rather than a high level of feelings of well-being. This positive change should nevertheless not be minimized, because the Life Satisfaction Rating tends to be quite stable and thus the average increase of 1.9 points in the score suggests a very meaningful improvement.

As the only change predictor of subsequent morbidity and mortality, the change in emotional states is particularly interesting because, as reported earlier, emotional states measured at preadmission did not predict 1-year postinstitutional outcome for the study sample, whereas these states were associated with survival for the long-term institutionalized sample. To further explore the association between change in emotional states and outcome, a global change score was developed. Five different measures were used. Four of these five measures were based on repeat data: change in (1) feelings of well-being (LSR), (2) hope (hope indicator), (3) anxiety (SCT), and (4) depression (SCT). The fifth measure related to gratification from the institutional environment after relocation.

The measures before relocation, as well as the change measures, were only minimally associated with one another. Because each measure appeared to tap a different type of negative reaction, a sign approach was used to identify those respondents who showed a markedly negative affective response. In this approach, the number of measures on which there was a negative change greater than that shown by respondents in the matched community control sample was assumed to reflect the intensity of the respondent's overall negative affective reaction.

On the measure of well-being, 1 in 5 respondents (20 percent) had become more depressed or had appreciably less feelings of well-being; 1 of 3 (32 percent) had either became more hopeless or shifted from hopefulness to hopelessness; less than 1 of 3 expressed more anxiety (28 percent); more than 1 of 3 more depression (37 percent); and about 1 of 7 (15 percent) were receiving no or at best minimal gratification from the institutional environment. For each measure taken separately, a significant minority showed emotional reactions that were measurable, although few respondents could be classified as having manifested a severe negative reaction. The distribution of the sample by number of signs revealed that, of the 78 on whom we had complete follow-up data, only 22 (or 28 percent) of the sample did not have any signs. Another 24 (or 31 percent), however, had only one sign. Thus a majority of the sample (46, or 59 percent) had only one sign or none. When two or more signs are used as an indication of a clear negative reaction, a large proportion (32, or 41 percent) of the sample can be said to have responded negatively to relocation during the initial adjustment phase as assessed 2 months after admission. That is, a large minority of the sample showed a measurable but subtle negative emotional reaction to relocation, a measurable change greater than respondents in the community control sample, but not a change that would be extreme enough to be immediately evident to the interviewer or to the staff (particularly considering that of the 32 with two or more signs, 20 had two signs, 8 had three signs, only 4 had four signs, and none had five signs).

Those that did show a noticeable reaction in emotional life also showed other indications of a negative reaction in the areas of cognitive functioning, behavioral symptomatology, and deterioration in physical functioning. For example, a group of 20 respondents were identified as manifesting decline from pre-admission to postadmission on four tests of cognitive functioning (the Mental Status Questionnaire, the Dana scoring of the TAT, the Pascal scoring of the Bender Gestalt Test and the estimation of 1 minute). Dichotomizing cognitive reactions ($N = 20$) and nonreactions ($N = 51$) revealed that a third of the respondents who manifested an affective reaction (11 of 31) also showed cognitive decline, as compared to only about a fifth (9 of 44) of the nonaffective reactors ($X^2 = 1.20$, $p = .27$, gamma = .34).

Similarly, a measure of behavioral symptomatology revealed a relationship between affect reaction and the presence of noticeable symptoms, as assessed by interviewers and staff during the 2-month initial adjustment phase. Symptoms used to place respondents into the category of adverse behavioral symptomatology included an extreme denial of institutional status, extreme apathy, increasing paranoia, severe depression, or further disorientation (Turner, 1969). The relationship between affective reaction and symptomatology was even higher ($X^2 = 6.89$, $p = .009$, gamma = .61) than the relationship between affective reaction and cognitive reaction.

A third measure of impact, deterioration in physical functioning, had the strongest relationship with emotional reaction ($X^2 = 13.62$, $p = .001$, gamma = .78). All available data were used in assessing this change in physical functioning, where a marked decline reflected either a worsening of a preadmission condition or the appearance of new functional deficiencies that substantially altered the respondent's functional capacity.

In looking at all four measures of changes or negative reactions, it was found that emotional, behavioral, and physical measures of impact tended to be highly associated, whereas cognitive decline appeared independent of the other three measures. The remarkably high association between ratings of behavioral symptomatology and physical functioning (gamma = .82) suggests the consistency within the data when impressions of interviewers and staff were used for judgments. A global portrait can be drawn from these data that describes both behavioral and physical symptomatology. For these very aged respondents, severe symptoms such as increasing suspiciousness and further disorientation are interwoven with deteriorated physical functioning, especially in mobility and general self-care. The particularly high association with physical symptomatology lends credence to the idea that emotional states are survival-associated psychological states. If this idea holds true, the degree to which self-consistency and other psychological attributes remain separate from the impact of survival-associated changes is remarkable. As shown earlier, those who markedly deteriorated or died did not manifest initial changes, other than in emotional states, that were more adverse in nature than those manifested by the group of intact survivors.

Early reactions are related to outcome. Physical reactions or changes, as expected, are most strongly associated with outcomes (as revealed by a measure of linear association, $H = .71$); emotional and behavioral reactions are also highly associated with outcomes ($H = .60$ and $.50$, respectively), but cognitive reactions are not ($H = .10$). These associations suggest that the processes that result in morbidity and mortality begin in the impact phase. On the other hand, a substantial group of respondents who did react to impact recuperated, a full one third, while a similar one third who did not react to impact did deteriorate later. An effort to clarify these pathways, however, did not shed light on why some respondents "bounced back" and others did not. In this analysis, various groups of respondents were classified by change and outcome ("rebounders," "masked reactors," and so forth) and contrasted on the many other measures assessed before admission. These contrasts did not reveal any information beyond what we already knew—specifically, that preadmission passivity and a change for the worse in affect states predict negative outcomes.

Psychological Changes Through the Adaptation Period

The study of psychological changes through the first year largely becomes the investigation of the psychology of intact survivors. Our exploration of the transition to becoming an institutionalized older person, in other words, is ultimately synonymous with the study of the psychology of those aged who have been admitted directly from the community who were more likely before admission to have been aggressive, to have possessed a high degree of functional adequacy, to have been better able to use others for self-definition, to have had more hopefulness, to have used less denial while awaiting admission; and, finally to have gained some therapeutic benefit after entering and living in the institution. Indeed, the residual sample that was followed throughout the transition, from the anticipatory phase through the adaptation phase, was obviously a select sample of the less vulnerable—as would be the case in almost all studies of the effects of relocation where a substantial proportion of persons could be expected to deteriorate or die by the time of the follow-up interviews. Yet it is important to identify the psychological changes for those who were the least vulnerable, in an effort to determine the pattern that characterized the psychological equilibrium of those aged persons who adapted best to the institutional environment.

One year after admission, complete repeat data was gathered from only 45 residents. These 45 residents represented a biased sample of the original 85 aged who were studied, in having a large representation of those aged persons who have survived and have remained intact during this first year. The sample of 45 includes 30 who were classified as intact survivors 1 year after admission and only 15 who were classified as not-intact (X^2 = 8.44, p < .01). The sample does not include all of the intact survivors because 14 refused to respond to the complete interview at this third or fourth contact. It does include about one third of the not-intact group—respondents who had appreciably deteriorated but who were willing to cooperate with the interviewer. Thus, the sample 1 year after institutionalization, while biased toward the more intact and less vulnerable, does include a significant proportion of the less intact and more vulnerable. This mix explains, in part, why the subsample of 45 obtained mean scores on most measures of psychological functioning that are comparable to the larger sample—both at preadmission and during the initial adjustment periods.

Adapting to the Home.   What typically happens after the first few months? In the initial adjustment phase, the major socializing agents were aged peers, primarily roommates and old acquaintances, and also administrative staff. Staff usually mentioned as resources during this earlier period are those personnel who have worked with the resident-to-be and his family members in helping the older person enter the institutional world. Other staff, either personnel or specialized professional staff, such as the physical therapist and the occupational therapist, have not yet become meaningful people. As daily living patterns become established in the institution, these personnel become more meaningful and administrative personnel tend to recede into the background.

Contact with peers also changes as the honeymoon period with roommates ends and as the social structure among the residents become more visible to the new resident. The new resident at first feels like an intruder in his own bedroom, not only because of its foreignness, but also because the roommate usually resents his intrusion. In time, the new resident establishes a part of the space as his own terrain, becoming comfortable and open enough to confront the roommate with needs for privacy and for personal comfort. Conflicts with roommates usually take the form of a confrontation about what appears to be a simple problem such as how wide should a window be open. This type of engagement between roommates is encouraged by personnel: feelings are not to be bottled up, and grappling, within limits, is not only acceptable, but is judged to be a sign of appropriate behavior within the institution. A rapprochement between roommates is usually achieved without active mediation by the staff and, with the establishment of a reasonably comfortable style of living in one's room, exploration of the larger environment begins. The public space outside the room becomes known and a familiarity is gained with the typical occupants of the varied public spaces: "That's where the men sit and play cards"; "The resident who looks out the window sits here"; "You can paint in Occupational Therapy"; and so forth.

With this growing awareness of the institution as an ecological system and of the range of other persons who people the home, both peers and staff become differentiated in terms of their function in the social system and in terms of the types of interactions that are sanctioned. The prescriptions, or etiquette, for relating to individuals who fill certain status positions become intelligible, and the more subtle varieties of positive and negative sanctions become less mysterious. The new pattern of different relationships with persons within the institution becomes as familiar as former and present interactions with significant family members.

By the end of 1 year, a personal style of relating has been established: some people have been sought out and a relationship established; relationships with some others have been avoided or circumvented because of potential conflict; still others have remained as an undifferentiated "they." Becoming an "old-timer" means that the small community of the institution is not seen as a monolithic bureaucracy but as an interpersonal world—the only world that one has, either for limiting or for expanding the potential for personal survival and gratification.

Systematic Changes. As shown in Tables 11 and 12, statistically significant changes occurred on only two measures for the subsamples of forty-five from the initial adjustment to the adaptation period. Within the area of emotional states, there was a lessening of body preoccupation, but no lessening of anxiety or depression. Body preoccupation had increased from the preadmission to the initial adjustment period, but now there is a

Table 11. Change in Status: Initial Adjustment Phase to the
Adaptation Phase (N = 45)

Area of Psychological Functioning	Means Postadmission		Statistical Test	
	2 months	1 year	t	p
Cognitive functioning	1.2	1.2	.00	—
Orientation (MSQ)	2.1	2.3	.09	—
Time orientation (60 seconds)	23.8	21.0	.96	—
Retention (Paired Word Association)	11.0	9.6	1.35	—
Organization (BGT)	32.8	32.4	.70	—
Perceptual accuracy (TAT[a])	22.5	20.0	2.92	.01
Originality (Reitman)	10.4	10.1	.00	—
Affective responsiveness				
Affective word count	4.4	4.5	.10	—
Introspection	2.0	2.0	.00	—
Emotional states				
Well-being (LSR)	16.3	15.7	1.90	(.06)
Hope	−.2	−.2	.00	—
SCT				
Anxiety	18.3	18.6	.34	—
Depression	13.3	14.2	.70	—
Body preoccupation	5.2	3.1	4.60	.001
Self-perception				
Self-care	3.2	2.7	.38	—
Self-esteem	20.0	19.0	1.24	—
Adequacy	−.48	−1.86	1.38	—
Self-in-interaction				
Dominance	−.05	.09	.82	—
Affiliation	.16	−.15	2.04	.05

[a]The statistically significant decline is similar to that of control samples, and is considered, therefore, as an artifact of repeat measurement.

"rebound" as body preoccupation lessens after continued living in the institution. A lessening of affiliation, or an increase in one's self-image as a hostile interpersonal actor, was found within the area of the self-perception. This increase in perceived hostility in interpersonal relationships is a continuous change, because there also was an increase from preadmission through the initial adjustment phase—a remarkable consistency over time.

It is surprising that despite the increased length of time in the institution, cognitive adequacy did not deteriorate, nor were emotional responsiveness or capacity for self-care perceived to

Table 12. Psychological Changes from Anticipatory Phase Through Initial Adjustment Phase to Adaptation Phase

Dimension	Anticipatory Phase	Initial Adjustment Phase	Adaptation Phase
Cognitive functioning	Cognitive constriction	Cognitive constriction persists	Cognitive constriction persists
Affective responsiveness	Constriction	Constriction persists	Constriction persists
Emotional states	Moderate feelings of well-being	Moderate feelings of well-being persist	Diminished feelings of well-being
	Limited hopefulness	Hopelessness	Hopelessness persists
	Anxiety and depression; low body preoccupation	Anxiety and depression persist; high body preoccupation	Anxiety and depression persist; low body preoccupation
Self-system	Perception of capacity for self-care	Perception of modest inadequacy in self-care capacity	Perception of modest inadequacy in self-care capacity persists
	Moderate to high self-esteem	Moderate to high self-esteem persists	Moderate to high self-esteem persists
	Moderate adequacy and high distortion	Moderate adequacy and high distortion persist	Moderate adequacy and high distortion persist
	Moderate dominance, and affiliation	Moderate dominance with a lessening of affiliation; more hostile and distant	Moderate dominance with a lessening of affiliation; more hostile and distant
Loss meaning	Abandonment	Loss predominates, especially mutilation and death themes	Loss and mutilation and death themes persist

have lessened! The classic descriptions found in the literature of the long-term resident, descriptions that are attributed to the negative effects of living in a total institution, usually suggest a deteriorated cognitive state, a disinterest in or lack of capacity for self-care, and a constricted responsiveness, usually described as apathy and withdrawal. While this description may be applicable to many of the residents in the institution, among those in this sample of forty-five, there is little evidence that such debilities are primarily a result of changes associated with actually entering and living in the institutional environment. By and large, the characteristics of "old-timers" were evidenced before admission. Psychological status, in other words, did not appreciably deteriorate during the first year of institutionalization.

Of special importance is the consistency of the self-perceptions: there was no lessening of self-esteem and there was also a consistency in self-description. That the long-term resident was able to maintain a consistent self-identification is an exceedingly important finding, because it flies in the face of most informed speculation regarding institutional effects. (See, for example, the portraits presented in Chapter One, which have been suggested by Goffman, 1961; Townsend, 1962; and others, of the "institutional personality" as being discontinuous with the past in major ways.) Not only was there consistency through the impact phase, but the consistency was also maintained throughout the first year. On the variable of perception of self in relation to others, however, there was a movement toward greater hostility but no change in dominance. There is thus a continuing change toward increased hostility toward others. Awareness of competitiveness among residents, narcissistic preoccupation of residents, and manipulation by other residents can be coped with by moving away from situations that provoke these reactions. Yet residents are forced to relate to others if the resources of the institution are to be available to them for personal gratification—which indeed is the staff's rationale for encouraging residents to be active and vigorous. Because the more aggressive residents were the ones who became overrepresented in the final sample of survivors, one could expect them to be actively engaged with other residents, albeit in increasingly hostile ways.

If there was continual engagement with ill aged peers, why did body preoccupation lessen? The earlier increase in body preoccupation from preadmission through the initial adjustment period was thought to be related to the adoption of the patient role. Does the resident cease seeing himself as a patient among other sick and aged people? Not entirely, but possibly he sees himself less as a patient because, among "old-timers," a distinction is made between "patients" and "residents." Residents who have become severely confused or who are in the infirmary are viewed by the more lucid ambulatory residents, as well as by the staff, as "patients." This perception helps the more competent residents cope with their own personal vulnerability. If competence can be maintained, as was the case for most of the forty-five in this select sample, a feeling of having escaped "patienthood" is probably engendered.

The underlying loss meaning of mutilation and death, of one's personal vulnerability, however, does persist. Becoming an institutionalized older person, and experiencing oneself as having survived, cannot dispel the underlying concern with one's personal vulnerability. Possibly the tendency toward a lowering of feelings of well-being (an average lowering of 0.6, $p = .06$, as shown in Table 11) is a consequence of not having been altogether able to work through the underlying concern with vulnerability. The lowered feelings of well-being, without, however, a corresponding increase in anxiety, depression, or hopelessness, offers a confusing picture. In adapting to the institutional environment, the resident appears to have had difficulty in maintaining a feeling of well-being but not so much difficulty as to have made him unable to contain anxiety, depression, and hopelessness.

The changes from the anticipatory phase to the initial adjustment phase for the two outcome groups suggest, however, a different constellation of changes in emotional state for the two groups. The intact survivors as a subgroup showed an improvement in feelings of well-being but not a lifting of hopelessness. The problems of sample attrition by the end of the first year do not permit a resolution of the ambiguities in the data. Nevertheless, the data are suggestive of therapeutic benefits in the area of emotional states for intact survivors who initially had an impressive enhancement in feelings of well-being and only a slight rebound thereafter (about a 2-point rise on the Life Satisfaction Rating from preadmission to the initial adjustment phase through the adaptation phase).

From the Anticipatory Through the Adaptation Phase

When the changes in the select sample of 45 are analyzed to capture the differences from before admission through one year after admission, the overall impression is of rather few systematic psychological changes. As shown in Table 12, there was only a minimal change in functional adequacy: the cognitive construction found during the anticipatory phase persisted throughout the process of institutionalization. Affective responsiveness remained at a comparable constricted level from preadmission throughout the first year after admission. Feelings of well-being persist at a modest level from the initial adjustment phase through the adaptation phase. Hopelessness, on the other hand, becomes pronounced after the actual entrance to the home and does not decline further. The anxiety and depression that is in evidence during the anticipatory phase does not increase. But body preoccupation shows an interesting pattern of first increasing during the initial adjustment phase and then decreasing during the anticipatory phase. Self-perception shows remarkable stability over time. There is only a modest shift in the perception of capacity for self-care. A systematic decline is evidenced throughout the transition, however, in affiliation.

These scattered and modest adverse changes do not suggest that the "unhappy" psychological portrait of the old-age home resident is primarily a function of entering and living in the institution. At a less manifest level, changes do occur for the sample that remains intact through the years, but these more covert changes do not appear to lead to further cognitive disorganization, affective constriction, painful emotional states, or distortions of the self. *The status of the "old-timer" appears to be largely a function of his status just before admission.*

A Case Study from Predecision Through Adaptation

The case of Mrs. B., "the sunshine lady," was presented earlier to illustrate the early stages of transition to institutionalization. Here some of the data presented earlier will be reviewed and related to other data that will help clarify the salience of the variables that predict ultimate adaptation or decline. Because Mrs. B. possessed traits before admission that helped her to resist the impact of institutionalization, she best illustrates those who are less vulnerable.

In the Community. After first contact, the interviewer wrote the following description of Mrs. B., a 79-year-old widow. "She is a short woman, about 5 feet, 1 inch in height, and a little heavy through the middle. Tense and hyperactive, she has bright, dark eyes and a very alert appearance. Her grey hair is short and is fixed rather attractively. The skin of her face is unwrinkled, makeup is nicely applied, she is nicely dressed, wears costume jewelry, and appears to be not a day over 60. Her voice is deep, vibrant, and commanding. She smiles easily and responds very well to encouragement."

Mrs. B. had a heart attack about 7 years prior to her entering the home and had been under a doctor's care ever since. The previous year she had had "a blackout," which she attributed to "eating something or taking too many pills." She now took phenobarbital three times daily and took other sleeping pills at bedtime. She said she "must not get excited" or she would "aggravate her female problem . . . . The vagina feels like a revolving machine. It started 8 years after my husband had passed away. One in a million, and I happen to be the one." In spite of the heart attack, she was able to get out, though she had some difficulty with stairs. Her eyesight was good; her hearing, excellent. She refused to compare her health to that of others, feeling in many ways in better condition. On the other hand, she was very concerned about her body and emphasized not overdoing things. She exhibited a great deal of anxiety about becoming sick and dying, saying that she "had dreams of dying."

She felt good about herself and told the interviewer: "I'm great. Other people say so. I've given so much of myself." The interviewer reported: "She gives affect easily and usually speaks as though dictating. She carefully selects her words and tries to make an impressive reply." Mrs. B. was noted to be compulsive in her need to brush off or pick up specks that to the interviewer appeared invisible. The interviewer also commented: "She is a gracious and alert old woman who is functioning well." That she was well defended is reflected in the interviewer's positive assessment of her overt feelings of well-being on the Life Satisfaction Rating: "She is enthusiastic about many of her activities and about her interpersonal relationships; in general, she feels she has done a good job of directing her own life and influencing those close to her; she feels she had to sacrifice herself to some extent in the interest of her family, but feels that they have come through. She thinks she is pretty great and that other people think well of her. As 'the sunshine lady,' she is always cheerful and smiling." She described herself as a healthy child who grew up in a warm and successful family.

Her husband was not as prosperous as her father. "My husband was successful until building the bridge took our business away. He went back to the tailoring business. We worked hard together. He didn't have time to visit with the customers, so I met them all and they came to me with their troubles. I also managed the house and the children . . . . My husband was a wonderful person—intelligent, self-educated. He read and read. He was very good and considerate of others."

After her husband's death 16 years earlier, she lived for a very short time with her daughter and son-in-law but "he got nervous because I was always picking something up. He suggested I look for an apartment of my own." She found her own apartment and had been living alone ever since in an efficiency suite of an apartment hotel. She had not considered any other arrangements: "I'll continue to do what I've been doing. I'm satisfied with my way of living and hope to continue this way for many years. I'm not obligated to anyone and I'm not a burden to my family." She was able to maintain this autonomous, somewhat luxurious living because she had "invested wisely."

She was a very active lady: "Time doesn't mean anything to me. If I'm tired I go to bed at 6:00 or 8:00, bathe, have a little breakfast, and then sleep for a couple of more hours. On Monday, Tuesday, and Thursday, I attend the senior groups from 11:30 to 3:30. I rest after that, and I may go out to supper, then back to rest. I read the paper every day and listen to the news." She played cards a great deal and visited her daughter on Fridays and often on Sundays. She wrote regularly to her son and grandchildren. "God blessed me with a wonderful family, so in case I should ever need help of any kind, every hand of my loving ones would be extended out to me."

Her gregariousness had a somewhat driven quality to it. "The mail brings me in contact with all people. They call me the *sunshine lady*! I'm always filled with kindness. I enjoyed my clubs immensely and I enjoy my friends immensely."

In describing her activities with the senior group, she said: "Last week we went to the home and since then I've really counted my blessings—beautiful! But not for me! Never! I like my way of living. I live by myself so as not to be obliged to children."

On the Waiting List. One year after this interview, Mrs. B. was hospitalized because she "took too many pills for my female condition." She stayed with her daughter for a short period after her discharge from the psychiatric hospital but "I knew I was a burden to her, so I decided to come here [a local nursing home] because I need constant supervision." When the interviewer asked Mrs. B. what room she was in, she said: "Oh, I don't have to tell you that. Just ask anybody around here. They all know me." Mrs. B. was still "the sunshine lady."

About living in the nursing home, she said: "I feel great changes have come over me since I'm not burdened with housekeeping. I feel much better and look much better." There was a remarkable consistency in her activities while in the nursing home awaiting admission to the home for the aged: "My activities here, and people here, are enough for me." She visited the day care center at the home for the aged once a week as she awaited admission and continued to visit her daughter on Sunday and Friday evenings. She continued to correspond with her family, as earlier, but did not play cards as much as she used to: "I find more pleasure in the little things." While she tended to maintain her activity pattern, she placed greater emphasis on getting enough rest.

What had happened to change things in Mrs. B.'s life? She said, "I had taken too many pills for my female condition." The record at the nursing home reported, however, that she had made a suicide gesture. This gesture gained her reentry into her daughter's house. But, again, there was a rupture in the relationship with her daughter and son-in-law and according to Mrs. B., "I knew I was causing her lots of trouble. It would be better for all of us if I went to the nursing home." Was there a specific precipitating event leading to her "taking too many pills"? Or, on the other hand, had she become overwhelmed as internal pressures had built up over time? If so, why after 7 years was there now a rather sudden change? We do not know. More clear, however, are the sequelae to the changes, so that she was now in a convalescent home awaiting admission to a home for the aged. From her interview, it is clear that her feelings of well-being had declined; she was much less zestful, blamed herself for what had befallen her, and evinced increased anxiety and depression. These feelings to a large extent are reactions to separation from family and her former life-style.

A year earlier, she had said that for any aged person, entering the home was a final separation from community and family. Furthermore, Mrs. B.'s feelings of concern about separation when on the waiting list were expressed in the shift in what she reported to be her earliest memory as compared with what she reported when she was interviewed in the community. In the first interview her earliest memory was: "I remember as a child that my father was very fond of cards, and that when the family would get together they would spend their time playing, which I myself resented very much even after I had been married." When asked for her earliest memory after she was on the waiting list, she cited an entirely unrelated event. "I was a child of about 12. I went to visit my mother's friend who had asked me to spend the night with her. I was miserable when I got there, really homesick for my mother. I couldn't sleep all night. My mother's friend had to take me home at about 5:00 in the morning. I guess I was pretty attached to my mother to be so homesick." This memory focuses on feelings of separation from a caretaker, specifically her mother. From the period of independent living to the waiting list, in other words, Mrs. B. shifted from a preoccupation with the attention of men to one of separation from her mother.

Another manifestation of this shift toward concern with feelings of separation appeared on the Personal Resources Questionnaire. Before application, for all areas Mrs. B. listed one or more persons, but when on the waiting list she could not list a specific person in five of the eleven areas. She apparently felt that she could not depend on her friends to respond to her needs as they had formerly.

Another perspective on how she was coping with the feelings of separation and abandonment is offered in her statement of her expectations regarding the move to the old-age home. Of the nursing home that she was in, she said: "I'm happy here and I hope to have the same results when I'm a resident at the home. I don't expect much there, only to give a little and take a little. I cannot live in a selfish world and be isolated from everyone else. If you are surrounded by people, then you have hope. You believe you will find someone you enjoy being with. I hope that will be the situation for me for the rest of my life. I won't participate in all of the activities of the home. Not all, but some. Only when I'm able to." When asked why she had applied, she responded: "I'd mentioned to my daughter before I came here that I'd hoped that home would be my home. I would want to go there in order not to be a burden to her. My daughter was pleased. She put in my application when I was so ill." She could not face her former feelings about how delighted she was that she did not have to give in to her feelings of illness and deterioration and could live independently in the community. The home was at that point perceived as a last resort. Now that there had been a change in relationship with the daughter,

as evidenced by her daughter's willingness to apply for her
admission to the home, there was no other alternative for her.
Thus, she needed to use the rationalization that moving to the
home was really something that she was doing for her
daughter.

Predictor Scores Before Relocation. Mrs. B. was well
above the mean on aggressiveness, especially on the individual
components that comprise the factor score, such as activity and
status drive. Aggressiveness in Mrs. B. is a trait that is consistent
with her hysterical character structure, a pathological structure
that apparently has persisted throughout her life. Her psychopathology did not limit her cognitive adequacy; she was lucid
and responsive to her environment. She was, indeed, hopeful
regarding the future. While she may have misinterpreted and distorted the motives of others, she did use others to support her
self-image. While the massive use of denial is characteristic of
her hysterical personality structure, she did not use denial to
avoid dealing with the impending event of relocation.

Initial Adjustment. The day after admission, Mrs. B.'s
son died and she had to be heavily sedated for a couple of
weeks. Six weeks later, however, she was her usual outgoing,
narcissistic self. She was not well liked but, being very active,
she felt that she was a definite asset to the home. Aware of the
attacks on her, she claimed that others were jealous of her
attractiveness and vigor. If anything, she was more "sickeningly
sweet" than before, as if she had a need to reassure herself and
others that any hostility toward her was uncalled for.

Long-Term Adaptation. The picture was the same at the
end of the year. She felt the staff had helped "take the pressure
off her" by reassuring her and by encouraging her to be active.
Also she had by now developed a "couple of good friends" who
shared her aggressiveness and who needed to disassociate themselves from the "sick old people."

Her status had remained remarkably consistent from preadmission to 1 year after admission. The apparent underlying
depression continued to be marked by her manic disposition,
with its flight into the hysteric where "everything is wonderful." While she had concern about her relations with the other
residents, she felt singled out for special treatment by the staff

and extolled them for the care and attention she was receiving. She was able to deny that the special treatment reflected the staff's effort to "hold her together." While, clearly, she had become increasingly hostile toward others during the year in the home, this behavior was not very different from her characteristic style. The home could tolerate this type of behavior and help her focus on her spry and active self. There was no evidence of any deterioration in physical, mental, or behavioral functioning 1 year after admission.

Mrs. B. is a good example of how aggressiveness can be maintained from preadmission to postadmission. As a trait that is congruent with the adaptive demands of the home, aggressiveness lessened her vulnerability to institutionalization. Because of her good cognitive functioning, the home was not a confusing experience. Her attitude that the home would offer her care and security, as well as her high degree of hope, facilitated her use of the environment for protective security. Although she tended to use denial as a major defense mechanism, she did not use it to avoid coping with the impending event. Once a resident, she was able to deal with the demands of her new life realistically, including becoming increasingly aggressive in interaction with others.

Summary

Passivity was the only psychological characteristic that could be isolated as a predictor of morbidity and mortality that was not associated with survival. The personality trait of passivity predicted outcomes for those who become institutionalized but not for matched samples composed of older people living in the community and living in the homes. Apparently, passivity hinders the development of adaptive techniques that facilitate using the environment to reestablish a viable equilibrium. The extremely strong relationships with negative outcome in the present study may also be partly a function of the lack of rewards in the institution to individuals who use this adaptive style. Because the rewarded style is assertiveness, additional stress is placed on passive residents to change their typical adaptational pattern.

Institutional life itself has only a modest role in causing excess morbidity and mortality. It must not be forgotten, however, that the institutions the study sample entered represent the best of facilities for the long-term care of the elderly. On the other hand, although outcomes appear to be largely a function of individual characteristics, morbidity and mortality were hastened for those with characteristics that sensitize them to stress. Initial emotional reactions, as well as behavioral symptoms, are likely to reflect the early physical decline. Surprisingly few other psychological indices were affected during the initial adjustment phase for those who underwent negative outcomes. Indeed, the general pattern of early psychological changes was very similar for both outcome groups including a slight decline in cognitive adequacy, an increase in bodily preoccupation, a perception of less capacity for self-care, the portrayal of self as more hostile in interaction with others, and a shift toward a focal concern with mutilation and death.

These early psychological effects tended to persist throughout the year—although, of course, two thirds of the sample now consisted largely of intact survivors and a smaller number of respondents who manifested marked decline. There were, however, some changes. Life satisfaction declined, but not to its preadmission level. Body preoccupation subsided and perception of capacity for self-care was enhanced, suggesting a more comfortable use of the institution to assure survival. Yet hostility in interaction increased beyond the level reached 2 months after admission, probably as a function of the engagement with peers within the institutional community. The focal concern with mutilation and death persisted, but self-consistency remained. The general picture became one of feeling personally vulnerable but of having survived.

Do these findings clarify the relative importance of environmental discontinuity and institutional life, in themselves, in causing institutional effects and, particularly, in causing the outcomes of marked deterioration or death? The findings suggest that both are causal factors that cannot be separated in the present study. Passivity as a predictor of severe outcomes under stress certainly supports the indication that environmental discontinuity is a critical factor. The need to adapt to any new set of environmental demands would be expected to be more taxing or stressful to those less likely to mobilize their psychological resources. This explanation is congruent with the finding that the older people who entered after living temporarily in nursing homes were more likely to have negative outcomes. For these people, entering the home was the second recent experience of environmental discontinuity.

Yet the impact of the discontinuity is not reflected in cognitive disorganization, because 2 months after entering the institution there was no essential difference in cognitive functioning. The effects of the physical differences in the preadmission and postadmission environments appear to have been overcome shortly after the disorganizing experience of the first few weeks after admission. The reestablishment of cognitive equilibrium may be related to the opportunity for residents to take with them personal belongings, the presence in the institution of acquaintances, familiarity with the environment from earlier visits, and the perceptual richness of the environment in non-profit homes for the aged. Cognitive functioning may be secondary to other areas of functioning as a reflector of discontinuity. To be specific, for those who showed extreme negative outcomes by the end of the first year, there was an initial emotional, as well as physical, reaction, a global adverse response to entering the new environment before it had become a useful one for the reestablishment of a viable homeostasis.

The importance of environmental discontinuity does not argue against the importance of institutional life as also critical in causing effects. Yet for those who survived intact through the first year, the impression is not of massive institutional effects. Rather, the most salient impression is of the persistence of the status at preadmission, a status that, to the largest extent, appears to have been a result of reactions to the losses that preceded admission.

5

Implications for Practice

Our investigation of the process of becoming an institution-alized old person has made amply clear that older people are likely to undergo profound psychological alterations almost immediately after they accept the reality that they will soon relinquish residential independence for the rest of their lives. The deleterious effects of the institutional process that have been documented by the present and earlier studies highlight the pressing need for practitioners, planners, and administrators of services to the elderly to reexamine a number of prevailing conceptions related to the delivery of these services. Long-term care of the elderly, for example, has been almost entirely equated with institutional care, with little consideration of whether the equation is necessary or even economically sound. With respect to such an issue, for example, the finding of the present study that the greatest psychological decrements oc-curred in anticipation of the dreaded institutionalization, rather than at the final stage of the process, is especially important. It dictates the conclusion that if planners direct their attention to options other than institutionalization, they may significantly delay not only the harmful effects of institutional life, but also those even more serious psychological and behavioral effects that have been shown to be associated with waiting for admission. Or, to take another example, those who make decisions about the care of the elderly have thus far exhibited a unidimensional concern with monitoring the quality of institutional facilities. Too often, what has been monitored are less critical facets of care, such as patient-staff ratios and conformity to building codes, rather than critical facets such as degree of interpersonal warmth, amount of individuation, and opportunities afforded for engagement. We have found these critical facets to be associated with well-being, as well as with surviving intact, for geriatric patients relocated from a state mental hospital to a wide variety of institutional settings (Lieberman and Tobin, in press). Also, it is of utmost importance for program redesign that planners begin to survey services available to the elderly throughout the community. Although the call for comprehensive service packages for the elderly was sounded forcibly at the 1970 White House Conference on Aging, it is still clear that few communities show any degree of coordination even between such integrally related agencies as hospitals and nursing homes. Even fewer examples can be identified of adequate coordination between these two types of service agencies and community-based care programs.

A Review of the Findings

Our investigation of the impact of the institutionalization process on old people was initiated to gain an empirical perspective on the widely held belief that institutional life itself explains the unpleasant psychological portrait of the institutionalized old as cognitively deteriorated, apathetic, helpless, and so on. It was reasoned that if other factors such as selection biases, anticipatory effects, or environmental discontinuity were also causally related to the portrait, then planners and practitioners must take account of these factors and develop interventions that go beyond upgrading the quality of institutional environments.

To identify the relative influence of the several possible

factors that might explain the rather bleak portrait drawn of institutionalized elderly, four phases in the process of becoming institutionalized were examined:

1. A period when one is *very old and living in the community,* which, for some, is a "predecision" period that antedates a decision to seek institutional care.

2. *An anticipatory institutionalization period* while awaiting admission to the institution, after having decided to seek institutional care.

3. *An initial adjustment period* lasting 2 months after entering the institution that follows the acute disequilibrium of the first month or so.

4. *An adaptation period* through the first year after admission.

The Relevance of Age.   Although only a minority of elderly live in long-term care institutions, the likelihood of becoming institutionalized increases with age. Although slightly less than 5 percent of all people 65 years old and over reside in institutions, of those 65 to 75 it is less than 2 percent, whereas of those 75 to 85 it is 7 percent and 85 and older, over 16 percent (Office of Nursing Home Affairs, 1975). Most very old people are able to live independently in the community in spite of having incurred a great many losses. The ability to cope with age-related losses was shown in the present study when older people living in the community were matched with the respondents who were followed through the institutionalization process. The matched community sample consisted of forty unattached elderly people, thirty-four women and six men, whose average age was 80 years and whose average educational level was eight grades. Half of this group lived alone; the others, in most cases, lived with their eldest daughter. These forty people represented a wide range of personality types, a variety also exhibited in the primary study sample. Thus, no one particular type of person could be seen as more likely to remain, on the one hand, in the community, or to seek institutionalization, on the other. Rather the data suggest that any type of older person may seek care in a home for the aged or may hold out against the forces of age and remain an independent community resident.

The psychological status of these very old community residents was impressively good, especially considering their physical status and the number of significant adverse changes they had experienced in the past 3 years. Two out of three, for example, reported the presence of two or more serious chronic diseases. Three out of five had lost some physical capacity in the past three years; two out of five had suffered the death of at least one significant other person; and an additional one out of five had experienced some other sort of decisive change in their relationships with significant others. One out of three had moved their place of residence, yet none had sought institutional care at this time. Many respondents in the community sample had discussed the possibility of institutional care with their families as a solution to the problems these losses had generated, but all had decided against giving up their independence. For all, institutional care was a feared or dreaded solution that would be taken only if necessary to assure survival. Although often physically impaired and having experienced many adverse changes, these community elderly were cognitively intact, in good rapport with themselves and the world outside them, and hopeful about the future. They recognized but were not preoccupied either with the losses they had already endured or with those that might lie not too far ahead, including the possibility of their own death.

Although they were apprehensive regarding deterioration in their personal functioning and decreases in the ability or willingness of responsible others to support noninstitutional living, they appeared not to have reached the threshold at which the seeking of institutional care seems the only answer. If, however, sufficient adverse changes were to occur to make institutional care seem the only pattern that assured the maintenance of residual capacities, while not prepared to welcome the eventuality, they would in all likelihood accept it as a necessary one to resolve the dilemma of independence and survival in favor of the latter value.

Anticipating Institutionalization. After the threshold is reached, the older person becomes transformed into what he has feared becoming: a person who needs institutional care. The term *threshold* is the most appropriate, because no single adverse change precipitates the transition. Rather, a decision in favor of institutional care is made because of a combination of changes that are compelling for this particular individual and responsible others, who reach a consensus that "it's time." Other older people may have undergone similar changes, but have not been brought to the threshold by these changes, so that for these people it is not yet time. Comparison of the primary sample when on the waiting list ($N = 100$) with the matched community sample reveals how unlikely it is that a single, particular precipitating event might explain differing capacities of the two groups to maintain independent status. Indeed, the largest difference between the two samples, which was evidenced in the area of adverse changes in relationships with significant others, suggests a change that probably occurs after other events have precipitated a decision to seek institutional care. That is, the deteriorated relationships are a reaction to the participants involved in the decision-making process.

Now that the decision has been made, changes ensue in rapid succession: application is made and, once accepted, admission is awaited. As the resident-to-be separates from independent community living and intimate others, his attention begins to shift to the gains that can accrue from becoming institutionalized—principally care, people, and activities. The meaning of the losses connected with giving up independent living is separation; the experience is that of being abandoned, and reaction to it is extreme. Increasingly, the person becomes cognitively constricted, apathetic, unhappy, hopeless, depressed, anxious, and less dominant in relationships with others. The older person in the anticipatory institutionalization phase already looks like an institutionalized older person. Indeed, when old people awaiting admission were compared to older people who had lived in homes for 1 to 3 years ($N = 37$), the latter looked more intact on several dimensions, suggesting the possibility of ameliorative effects that may take place after living in the institutional environment has been a reality for some time.

The effects of the anticipation phase are well illustrated in the cases of three women first described in Chapter Two. Each of these very old women was interviewed before a decision for institutionalization had been made and again during the waiting-list period after applying to a home, as well as during the 2 months and, finally, 1 year after admission to a home. The changes in psychological functioning from the "predecision" period to the period while awaiting admission were dramatically similar to those generally cited as induced by the harmful qualities of institutional life itself. This finding amply demonstrates how separation and anticipation of loss can affect psychological status, eventually painting a portrait no more desirable than that of institutionalized elder people.

Initial Adjustment. Once the older person actually enters the home, he usually enters a period of acute disequilibrium lasting 1 or 2 months, and then an initial adjustment is made. The changes in psychological status from preadmission until 2 months after admission are minimal. There are no additional decrements in cognitive functioning nor in emotional responsiveness; well-being does not diminish, and depression or anxiety do not increase. The changes are specific: less hope, more body preoccupation, and a perception of self as possessing less capacity for self-care, and as more hostile in interaction with others. Essentially, the new resident has become one patient among many old, sick, and frail elderly. In identifying with other frail elderly, the resident develops increasing preoccupation with body functioning and incapacity sets in. Mood is not affected, but the future is perceived as foreshortened. When the new resident becomes actively engaged with other residents in the care-giving environment, he or she engages in conflict and increasingly perceives himself or herself as being more abrasive in interactions. Family members recede into the background, becoming mythicized characters who have less relevance for the present than for the past, and for their usefulness in assuring oneself of a retained personal meaning when confronting one's own mortality.

Although the feared losses are further deterioration and death, and the sense of being personally vulnerable is inescapable, there are no further encroachments on cognitive functioning, affective responsiveness, self-esteem, ability to use others for self-definition, and feelings of well-being, depression, anxiety, and of dominance in interaction. Indeed, the new resident is quite able to retain a remarkable continuity in self-definition—as is clearly seen in the profiles of Mrs. A., Mrs. B., and Mrs. C.

The portrait 2 months after entering and living in the institution environment is, with only minor exceptions, like that before admission and, thus, is best explained as induced by the waiting-list period rather than by the entrance period.

Through the First Year.   By the end of the first year after entering the institution, some residents show no serious adverse changes, while others have either markedly deteriorated or died. Of the eighty-five respondents who entered the institution, forty-four suffered these extreme outcomes. Among the latter are those whose deterioration or death was hastened because they entered and lived in the institution. A comparison of the two outcome groups—the intact survivors and the seriously debilitated or dead—revealed that those who had lived temporarily in nursing homes while awaiting admission to the permanent home were more likely to endure severe outcomes, although preadmission psychological status of these elderly was the same as those who maintained their usual living arrangements prior to entering the permanent homes. The deteriorated and dead were more passive, less able to attend to daily functions, less hopeful, and less able to use others for self-definition. They also showed more denial in dealing with the impending event of entering the institution. Among the five predictors, only passivity was not associated with survival. As a trait that is not associated with survival, passivity is, thus, a predictor of vulnerability to the stress of entering and living in an institution. This finding suggests that the inability to reorganize psychological resources to meet new conditions may be of particular importance when confronted with environmental discontinuity. However, because aggressiveness is the rewarded style in the homes studied, the relationship between passivity and severe outcomes may also be explained as an artifact of the demands of institutional life.

Since those who manifest severe outcomes by the end of

the first year also show more extreme emotional and physical changes after the first 2 months, environmental discontinuity may have adverse effects. For those with more favorable outcomes after a year, the reactions 2 months after admission were usually less severe—they improved in life satisfaction and exhibited lessened anxiety, but they, too, were affected by the change to institutional life: hope decreased, although less so than for the more vulnerable; body preoccupation increased; and they perceived themselves as less capable of self-care and as more hostile in interaction with others. Apparently, in the first 2 months there is no escaping from the meaning of institutional living as a severe loss expressed symbolically by themes of mutilation or death, so that the experience for all is that of being personally vulnerable. From the initial period through the end of the first year, those who showed no marked negative effects nevertheless showed diminished feelings of well-being and a further heightened perception of themselves as hostile in interaction with others. On the positive side, body preoccupation decreased for this group. The absence of any other changes reflects the remarkable consistency in psychological status from preadmission through 1 year after admission.

Other Pathways. Not all elderly enter long-term care institutions after a lengthy anticipatory period, nor do they necessarily come from the community or other long-term care settings. Indeed, it is now more common to enter homes for the aged without a lengthy waiting-list period and, increasingly, to come directly from the acute hospital. This pathway is encouraged by the current regulations regarding reimbursement for care in long-term facilities. Still, over one half (55 percent) of admission to long-term care facilities come directly from community dwellings, with the other one half divided between other long-term care settings (13 percent) and general hospitals (32 percent: 10 percent from state mental hospitals and 22 percent from general hospitals) (Office of Nursing Home Affairs, 1975).

When a patient is admitted from the general acute hospital, his or her anticipatory period is likely to be very short. A catastrophic illness, a stroke, or a broken hip leads to acute hospitalization. When survival is assured, during recovery, the elderly patient may be more hopeful of improvement than is the family or physician. Together the family and the physician may arrive at a decision that the aged person can not be cared for at home. At this point, the elderly patient is probably physically depleted and too mentally upset and confused to comprehend the situation. As lucidity returns, the patient may sense that something is not being said. Most often the physician informs the patient that there is a need "to go to a nursing home for a while until you get better." The upset family, who now has the task of selecting a nursing home, may rely completely on the suggestions of the physician or social worker. The elderly patient is then abruptly transferred; but even before the physical relocation the patient's condition may worsen. The anticipatory period has already established negative effects. Moreover, the presence of a spouse may intensify critical moments. The spouse, usually a wife, is anxious, on the one hand, because of the possibility that her husband's health will not improve or that he will die, and is anxious, on the other hand, because of the need to change her life-style, which may require moving in with a child.

Although the type of situation just described is quite different than the one we have studied—in its apparent immediacy and more acutely painful quality—nonetheless, the situations have aspects in common. One or another explanation for effects may indeed be more relevant for a particular situation, and certainly the focus of intervention will vary. Yet the presence and the effects of the process that we have described, as well as the explanations and practice implications, can be sufficiently generalized to be meaningful for all situations in which old people become institutionalized.

Explanations for Institutional Effects

Let us review the four explanations incorporating our findings. These explanations relate to selection biases, process effects before admission, environmental discontinuity, and institutional life.

Selection Biases.   Essentially, we have controlled for selection biases. In following those persons studied from before
until after admission, for example, we have avoided the pitfall
inherent in cross-sectional designs in which institutionalized and
noninstitutionalized samples have been compared and the differences interpreted as change. Assessments of the same individuals over time have revealed little adverse change *in those who
survived*; in fact, remarkable stability in functioning is associated with entering and living in the institution.

Also, apparently no one type of person seeks admission. A
wide diversity of personality types was present in the group
who entered the homes studied, as well as in the population
from whom they came, as suggested by the diversity of types
among the matched community sample.

Process Effects Before Admission.   The psychological
portrait of the institutionalized older person who enters one of
the better long-term care institutions is sketched in before the
person actually enters and lives in the institutional environment.
The psychological effects of institutionalization are less attributable to institutional life than to reactions to the waiting
period preceding admission. The effects are particularly attributed to the loss meaning of separation imparted to the process
and to the experience of being abandoned that reflects both
separation and the dread of the impending event. Our findings
suggest that reactions or effects occur in response to meanings
of loss and anticipated loss and not to the events that precipitated admission. The matched community sample had experienced almost as much adverse change in the 3 years before they
were studied as those who applied for institutional admission.
The largest difference between these two populations was
shown to be in relationship to attitudes toward significant
others, a change that appears to be more a result of deciding to
resolve the dilemma of independence as survival by seeking
institutional care than a precipitant for seeking care. Among the
very old, personal and social disequilibrium is ubiquitous. Those
who seek institutional care as the solution to these points of
disequilibrium are likely to characterize the relationships between themselves and significant others in terms of feelings of
separation, rejection, and abandonment.

Environmental Discontinuity. Although environmental discontinuity can not be easily disentangled from the effects of institutional life, the data suggest the critical role of discontinuity, particularly in relationship to outcomes 1 year after admission. Those who manifested the extreme outcomes of marked deterioration or death were more likely to have lived transitionally in nursing homes, to be more passive and to exhibit physical deterioration, as well as emotional reactions, shortly after admission. These several findings taken together suggest that the move itself is taxing. Supporting evidence comes from three additional studies (Lieberman, 1974) in which elderly people, on the whole, showed extreme adverse effects when relocated from one environment to another. Independent of prerelocation and postrelocation environments (for example, community to institution, institution to institution, or institution to community) and independent of situation characteristics (for example, voluntary or involuntary relocation, variable waiting periods, relocating alone or with others) moving from one environment to another is associated with excess negative outcome.

Those who are most likely to manifest the effects of environmental discontinuity are the most passive individuals, those least able to mobilize psychological resources to cope with the new adaptive demands. Less critical are the meanings of the impending event or of the degree of felt personal control over one's destiny. As expected, when these more physically debilitated elderly were studied under conditions of relocation, the outcomes associated with the move were more likely to be extreme morbidity and death. The weaker the biological substrata, the more unlikely it is that the original taxation of environmental discontinuity will be overcome and a viable homeostasis reestablished.

Institutional Life. Even the best of long-term care institutional environments for the elderly induce harmful institutional effects. To be sure, these adverse effects are less pronounced than was previously thought to be the case. Still, after separating the effects of the process that precedes admission from the effects of environmental discontinuity, some institutional effects do remain. Since the frail elderly are gathered within one environment, the newcomer cannot escape the dreaded identifications that include being sick, being in need of care, being closer to death, and possessing a limited and uncontrollable future. Participation with other residents in the care and activities that are provided is essential to adapting to this new world. But participation involves unavoidable conflicts with others and an ensuing awareness that one has become more hostile in everyday relationships. At the same time, family members recede into the background to become mythicized characters. The meaning of the environment unavoidably becomes that of mutilation and death and an underlying experience of being personally vulnerable, but of having survived.

Early Intervention

How early can we intervene to facilitate a beneficial adaptation to institutional living? Can we begin before the actual decision to seek institutional care? Can we be helpful when the older person is first threatened with the possibility of having to seek such care? To people in their late 70s and 80s, a further loss of capacity for self-care or a lessened ability of others to support independent living can quickly change the equilibrium. Older people, as well as responsible others, are only too acutely aware of the precarious balance, because crises have already thrown their lives out of equilibrium and new crises will probably occur, again threatening their precarious equilibrium.

For Mrs. A. ("I'm a busy lady"), for example, the death of her husband was followed by a decision to leave Los Angeles for Chicago so that she could be close to sister, son, and daughter-in-law. The family had debated a variety of living arrangements, including convalescent homes. Fortunately for Mrs. A., her relatives were able to locate an apartment near her sister. A balance was reestablished and Mrs. A. was able once again to live a comfortable, independent life until the death of her sister and rectal surgery precipitated her application.

Mrs. B. ("They call me the sunshine lady"), similarly had her viscissitudes. Sixteen years prior to our study, she had lost her husband and thereafter lived with her daughter and son-in-law. When this arrangement proved unworkable, after 8 years of living together, she moved into her own apartment. One year later she had a heart attack from which she recovered and she continued to live alone for 7 additional years until she took "too many pills." After her discharge from a psychiatric hospital, she entered a nursing home. During the several years that preceded her entering the nursing home, she manifested symptoms of psychological debilitation. Yet she persisted in living in the community.

Mrs. C. ("I want people"), shared an apartment with a close friend for the 9 years that preceded her application to the nursing home. When her friend became too hard of hearing to carry on conversations, Mrs. C. chose institutionalization as preferable to the isolated condition afforded in the apartment.

The events leading these three elderly women to apply for institutionalization are not unusual in the lives of elderly people. Several aged in community sample had undergone similar losses but had not sought institutionalization. Indeed, it is difficult to identify the precise differences between those who seek institutionalization and the larger number of their aged peers who, although experiencing quite similar events, did not apply. Certainly the changes in the capacity for independent living of the three elderly women followed from a predecision phase to the anticipatory phase were not remarkably different from those who did not apply. All three had family members who felt a responsibility for their care and comfort; none was "dumped" into the institution; and each felt that it was her decision.

Like others who sought institutional care, as contrasted to those who did not, the critical change was in relationships with others. For Mrs. A., it was the loss of a sister; for Mrs. C., it was the increasing inability of her roommate to communicate and to be a companion to her. These two women are not atypical. Either sudden or gradual losses of intimate social supports can lead to the appraisal that it is impossible to manage independently in the community. The aged person turns to responsible and caring children for help and, in discussions with these confidants, makes the decision to seek institutional care.

Thus it was not the absence of responsible others or confidants that led to institutionalization. Nor was it because the resident-to-be was a particular type of person. Mrs. A. was clearly not a "dependent personality type," although Mrs. C. may have been. Mrs. B., on the other hand, was chronically mentally ill and apparently it was intrapsychic and not interpersonal changes that led to her suicide attempt.

Each of these very different women perceived the institution as necessary to maximize comfort. Mrs. A. was terribly depressed, Mrs. B. was self-destructive, and Mrs. C. was extremely nervous. All three were unable to envision viable independent living in the community. Yet it can be argued that alternatives could have been developed that would have assured a modicum of comfort and security outside of the institution. For each, a congregate living arrangement that was less than total institutional care may have sufficed. We may ask: Were all three prematurely institutionalized? Did their status warrant institutional care at this time? Did we, to use Margaret Blenkner's term (Blenkner, Bloom, and Nielsen, 1971), "overdose" these three elderly women? Could supports have been sufficiently stabilized to facilitate an adaptation to the community?

For Mrs. A., Mrs. B., and Mrs. C., vigorous efforts were not made to help them live in the community. They, as others among the very old, perceived the home for the aged as a resource readily available to them and selected this option when adverse personal and interpersonal changes did in fact occur. Unfortunately, at the time we first interviewed these three widows, alternatives to institutional care were relatively nonexistent. The choice then was either to enter the home for life or to remain in the community and receive virtually no assurance of help from providers of social and health care. Time has begun to develop what might have been other options, at least for some of those elderly persons who entered homes for the aged during the period studied. In this decade, a network of community-based services to the elderly has emerged that has afforded many the opportunity to meet social and physical needs through living arrangements that can offer far more autonomy than the total institution. In part, the impetus for the development of one of these networks was a result of the study reported here and, more specifically, a further study of elderly on the waiting list to one of the three homes. This latter study—to be reported in the following section—was designed to explore the types of services needed within a viable geriatric care system that could prevent unnecessary, premature institutionalization.

Services to Prevent Premature Institutionalization

As a vehicle for the exploration of services that would be helpful in preventing unnecessary premature institutionalization, Tobin, Hammerman, and Rector (1972) studied the preferred disposition for aged who had already been placed on the waiting list. Thirty-eight judges, professionals in the institutional referral and care system as well as board members of the institutions, were asked if disposition for ten waiting-list aged would have been different if ancillary services had been available; and, if so, what ancillary services would have been necessary for each of the ten waiting-list aged.

Of the ten cases, for only two did one half or more of the judges recommend that the resident-to-be actually be admitted at this time. For the others, a variety of recommendations was made. These recommendations encompassed eight general categories of services: counseling, activities, vocational rehabilitation, day care, home health care, noninstitutional residential care, money, and medical diagnosis. These service categories are not in substance different from categories developed by other investigators, such as by Lissitz (1970) and by Lawton (1970). Professionals, as well as informed lay people, can thus readily identify the types of supports that can facilitate independent community living. Moreover, the Tobin, Hammerman, and Rector study showed that these are the very services that could reduce the frequency of institutionalization by focusing on elderly people who have already applied, been accepted, and are now awaiting imminent admission to the long-term care institution.

If these services had been available to Mrs. A., Mrs. B., Mrs.

C., and their families, the services may indeed have been perceived as capable of assuring a more satisfactory way of living
than could be offered by the institution. Mrs. A. and Mrs. C.
certainly could have benefited from a mix of services that
would have assured a noninstitutional solution. Some other
type of living arrangement, short of the total institution, could
have been considered. Most likely the total costs of living in
another residential arrangement would have been less than institutional living—although the latter covers costs of medical and
social service as well as of food, clothing, and shelter. For Mrs.
B., as contrasted with Mrs. A. and Mrs. C., the costs to structure
an environment in the community—that could offer her the protective security she needed—might have been greater than the
costs of institutionalization. Even if costs had been less, this
alternative solution may not have been advisable for her. Obviously, economic costs can only be one consideration in planning for people. Human costs are certainly of more importance.
Nevertheless, until extensive home health care is needed, costs
are less when older people remain in the community (see, for
example, Pollack, 1973). Relevant to human costs, as our study
suggests, the institutionalization process itself is associated with
damaging psychological consequences and, for some, with a
hastened mortality. We argue, therefore, for the development of
alternatives to institutional care. At the very least, alternatives
must be available so that older people and their families have
options.

Toward this goal of generating options, many (see, for
example, J. Kaplan, 1974, and Shore, 1973) have argued for parallel services rather than for "alternatives." The term *alternatives*
has become associated with keeping older people out of institutions no matter what their needs or wishes. Such an attitude
would limit the options of those who might choose to live in a
humane and care-taking total environment. Yet it would appear
from the data presented here that institutionalization, even in
homes of the highest quality, should not be considered a first
choice, but should follow only after serious efforts have been
made to determine whether continued independent living might
be possible if specific deficiencies were corrected through ancil-

lary services. Stated another way, all efforts need to be made to prevent unnecessary or premature institutionalization. In practice, however, the distinction between unnecessary and necessary institutionalization is not easily made. Thus, it is essential that service providers become versed in the use of flexible service packages in order to help older people and their families understand and explore the available options.

One approach to options, or parallel services, is to consider three somewhat different ways of structuring their delivery. As shown in Table 13, three approaches to service delivery can be constructed that cover the range of needs among the elderly population, from services for the comparatively well elderly through services that provide alternatives for preventing premature institutionalization to services for those whose needs may demand institutional care or its equivalent. For older people anywhere along this continuum, services can be organized around an individualized home-delivered approach, a congregate-organized approach, or a congregate residence approach. In the first two approaches, older people who live in their own home or in a home of others are helped to remain in this setting by providing services delivered to the home or by facilitating travel for providers of services to individuals or families. In the congregate-delivered services, older people are served in group settings that can maximize their participation with others and that can be more efficient, as well as economical, for the integration of services such as occurs in the multipurpose senior center. Note that some forms of group services are likely to be open to all ages, such as courses at local community colleges, whereas others are likely to be age-segregated, such as programs at the senior centers. In the congregate residence approach, older people reside together. This approach apparently affords important benefits for the comparatively well elderly (see, for example, Rosow, 1967, who found that age-segregated housing enhances social interaction, and Hochschild, 1973, who found that older people in such living arrangements gained a sense of meaningfulness through developing their own activities). Whether similar benefits can accrue for age-segregated residences for the more impaired elderly is open to question. Our

Table 13. Alternative Ways of Structuring the Delivery of Services

A Continuum of Service:	Individually Delivered	Congregate Delivered	
	Home-Based	Congregate Organized	Congregate Residence
from services for the comparatively well elderly	Out-Reach Information and referral Telephone reassurance Friendly visiting Work at home Senior Wheels to shopping, doctor, dentist, and social functions	Adult education Recreational senior center	Senior housing (includes retirement hotels) Senior housing with recreation Senior housing with recreation and social services
through services that provide alternatives for preventing premature institutionalization	Escort service Homemaker service (housekeeping, handyman, and so forth) Meals on Wheels	Nutrition sites (Wheels to Meals) Sheltered workshop Multipurpose senior center (all of the above plus outreach, and health and social follow-up)	Sheltered care Halfway house
to services for those whose needs may demand institutional care or its equivalents	Home health care (visiting nurse, rehabilitation, speech therapy, dentist, and doctor) Foster home care (complete social and health care for bedridden person in a home)	Out-patient day or hospital care	Mental hospital Institutional care (nursing home and home for the aged) Intermediate nursing care Skilled nursing care Short-term crisis care Vacation plan Terminal care

study suggests that grouping together the more impaired elderly works to their detriment by forcing an identification with others who are similarly frail and unable to care for themselves, an identification that reduces their own capacity to transcend physical and mental incapacities. Possibly new forms of congregate residences can be developed for the more impaired elderly that could limit the effect of this adverse peer identification. This possibility will be considered in the last section of this chapter.

Given the potentially adverse effects of congregate living for the more debilitated, individualized home-based and congregate organized services become important therapeutic tools. Maintenance in the community, however, with home-delivered or congregate organized services is simpler to recommend than to do. The caseworker must be able to tolerate the anxiety that is associated with encouraging an older individual—who may be debilitated, angry, depressed, and confused—to live independently in the community rather than in a more protective environment. Also, the caseworker must be able to tolerate the difficulty of asking younger family members, who are themselves middle-aged and older, to take on or keep a burden that can only grow heavier. Yet the stabilization of the intimate support system on behalf of the elderly person must be a primary thrust of early intervention (see, for example, Lowenthal, 1964). The competent worker must not only possess skills that can facilitate communication and resolution of conflicts within a family but also must be able to generate extrafamilial resources for the family when it is in crisis—including helping the family to select congregate noninstitutional housing replete with home-delivered services when such a solution is possible.

Institutional care may still be necessary even after efforts are made to stabilize the support system. Throughout this process, the older person must participate as fully as possible. Older people must not be "brain-washed" to feel that it is their decision when it really is not. Many in the sample we have studied may have been misled in this way. Lieberman and Lakin (1963) found that residents who entered one of the three homes tended to shift, when telling stories to the Institutional TAT cards the researchers had developed, from portraying the move as voluntary when on the waiting list to portraying the move as coerced by family after entering the home. The elderly resident-to-be may have had no other choice but to agree with family that the decision was voluntary, for fear of further conflict with the family at a time when no other alternative was perceived as available. If so, the subterfuge did not work, as it rarely does, although it makes family members feel more comfortable. Painful as it may be, the decision-making process must include as active participants the aged parent who is feeling abandoned (possibly without just cause) and family members who do not wish to abandon their aged parent but feel they are doing so. The most family members can do is what is best for their parent, which usually leaves them with a sense of impotence and guilt. When institutional care is necessary—after all efforts have been made to prevent unnecessary, premature institutionalization—three types of interventions must then be considered: selection of the candidate for institutional care and determining the most appropriate institutional setting; crisis management during the preadmission period; and preparation for entering and living in the institution.

Selection

Selection has at least two aspects. The first aspect relates to the appropriateness of institutional care for a particular older person. The second aspect relates to the appropriateness of a particular institution for an older person. Given that many efforts may have been made to prevent premature institutionalization and given that the judgment has been made that institutional care is necessary, is there any choice but to provide institutional care? Often we are confronted with an elderly person and his family who are seeking institutional care because they perceive such care as the best or only solution. Yet the older person may be extremely physically and mentally deteriorated, as well as passive. The combined deterioration and passivity, however, are the very characteristics that sensitize the older person to the severe adverse effects of environmental discontinuity. The paradox is that frail, confused, and passive elderly people who are judged to need institutional care the most are also those most likely to have their deterioration and death hastened by the move. Yet if these elderly people remained in the community it may also be the case that their deterioration would be hastened because of the lack of physical care and a viable intimate support system. In current practice, there is usually no solution other than providing institutional care, appraising the family of the risks involved, and making every effort to minimize the risk.

Risk can be minimized by selecting an institutional environment that harmonizes with the personal characteristics of the individual. Matching individuals to environments does not only involve the quality of institutional environments, but also involves the fact that institutions of the same quality may differ greatly in the adaptive demands made on the newcomer. Some institutions, for example, foster a more gentle, others a more aggressive style of intervention among residents. These differences are usually a product of the characteristics of the resident population and of administrative philosophy and style. The homes studied here, for example, foster and reward aggressiveness. In a similar institutional environment, the Philadelphia Geriatric Center, it was found that aggressiveness was related to successful use of therapeutic programs (Kleban, Brody, and Lawton, 1971). Corroborative evidence for the effectiveness of placing individuals in environments that harmonize with their personal style is afforded by a study of the relocation of physically intact elderly residents of a state mental hospital to nursing homes and boarding houses (Lieberman, Tobin, and Slover, 1969). When a division was made, for example, between high and low responders, based on diverse assessments of personality, decline for high responders was associated primarily with the interpersonal warmth of the relocation environment, whereas decline for the low responders was associated primarily with the amount of interaction before discharge. Responders thus benefited most from a warm environment, whereas benefit for the nonresponders was more independent of the relocation environment and more a result of having less interaction before relocating. These findings suggest that the primary explanation for the effect of this relocation among low responders was how much the individual would lose in the move. Additional evidence for the importance of matching, or congruence between resident need and environmental demand, has been generated by Kahana (1974). Further studies should be undertaken to clarify the variables that are most critical to match and to clarify to what extent matching can reduce the excess morbidity and mortality among the most physically debilitated. What evidence we do have leads us to conclude that, by reducing environmental discontinuity, matching makes a marked difference for the less deteriorated but less difference for the most debilitated for whom any relocation may exhaust meager resources (a study conducted by Marlowe and Lieberman, reported in Lieberman and Tobin, in press).

Managing the Crisis

Before admission and after the decision, the older resident-to-be, as well as the family, is in a state of crisis. Family members feel guilty and the older person feels rejected, abandoned, and often enraged. The case of Mrs. B. illustrates this pattern. Her rage at being abandoned was only thinly veiled. She repeatedly stated that she was going to the home so as not to be a burden to her family. Yet it was only too clear, because she saw herself as so "loving toward," and "sacrificing for" others, that if her own mother had been dependent on her she felt she would have certainly and readily take on whatever burden was necessary to assure the mother a comfortable life.

Containing the breakthrough of Mrs. B.'s underlying rage, as for many others, are the dual fears of destroying the precarious balance within the family and of antagonizing the staff who might have responded to her anger by rejecting her as a resident of the home. The resident-to-be cannot afford to be rejected, because the home has been determined to be the best, if not the only, solution available. To handle the rage and to maintain self-esteem, the resident-to-be usually emphasizes that the decision to apply to the institution was wholly his own. The decision is often phrased, as it was by Mrs. B., as being "for the good of the children . . . I don't want to be a burden on them." Possibly this is the best way to cope with the underlying feelings. The rage at being abandoned cannot simply be dismissed and it is far better that older people do not withdraw, turn the anger inward, and blame themselves. Blaming others, even if they do not deserve the blame, or rationalizing that the decision is wholly one's own may be fine mechanisms for containing debilitating rage and for mobilizing psychological resources that will be helpful in dealing with the demands of the new environment. For many older people, however, these types of mechanisms are dystonic or incongruent with their typical coping styles. For them, other mechanisms must be encouraged so that they do not slip into self-disparagement and passivity.

Family members have to be helped to accept the resentments and anger but without being overwhelmed by guilt. Too often, an effort is made to reduce the guilt of the younger person at the expense of the older person. Younger family members must be able to tolerate abuse or, when necessary, to withdraw gracefully when the interaction with a parent is dysfunctional for both. Communicating our understanding that children will be mythicized after the older parent has accomplished an adaptation to institutional life may be helpful. That is, the relationship between the parent and children—independent of its earlier history—will have been modified by the decision-making process and will continue to be modified after an adaptation to the Home. The children will become important in different ways. Reports of successful children—real or imaginary—become the mainstay of resident interaction, provide status among elderly peers. Also, children who carry on traditions and values help the elderly achieve a personal resolution with death, a feeling that one's life has been a meaningful one.

Preparation

Preparation is usually thought of in terms of information about and exposure to the future situation. Although this type of preparation may reduce psychological symptoms such as anxiety during the anticipatory period, the evidence is unfortunately great that it will not reduce the rate or degree of severe sequelae (Lieberman, 1974). More crucial in minimizing these sequelae are efforts to reduce or contain passivity and to support or stimulate aggressive mobilization of psychological resources. But first a few comments on traditional preparation.

Apparently a sound appraisal of one's situation, including knowledge about the institution, is beneficial for the resident-to-be, whereas avoiding dealing with the impending event, which may take the form of avoiding thinking about the event, is not. Exposure to the future environment, visiting the institution, or even living there on a trial basis, does not of itself assure a willingness to cope with the environment or a realistic appraisal of it. The resident-to-be must be helped to do both, so that the losses of freedom and privacy become perceived as balanced by the gains of security, activities, and people. Even then, appropriate appraisal of and preparation for the new environment is in no way synonymous with the actual experience of entering and living in the new environment. Exposure may indeed limit the impact and facilitate adjustment but it cannot be expected to do away with the effect of the actual relocation. Only when the resident-to-be is actually a resident in the home will he or she meet the full impact of a foreign world with all its attendant consequences and meanings. All procedures, however, that will minimize discontinuity are helpful, such as having the person visit the institution and assigning a caseworker to be actively engaged with him or her from before until after admission.

Yet if excess morbidity and mortality is to be diminished, the critical type of preparation relates to increasing aggression. Obviously, for some older people aggressiveness is so alien to their make-up that there is little possibility of increasing their assertiveness. Still, this is what must be done if the institutional environment is to be used to reestablish a viable equilibrium. This therapeutic task is not in substance different from that advocated by others. Goldfarb (1974), for example, argues that the basis of therapy for older people is to heighten their sense of mastery, a characteristic opposed to passivity. When an older person is confronted with the feelings of abandonment and outrage that often accompany entering and living in an institution, heightening mastery may be a difficult task. Nevertheless, the mobilizing of psychological resources must be a primary goal preceding the actual relocation.

Institutional Life

By its very nature, institutional living is physically and socially discontinuous from autonomous community living. The best of long-term care institutions is still a foreign spatial environment inhabited by other old, sick, and needy people. While the caretakers may be able and loving, they are not one's own family. If the new resident is to receive the maximum benefits from this relocation, he or, more likely, she must become a part of the institutional fabric. In so doing, he or she experiences unavoidable negative effects such as a focal concern on mutilation and death that reflect an underlying experience of personal vulnerability and a deepening of hopelessness. Can we intervene to stop the development of such effects? Probably not. Even for the resident who is most successful in making the transition from preadmission to postadmission, as was the case for Mrs. A., there is an apparent unavoidable shift toward a focal concern of mutilation and death. Yet at the same time a sense of self was maintained, and the sought-after gains of care, people, and activities were achieved. Indeed, by the end of the first month or so, Mrs. A. was her old self in many ways. To be sure, individualized efforts were made to help her weather the impact of the relocation. Because a reaction was expected, she received help that reduced its intensity and foreshortened its expression. If appropriate help had not been available, the initial reaction might have crystallized into a permanent negative trend.

The new resident must thus be helped through the transitional acute period with minimal negative effects. All people and objects from the former world that are incorporated into the new institutional world become anchors for the new resident. Family and workers, as well as personal belongings that have special meanings, offer continuity. People and things that give continuity can offset some of initial sense of abrupt change, but the balance is tipped toward what the newcomer experiences as unpleasant because of having to learn new rules and to puzzle out the attitudes of a new environment when cognitive and perceptual functions may be weakened by age and anxiety. For some, the anxiety can be reduced by the assurance that strange or different behaviors during this period are expected as well as tolerated, and that there will be neither punishment nor expulsion from the home for these behaviors.

Once the initial impact of entering and living in the institution has been weathered, the new resident can go beyond merely accommodating to the foreign world. A rewarding and life-enhancing adaptation can be achieved within the constraints of congregate living if the environment is sufficiently flexible and individuated. If a range of life-styles is actively encouraged, the heterogeneous population of residents play out the diversity of their idiosyncratic selves. Efficient operation obviously conflicts with maximum development of a flexible and individualizing environment. But if human losses are to be minimized, the struggle must be to help each individual express those aspects of self that yielded satisfaction in independent living. Self-continuity can be achieved and benefits can be accrued—as was generally the case for respondents in our study sample 1 year after admission to long-term care facilities.

Can psychological costs be reduced to an inconsequential amount? Should we interpret our findings about intact survivors to mean that an inconsequential cost was paid? Did they not maintain a continuity in self-image? Did they not, additionally, show an initial improvement in feelings of well-being and a lessening of body preoccupation? Finally, did they not maintain their functional capacity? Still, the case for unmitigated maintenance of self is not that simple to argue. Just as there are unavoidable negative consequences associated with entering and living in the institutional environment, there appear to be unavoidable negative consequences to continual living and adapting to the environment.

In a sense, the shift to institutional living involves a series of tradeoffs. For example, feelings of well-being are increased, but so are those of hopelessness. This seeming paradox in emotional states is readily understandable. In accepting the institution, and in gaining care, people, and activity, the new resident develops feelings of protection and security, and perhaps even pleasure over personally rewarding events in the new life-style. Yet there can be no escape from the identification as a resident of an old peoples' home, a congregate living arrangement that will be a home till death, a home that would not have been the first choice as the place to end one's life. While the original decision to seek institutional care may now appear most sensible, the home departs markedly from what most consider to be really a home. The institution is too much a world of sickness and death, of schedules and staff, to be that comfortable, warm, and relatively free and unstructured place properly called "home."

For the elderly resident, the task of accepting the institution as one's home—when, only slightly below the surface, is the awareness that it is not really the wished-for home—is not unlike the task of accepting unwanted realities that confronts their age peers living in the community. Acceptance of physical deterioration, social losses, and impending death is a feat that apparently many, if not most, very old people are able to accomplish through a variety of mechanisms. Contrasting one's current life to that of others of a similar age, for example, helps to reassure the very old person that he is indeed more fortunate than most, especially if those in his reference groups are now dead or more incapacitated than himself. Using magical mastery to control the inner and outer world (Gutmann, 1964), using subception (the unconscious screening out of unpleasant stimuli) to prevent troublesome stimuli from registering (see Weinberg, 1956), or denying stimuli are mechanisms that are equally helpful for the very old both inside and outside of institutions. An appreciation of the availability and utility of these mechanisms is most helpful in avoiding "overdosing" or creating "excessive disability" (Kahn, 1971) among the very old.

On the problems and challenges of working with institutionalized elderly, Perlman, Hammerman, and Tobin (1969, pp. 6-7) have warned:

> *Clients are usually poorly motivated. Generally, in their earlier years they had not asked for social*

work help because they did not need it. If they now identify a problem, they see its causative factors as being outside themselves and, as a result, behave as though they no longer have any control over how life treats them. They are really quite fatalistic. How one determines where the client really is, not where he says he is; how one determines what is a valid pace for the aging; and where to find health amid so much pathology, are everyday exercises for the student. His judgment is tested constantly, too, as he determines how much he should do for his clients, how much he should do together with them, and what they must be urged to do for themselves. He is torn on the one hand by the frailty and lack of energy he sees in his clients, and, on the other hand, by an awareness that he must help them to help themselves whenever possible; and that, unless he can somehow involve them in the helping process, self-dependence cannot be fostered and regression assuredly will take place. At the same time, if he places too heavy a demand on them, their waning self-esteem may be further damaged. He must be ready to settle for minimum realistic goals, such as preventing regression. Above all, he must keep his clients involved in some form of problem-solving and not allow them to settle for the status-quo. All of these experiences are particularly difficult when working with the aged; yet, with some modifications, they represent the common tasks of the casework practitioner.

Active engagement of staff is most necessary for the well-being of the frail elderly. Indeed, engagement with others is one of the opportunities afforded by congregate living. Nevertheless, the study findings on the dynamics of the respondents' interpersonal relations again raise a paradox. Interacting with other residents in the home may reduce alienation and withdrawal but may also increase interpersonal conflict. That indeed it does is reflected in respondents' portrayals of themselves as more hostile in interaction with others. If engagement is encouraged, as it should be, then it is to be expected that conflicts will occur among a heterogeneous population of individuals whose idiosyncracies have had a lifetime to develop, and who are now thrown together with strangers on whom they are dependent for care and security. Still, there is no alternative to the encouragement of interaction, abrasive as it may be at times, because any other course is to encourage the onset of the debilitating effects that unquestionably accompany isolation and withdrawal. Other courses are everpresent temptations in even the best of institutions, where the propensity of staff is unwittingly to discourage engagement in order to maintain efficiency of organizational procedures. The wished-for orderliness in scheduling and serving meals is only one of many poignant examples where interaction among residents may be hindered to preserve efficiency.

The major paradox from a psychological perspective relates to the difference between manifest and latent levels. At the manifest level, there is stability in most psychological functions and improvements in others after entering the institution, especially for the intact survivors. At the latent level, however, becoming a resident among people who are seriously ill and often close to death deepens hopelessness. The context means being personally vulnerable because the institution fosters a focal concern with mutilation and death. Thus even in the best homes, which do the most to facilitate the transition, even the least vulnerable residents pay a big price. We need not speculate on the effects of homes of lesser quality. Anecdotal and empirical evidence substantiate their deleterious effects.

New designs must be drawn for the programs of existing facilities and new facilities may be needed to accommodate the addition of services where gaps have been identified. Of even greater importance, however, are the needs for redesigning the system itself. Any geriatric care system by necessity will include institutions. Thus, attention will have to be given to the unavoidable effects of transitions and the necessity for, as well as the limits of, assistance throughout the process of becoming institutionalized. The meaning of each phase in the process, and the consequent critical intervention needed during each phase, as shown in Table 14, must form the basis for revised procedures. It is toward the future that we now turn.

A Forward Look

The home for the aged as we have known it and the institutions of this study no longer exist. Today's homes for aged are more nearly chronic disease hospitals for physically and mentally impaired elderly than care centers and homes for ambulatory aged who are not totally self-sufficient. This transformation has resulted in large part from the availability of options. Many elderly who in the past would have needed to enter homes for the aged are now being helped to remain in their own home or in quasiinstitutional settings. The residual population, therefore, who make up the population of old peoples' homes is older and sicker than before. Because the residential population has shifted toward the more infirm and more mentally incompetent, the balance in care has increasingly tipped toward medical service and away from social and psychological services. This trend is fraught with dire consequences unless new ways can be developed of attending to the social needs of the very debilitated. The loss of physical or psychological self-sufficiency does not automatically mean the loss of social needs, the satisfaction of what can be distinctly therapeutic. The consequences will indeed be dire if we retreat to "warehousing" these most needy elderly and do not make every effort to provide life-sustaining social as well as physical supports. The "therapeutic community"—which was the essence of the home for the aged when the population was more ambulatory—may not be the most critical approach for the new debilitated population who are more bedbound, but the principle remains the same: individualizing care to assure maximal restoration of residual potential.

Although increasing numbers of the very old are being helped to remain longer in the community, a comprehensive system of long-term geriatric care still does not exist in any community, although rudimentary forms are now in evidence.

Table 14. Phases: Meanings, Interventions and Consequences of Not Intervening

Phase	Period	Psychological Meaning of the Phase to the Elderly Person	Critical Intervention by Practitioners	Primary Consequence of Not Intervening
Predecision	Before application for institutional care	Being threatened with loss of independence	Stabilizing supports	Premature institutionalization
Anticipating institutionalization	After application, while awaiting admission	Being abandoned	Selecting the appropriate setting, managing the crisis; and preparing the resident-to-be	Severe psychological effects
Initial adjustment	First few months after admission	Being vulnerable to physical and psychological deterioration	Reducing discontinuity	Hastened deterioration and death
Adaptation	The first several months after the initial adjustment	Being vulnerable to further threats to survival.	Humanizing the institution	Additional excessive dysfunction and deterioration

People persist in viewing long-term care as synonomous with institutionalization, often provided by proprietary nursing homes that offer little beyond custodial care. Homes for the aged remain embedded in a social and health system that can best be characterized as a *nonsystem.* The Webster Unabridged Dictionary defines *system* as a "complex unity formed of many often diverse parts subject to a common plan or serving a common purpose." There may be agreement on a common purpose among the providers of social and health care to the elderly, such as promoting optimum functioning, but in no sense is there unity on the means to achieve such a purpose. The lack of unity is quite evident when long-term care institutions for the elderly are examined as part of the health care network. The work of the contemporary long-term care institution is seldom coordinated either with community-based programs or with the work of general hospitals for acute illness.

Offering older people and their families meaningful alternatives to total institutionalization requires a comprehensive health care system. At least four general objectives would have to be fulfilled if we are to establish a coordinated system:

1. Access to quality social care as a right, with safeguards for the financial stability of families, incorporating guarantees of the satisfaction of the social needs of each client through involvement, to the greatest degree possible, of the client in making decisions that affect him and in planning the regimen of care—a blending of need and demand, or of professional judgment and client preference.

2. Access to a range of services for all socioeconomic levels so that service can be selected or modified according to the condition and needs of the client rather than demanding that he wholly accommodate himself to what service is available.

3. Coordination of services through centralized responsibility for planning, mobilizing, delivering, and monitoring resources with, and in behalf of, clients including the

development of normative goals for who is to be served, what resources are to be used, and to what end such resources are used.

4. The establishment of a continuum of social and health services with effective linkages among preventive, acute rehabilitative, and maintenance services, and the establishment of principles for the use of manpower on behalf of the whole spectrum, rather than on behalf of segmented aspects of human needs.

Meeting these objectives (see Hammerman, 1974, for a more detailed list of objectives) would obviously necessitate a sweeping modification of the health and care system.

A viable geriatric care system that fulfilled these objectives would care for a much larger number of older people than is typical today, especially of those 75 years of age and over. The future elderly will be better educated and have greater expectations of themselves and of service providers. They will make increasing demands on the social and health system. It is those above 75, however, who will most need a system that assures maintenance of functioning. For the coming group of "old old," whose children are themselves likely to be "young old"—in their 60s and 70s—a social and health system must be developed in which direct services are synchronized with emotional and practical supports that can be offered by the aging family. The long-term institution or facility would be an important component in a viable geriatric social and health system. Equally basic to the system would be a community social and health organization, under one auspice, that attempts to integrate a range of services. The saliency of this approach is reflected in legislation that was first proposed by Kennedy and Mills in 1974 and then again by Kennedy and Corman in 1975. This legislation included a modification of Medicare that would cover the costs of providing those social and health services that would help older persons avoid institutionalization for as long as possible, and that would also cover institutional care when such care becomes necessary. The proposed legislation incorporated the Morris (1971) proposal for local personal care organi-

zations to be developed and funded through nonprofit corpora-
tions that would purchase care for all beneficiaries within a sub-
state area. The intent of the Morris proposal was to create for
each beneficiary a package of social and health services that
would be tailored to meet his particular needs.

In its most complete form, the tailoring of individual personal care packages would necessitate a professionally trained
case manager who could facilitate the integration of services,
balancing client preference and objective assessment of need.
The range of diagnostic specialists and therapeutic modalities
would be available to the case manager. An efficient centralized
intake setting for these activities of the manager would be the
multipurpose senior center, to which varied consulting specialists would come for diagnosing and providing therapy to individuals. When diagnostic or therapeutic referrals were made to
outside sources, continuity of care would have to be assured, so
that the client would not simply be shuffling back and forth.
Beyond using the case manager as the integrator of service,
social and health service providers would have to form agree-
ments incorporating client preferences, if the older person is not
to be excluded from the human service systems. These are only
some of the ingredients for a sensible community social and
health provision system. (See Tobin, Davidson, and Sack, 1975,
for a fuller discussion of this and other models for effective
social services to older Americans).

Adopting the Morris proposal would be a necessary first
step in developing an effective geriatric long-term system where
community services are fully articulated with acute care hospital settings that provide specialized care to the general public
and with long-term care institutional settings. How extant types
of institutions can be made congruent with these objectives,
through modifications that are in no way visionary, will become
clear in the following examples.

The Community-Oriented Institution.   The contemporary
long-term care institution can be transformed into a community-oriented one that undertakes the traditional function of
maintenance and stability of a severely disabled, chronically
sick population as only one of many objectives. The institution

could also function as a diagnostic center responsible for evaluation and creation of a client care plan, subject to periodic review and change—as a short-term crisis care resource where immediate needs can be provided or while attention is given to restructuring the client's environment to provide whatever supports will allow him to remain in the community. Why, for example, cannot the institution function as a resource to families even under such benign conditions as when the family wish to take a vacation by themselves and need a place for the elderly family member to stay? Must institutions restrict themselves to help-giving only when individuals or families are desperate? Residential facilities surely can function as day and night hospitals, as well as for intensive rehabilitative or convalescent services during and following acute episodes.

The institution, therefore, would have a role to play in many aspects of social and health care for the elderly. In this expanded view of its functions, the institution would move from "single service operations to campus style service centers . . . toward becoming true geriatric multi-service centers" (Shore, 1973, p. 34). This approach is not a new one; indeed, there are many such multiservice centers and geriatric campuses in existence. Moreover, if proprietary nursing homes evolve in the same way as proprietary hospitals have in the past, we shall very likely witness their becoming nonprofit, community-based institutions from which a range of community-oriented services emanate (Gaynes, 1973).

The Small Institution. The small local institution is not yet a broadly represented reality. Although small institutions are potentially less dehumanizing for their residents than large institutions, they are not perceived as economically feasible. Professionals have not yet been able to mobilize sentiment for constructing more humane institutional facilities if such facilities are likely to be costly. If, however, local care *systems* are developed, the administrators of these systems might play an important role in developing more desirable institutional environments for those elderly people who need them. If a continuum of care is created that includes both community and institutional components, older people who reside in institutions might be regarded as the continued responsibility of the comprehensive local system. If the local system has delivered services to an older person with the intent of maintaining him in the community, it is reasonable to assume that it could be encouraged to enlarge its responsibility to include assurance of optimal institutional care if and when need for such care arises.

What types of institutions for older people are likely to prevail as time goes on? Will there be no choice but to send the infirm older person to a "warehouse"? Many argue (see, for example, Anderson, 1974) that our society will not allocate sufficient funds for therapeutic institutional care for the very old, saying, among other things, that it is very costly to provide sufficient personnel for more than minimal attention to the unpleasant task of caring for the chronically ill aged. Yet, it may become feasible to limit costs, if small institutions can create or adopt techniques that lower costs, such as the greater use of volunteers in implementing modern concepts of human service delivery. If, moreover, the local care system is effectively linked to general hospitals and to the specialized services offered by other medical centers, it would be less costly to design small prosthetic environments for the impaired older person. Such prosthetic environments could make use of sophisticated electronic devices that, for example, prepare and serve prepackaged foods, efficiently clean floors and other spaces, and telemetrically monitor vital physiological functions. These devices could decrease the burdens related to the tasks of everyday living and thus afford greater physical and emotional independence. One device now being adapted for hospital use permits an immobilized patient to dial a telephone, turn pages of a book or magazine, or change television channels by simply moving his or her eyes across a monitoring screen. The attitudes of the emerging elderly will make these innovations more feasible. In the future, aged people, who will have experienced the increased benefits of science and technology, are likely to be comfortable with sophisticated medical technology and advanced electronic gadgetry. (See Tobin, 1975, for a further discussion regarding the feasibility of using these technologies in developing institutions for the elderly of the future.)

This type of institution—housing as few as 60 frail and impaired elderly—appears unrealistic in terms of our present orientation to the allocation of economic and other resources. Current thinking is that about 180 beds is the efficient size for a long-term care institution, given the costs of operating a combination hotel, hospital, and social community. An optimal size, from the perspective of the resident, however, is much smaller than 180. Small institutions could be efficient if professional expertise of a wide variety of types were used to develop and coordinate the delivery of diverse, high-quality services. The "decentralized" long-term care facility would also become more realistic if legislation were passed that assured both services to prevent premature institutionalization and quality care when institutional care becomes necessary. Indeed, if the small institution were embedded in a community system that prevented premature institutionalization, the case for high-cost small institutions could be more cogently argued.

Current social and health services are generally more economical to deliver through the community than through long-term care institutions. But this might not be so if community services were to become more widely available and if programs were coordinated. The strains on the system would then be very different from those that arise from organization of the "hit-or-miss" programs that now operate. Coordination would very likely increase the visibility of services and therefore the demand for them, so that costs of delivery would rise. The homebound and the bedridden, who now all too often suffer in silence, would doubtless receive increased service. Reorganizing to offer extensive services to all who could benefit from them would be costly indeed; but such services might cost less in the long run, because they would prevent or delay the potentially great economic and social costs that accrue from allowing the individual to deteriorate seriously. At present, the absence of broad-scale preventive programs means that more older persons than necessary are being placed in total institutions. If social and health systems for the elderly were more efficient, institutionalization could be warded off for many more people and could be offered more selectively. Examples of selective use of institutions include posthospital residence while realistic efforts are made, from the outset, to return the person to the community or to a quasiinstitutional environment, as well as brief stays during crises, or when family members who usually care for the older person are temporarily unable to do so.

In sum, the local institution could become a flexible resource for the community provision system. If it were effectively linked to other components of the general health system, it could be less costly than other forms of care in the long run.

The Geriatric Restoration Center. This approach, like the previous one, begins with the assumption that many of the "old old" need care within a total institution. The geriatric restoration center, however, does not provide care for long periods of time. It is basically a short-term convalescent and crisis center for those elderly who have been discharged from the hospital or who are currently living under duress in the community, but who can be restored to perform daily functions without constant help. The thrust is, therefore, toward helping the person to master the prerequisites for daily living in noninstitutional settings. Admission is selective and is based on the ability of the center to restore the person to independent community living. The assumption is that other community-based institutions can offer custodial and supportive care to those who seek admission but who cannot be so restored.

This approach has been studied by Cosin (1947) in England, where the geriatric center, as part of a medical center, is selectively used by the general hospital and by community social and health service agencies. That center's ability to discharge patients back to the community is facilitated because English physicians frequently make home visits and because efficient programs for the delivery of services to people's homes are generally available.

One of the few efforts in this country to develop a center somewhat comparable to the one developed by Cosin is the Johnston R. Bowman (JRB) Health Park of Rush-Presbyterian-St. Luke's Medical Center (as conceived by Jerome Hammerman). The JRB Health Park, comprising 180 hospital beds and 43 independent apartments, is to be part of a tripartite care complex (a postreferral hospital, research institute, and teaching center). The population base for the network is projected to be 2,000,000 people, of whom approximately 200,000 would be over 65 years old. This base would be served by out-patient clinics, a series of ten or so general hospitals, and the center. The center, as the service component of the JRB Health Park, would facilitate the Health Park's goals in the areas of training and research, and, hopefully, vice versa.

This facility should, in turn, be able to influence the general hospital from where patients are referred. Functioning properly, the geriatric center could become the initiator and coordinator of services throughout the system. Because of its strategic location as the end service in the health delivery system, the geriatric center could emerge as a sophisticated mechanism for providing linkage between the facilities available to the client on his return to his community and those catering to his acute medical needs. Planning for readaptation to the demands of daily living in the community would begin at the time of admission to the hospital; by working with the client, family, hospital staff, and so forth, it would be possible to develop a restoration program that accelerated the client's return to independent living. Over time, a smooth flow of clients from the hospital to the restorative geriatric center would be developed through staff interaction. Various services available in the hospital would also be made more useful by the availability of geriatric consultation from the center. Along with affording a geriatric perspective on the more traditional medical problems, such as those related to drug dosage and drug interactions among geriatric patients, geriatric specialists could advise on the psychosocial components that are dictated by the special characteristics of the elderly as patients. Clients could also return directly to the center for in- or out-patient services, if those types of care were not offered by the community-based institution discussed under the first approach.

The geriatric center could also play a critical role in the area of training. The staff of the center would form the nucleus for geriatric teaching, and an active geriatric service would provide a training ground for a diverse array of students and practitioners who wish special sensitization to the needs of elderly clients. Such a program might alter the currently prevailing attitude toward older patients, an attitude similar to that toward chronically ill patients, where the permanence of the condition is assumed. If so, all personnel would generally become more sophisticated regarding care for the aging. At the professional level, there might be an increase in the number of geriatricians, geriatric psychiatrists, and so forth.

The range of opportunities for knowledge-building would be enormous. The presence of a geriatric center that coordinated its activity with the entire geriatric care system would offer a fertile terrain for social health experiments in the financing and delivery of care to the elderly. More concrete projects would also become possible, such as restorative-oriented treatment of specific disease entities.

The Terminal Care Facility.   Another institutional form that must be considered is the terminal care center, the hospice modeled after Saunders' (1972) center in England, in which terminal patients are helped through the dying process by the careful management of pain and the maintenance of maximal social supports. Because Saunders' hospice is embedded in a hospital complex, it becomes a legitimate and specialized service, much like a surgical or internal medicine service. One most relevant practice of the hospice is to encourage visits by the family and render help both to the dying person and the family at the "bedside." In the English example, the staff of the hospice also go into the community to help the dying patient and his family.

Hospices are beginning to be developed in this country, sometimes in hospitals where a fixed number of beds is designated for terminal care. The development of these centers is possibly a reaction to the increasing preoccupation in our society with euthanasia, as well as to the growing awareness that current hospital practices do not ease the crisis of death for the patient or his family. At present, over 60 percent of all annual deaths occur in hospitals and other institutional settings, a steadily increasing trend that can be traced back to 1937 (National Center for Health Statistics, 1965). Furthermore, deaths are now increasingly concentrated in old age rather than being spread more evenly across the life span. Three of four deaths in 1967 (77 percent) occurred in the 55 and over age group (*Vital Statistics of the United States, 1967,* 1969). As more people live longer, more people are likely to die in settings that are presently not engineered to ease the dying process for them and their families.

The development of terminal care centers may be hastened by the evidence that is being amassed that the process of dying can indeed be eased for the person as well as for close family members. Students of thanatology believe that sensitive and trained personnel can be helpful to both the dying patient and the family. The work of Kubler-Ross (1969) and others emphasizes the importance to the dying person of completing a series of psychological stages in preparation for death. These stages, if worked through, eventuate in a final resolution in which death becomes more acceptable. However we may conceptualize the "best death," or even the "successful death," the aged of the future will, in all likelihood, manifest a different set of attitudes and expectations regarding society's responsibilities for easing the dying process. They may well demand more fulfillment of their needs at the end of life. There is likely to emerge also the demand for a wider range of options for the family in maintaining some degree of control over the management of death. These issues are already under discussion in various voluntary organizations that are now developing hospices.

The trend toward establishing hospices is also related to the current misuse of institutional settings. Some mental hospitals, for example, have been admitting increasing numbers of terminal patients who are simply identified as mentally ill (Markson and Hand, 1970). If the patients so misclassified were treated as "dying," it might be possible to improve their terminal experience. In other institutional settings, patients are labeled *terminal*, and then ignored. Efforts to reach these patients have at times proved successful. Kastenbaum (1972), for example, used a "reach out" procedure for mental hospital patients who were treated by staff as if they were already dead. He identified half such patients as capable of sentient experiences and responses. Efforts such as these have illuminated the possibilities for more humane practices in the care of the dying patient.

The creation of specialized terminal care institutions within the hospital system would make it possible not only to provide better care for patients in the terminal center itself, but also throughout the hospital system. Professionals and paraprofessionals from the center could be mobilized to provide terminal care and counseling in the same way that other therapies are now ordered for patients in hospitals. With these personnel being used throughout the hospital, practices in caring for the medical and psychological needs of the elderly patient would be improved. At present, efforts to change practices for the terminal patient in hospitals—usually limited to offering seminars to change the attitudes of service personnel—have not been very successful. The presence of a terminal care *service* may, however, yield a much better outcome.

The hospice could make an even further contribution to the efforts of other community agencies if its personnel could also go into people's homes to ease the dying process. The hospice, however, may have a limited value for the very old, for whom the process of dying is more drawn out than it is for younger terminal patients. Indeed, the admission policy at St. Christopher's is to provide care for patients with 3 months or less to live, a specification that is appropriate for the younger cancer patient where the brief and final course of the terminal illness can be specified. For the older patient, a longer period of terminal dependency may be expected—extreme physical and mental incapacities may linger for months or even years. For these elderly, special institutional environments may have to be developed that maximize residual functioning and also facilitate the older person and his family in coping not only with death, but also with the indefinite boundaries of the illness. Thus, the terminal care center again draws attention to the need for a coordinated *system* of social and health services for older people.

A Final Word. The forms of social and health services that have been discussed may become more visible in future years than they are at present. Currently there is a broad array of services for the elderly, but they lack articulation with each other. Fortunately, however, these issues are now being seriously confronted both by service providers and legislators. A better understanding is growing of the problems inherent in developing services that can be delivered either simultaneously or sequentially—currently referred to as the issues of "continuity of care," "service integration," "unnecessary duplication of services," and "appropriate level of institutional care." As people age, their needs shift; so must the package of services shift from general, life-enhancing services to services that maintain the individual as a viable member of the community, and, finally, to services that meet survival needs, including but not limited to institutional care. Only through efficient linkages will there be a fit between changing needs and available services. Linkages, however, will only be useful for individuals if we apply the knowledge that we have gained regarding diverse psychological processes including the psychological process of becoming institutionalized when old. To the extent that practice flows from this knowledge, the future social and health system will be an effective vehicle for assuring the most frail among the elderly of an optimum quality of life.

Appendix:
Measurement

Standardized measures will be reviewed only briefly to clarify their modification and use in this study. The measures to be elaborated on are those developed specifically for the present study such as the hope measure, the SCT anxiety and depression measures, the Self-Sort Task and measures, and focal concern using as data the earliest memory. Following clarification of measures is a brief discussion of statistical analyses of data.

Area 1: Cognitive Functioning

Because cognitive adequacy (or its converse, cognitive impairment) was conceptualized as a complex attribute and not as singular and static, six different measures were used: (1) the Mental Status Questionnaire (MSQ) to assess orientation in time and place; (2) the estimate of 60 seconds to assess orientation to the immediate present; (3) the paired-associates word learning task to assess learning and retention; (4) the copying of three designs of the Bender Gestalt Test to assess cognitive organization; (5) the organization of Thematic Apperception Test (TAT) stories to assess perceptual organization and accuracy; and (6) the Reitman Stick Figure Test to assess the capacity to vary responses (originality versus rigidity).

The Mental Status Questionnaire (MSQ).   Kahn, Pollack, and Goldfarb (1961) developed the MSQ as an index of the presence and degree of organic brain syndrome by using samples of aged persons who were evaluated by more extensive evaluations. This questionnaire consists of ten simple questions that reflect the respondent's orientation to time and place, such as "What is the name of this place (street)?" and "Who is the President of the United States?" It is scored for the number of wrong answers; a score of four or more is presumed to be evidence of organic impairment.

Clock Time.   The estimation of the passage of 1 minute (60 seconds) was originally included in the present study as a measure of futurity because Fink (1957), among others, related underestimation to lack of futurity. The present sample, however, showed extreme underestimation (mean = 22.1 seconds), which suggests that such error may be a function of cortical deficit related to alterations in speed and timing of the central nervous system. The correlation of −.40 with errors on the MSQ suggests a common dimensionality.

Word Learning.   The Inglis Paired Word Associate Learning Test was adapted for the present study. Inglis (1959) and Caird, Sanderson, and Inglis (1962) reported discrimination between groups of elderly psychiatric patients with and without memory disorder. Three pairs of words were used for a maximum of ten trials each. Thus the maximum error score was thirty, as compared to Inglis who continued presenting the stimulus word for thirty trials giving him a maximum score of ninety. The reduction in the number of trials was based on our pretest, where it was found that when correct recall did not occur in ten trials for each word, or thirty trials overall, frustration mounted and learning to criterion was not achieved. Two sets of word pairs were used so that forms could be alternated at follow-up interviews to reduce the practice effect. The first set was *cabbage-pen, knife-chimney,* and *sponge-trumpet.* The second set was *flower-spark, table-river,* and *bottle-comb.*

The Bender Gestalt Design Copying Test (BGT).   The

Bender Gestalt Test was devised by Bender (1938) to evaluate visual-motor dysfunction. Nine designs of varied shapes and complexity are copied on a single 8½ × 11 (inches) sheet of paper. The Pascal scoring system (Pascal and Suttell, 1951) is an empirically derived system based on qualities of design copying that discriminated between known brain damaged and normals. Each design is scored for salient types of errors, such as extra dots or circles where the design has a total of twelve dots. High scores are associated with psychiatric disability, organic brain damage, less adequate reactions to physical stress, and inability to cope with cognitive complexities of the physical environment (Bender, 1938; Billingslea, 1948; Hutt, 1945; Pascal and Suttell, 1951). Decreased level of inner organization as measured by adequacy of the Bender Gestalt reproductions is also associated with imminent death (Lieberman, 1965).

The BGT was administered to a comparable population in a previous study (Lieberman, 1965) and scored by the Pascal system. The total score was the sum of scores for the nine designs. A regression analysis of the nine individual design scores on 278 records revealed that designs 1, 3, and 8 accounted for 89 percent of variance. Design 3 correlated highest with the total score—.70 (Design 8, .64; and Design 1, .50). Thus, only designs 1, 3, and 8 were used for the present study. Reliability of raters on this study with the Pascal and Suttell's ratings of protocols in their book was .92; and the correlation (*rho*) between two raters on twenty cases in this study was .97.

In our adaptation of the test and scoring, the three designs were administered in succession and each design was in full view of the respondent as he copied it. No help was given by the interviewer and erasures were not permitted. Scoring was eliminated for some of the most ubiquitous errors among the very old such as tremor and rotation. By placing a ceiling on types of errors, the maximum error score for Design 1 was ten; Design 2, twenty; and Design 3, thirty. Thus the range was from zero to sixty, where sixty reflects gross distortion of all three designs.

The Thematic Apperception Test (TAT). Five Murray TAT cards (1, 2, 6BM, 7BM, 17BM) were scored by the Dana (1959) perceptual system to test for perceptual organization.

These five cards were selected because of their extensive use with community elderly in the Kansas City Study of Adult Lives (see Neugarten and Associates, 1964, for various measures using these responses to these five cards, particularly Gutmann, 1964, and Rosen and Neugarten, 1964). The Dana system has three components: perceptual organization (PO); perceptual range (PR); and perceptual personalization (PP). The PO score is made up of a point for the presence of each of seven elements (card description, present behavior, past events, future events, feeling, thought, and outcome) that demonstrate that the respondent followed standard directions to tell a story. The PR score measures the number of selected stimulus properties the respondent includes in the TAT stories. The PP score measures the number of personal references the respondent introduces in telling the story. The personalization measure proved to be inappropriate for this sample. Many of the most intact aged introduced personal references, whereas constricted respondents tended not to. That is, personalization was actually inversely related to perceptual organization ($r = -.16$, $n = 112$) and perceptual range ($r = -.10$, $n = 112$), whereas PO and PR were positively related ($r = .55$, $n = 112$). A total perceptual score was obtained, therefore, by adding PO and PR. Rater reliability for ten cases for PO was rho = .65, and for PR, rho = .72.

The Reitman Stick Figure Test. The Reitman test was developed to assess cognitive thinking (Reitman and Robertson, 1950). There are twelve solitary figures in all, each in an obvious physical pose or postural stance, such as slouching, running, jumping, and so on. The instructional set encourages the respondent to construct a story about the stick figure that tends to be descriptive of action or affect. Lakin and Eisdorfer (1960) have used the test to measure affective expression in the aged.

Because each stick figure is in a different pose, the respondent is expected to vary each description. Respondents often perseverate, however, unable to give a different description for each figure. A measure of the ability to vary responses when telling stories to the twelve Reitman Stick Figures was developed for the present study (Slover, 1967). For each respondent, a score was computed for the number of original descriptions.

The stories were considered not to vary when the described activity and affect were the same as offered for any other figure. The preadmission range was 3 to 12, mean = 9.3, median = 10.

This measure of originality, or ability to vary response, is related to the concept of rigidity. Most researchers have tended to agree that rigidity refers to a "relative inability to change one's action or attitude when the objective conditions have changed and a resistance to undertaking a new type of response" (English and English, 1958, p. 467). There is less agreement, however, regarding whether the concept of rigidity is a unitary one, or, if not, how best to assess varied types of rigidity (see reviews by Chown, 1959, Goins, 1962). The centrality of the concept is supported by Kounin (1941), Mangan and Clark (1958), and Schaie (1958), who have suggested that rigidity increases with age in the latter part of the life span. A sensible measure for the assessment of rigidity appeared to be the originality measure that uses as data stories told to the stick figures.

Signs of Cognitive Impairment. The six measures of cognitive inadequacy were positively correlated with each other (range of correlations, .08 to .47; the mean of the fifteen correlations was .29). The interrelationships among the measures, while suggesting commonality, are low enough to reflect their relative independence. For each of the six tasks, a level could be determined that reflected cognitive dysfunctioning and was greater than appeared in the community control sample: two or more errors on the MSQ; the word pairs not learned in thirty trials; a BGT Pascal and Suttell score of fifty or more; a TAT Dana score of seventeen or less; the 1-minute estimate of 10 seconds or less; and a Reitman originality score of seven or less.

A score was then computed for each respondent of the number of the six tasks where this level of dysfunction was reached. For the primary sample of eighty-five on first administration prior to admission, one of three (34 percent) had no signs, less than one of three (28 percent) had one sign, less than one of the two (13 percent) or three (16 percent) signs, and only a few (8 percent) four to six signs. The large percentages of

the sample with no or few signs reflect one criterion for inclusion in this study.

Area 2: Affective Responsiveness

Two measures were used to assess affective responsiveness:
affect range and willingness to introspect.

Affect Range. Affect displayed in stories told to the
Murray TAT cards was used to assess affective responsiveness.
The score was made up of the number of different affects, of a
possible total of seven, that were introduced in stories told to
the five Murray TAT cards. The seven different affects were:
hostility, unhappiness, dislike, joy, affection, interest, and trying. Each TAT card was analyzed in order for emotional or
motivational words or expression, and each such word was
entered into the one most appropriate category of the seven.
Reliability between two raters was $r = .93$. The preadmission
range was 1 to 7; the mean was 4.2; and the median was 4.0.

Willingness to Introspect. Gendlin and Tomlinson's
(1967) measure of the ability to experience was used to measure willingness to introspect. This scale is structured so as to
discriminate seven levels for the introspective exploration of
feelings. High scores apply to self-reports that include direct
reference to intense feelings and introduce diverse introspective
strands to further self-understanding. Scores at the low end of
the scale apply to verbalizations that indicate that feelings are
being ignored or described in an impersonal, unfocused, or
externalized fashion.

Ratings were made at preadmission to responses to open-
ended questions on eight affect states: loneliness, depression,
anger, shame, guilt, happiness, satisfaction, and pride. Because
only the affect of "loneliness" (e.g., "Could you tell me about
the times when you feel lonely?") was repeated at all times for
all samples, willingness to introspect on one's feelings of loneliness was the measure used to follow respondents over time.
Scores on loneliness correlated highly with the total score on all
eight affects ($r = .73$). The total score was highly correlated
(.92) with experiencing as assessed by the Focusing Manual and

Post-Focusing Questionnaire for ten respondents in the community sample. The manual and questionnaire consists of a series of instructions requiring the respondent to focus in silence on inner feelings and then to evaluate the experience. The pre-admission range for loneliness itself was 1 to 7; the mean was 2.2; and the median was 2. These findings suggest affective constriction, with only a few respondents (7 percent) receiving scores of four or more.

Area 3: Emotional States

Three different dimensions of emotional states were measured: feelings of well-being, hope, and the painful states of anxiety and depression.

Well-Being (Life Satisfaction Rating—LSR). The LSR was developed by Neugarten, Havighurst, and Tobin (1961) for use in the Kansas City Study of Adult Life. Its five scales measure: zest versus apathy; resolution and fortitude; congruence between desired and achieved goals; positive self-concept; and mood tone. Each of these five components is rated on a 5-point scale (5 being high); the ratings are summed to obtain an overall rating with a possible range from 5 to 25.

Hope. Five measures were combined in a total score to develop an index of hope: the Srole Anomie Scale (1956); a measure of time orientation, using responses to three open-ended interview items; a measure of time orientation, using the Sentence Completion Test (SCT); willingness to introspect; and the measure of self-esteem, using the Self-Sort Task. The weights for each of these measures was determined by a regression analysis against a criterion hope score for thirteen respondents (Haberland, 1972). The criterion hope score was based on responses to an intensive battery of instruments used to measure seven attributes of hope: density, direction, extensionality, focus of control, affect, gratifying change, and purpose in life.

Of the five measures, the Srole Anomie Scale is most directly related to the lack of confidence in gratification from the environment. Higher scores reflect greater feelings of alienation.

The interview time orientation measure was based on ratings of the responses to three items: "What does time mean to you, nowadays?" "How much do you plan ahead?" and "What does the future mean to you?" Low scores suggest answers such as "Time means nothing," "All is routine and monotonous" and "There is no future for me." A high score suggests emphasis on accomplishment and futurity with planning ahead and expectation of gratification for self and others. Rater reliability on fifteen cases was 88 percent exact agreement. The codings are as follows:

Responses to "What does time mean to you, nowadays?" were rated from 1 to 4: (1) "Time means nothing"; (2) "Time means something to fill up"; (3) "Time is 'nice' to have" (grateful to have time), "Time is nice for me," "I'm glad to get up in the morning and have something to do," "Grateful for every day I can get up and do my duty"; and (4) "Time means opportunity," or "time passes quickly." Responses to "How much do you plan ahead, the things that you will be doing the next week or the week after?" were rated from 1 to 4: (1) does not plan ahead; (2) does not plan ahead, but enjoys current activity, (3) makes plans for 2 or 3 days, or a week ahead, and (4) makes plans for more than a week in advance ("Plans—have my calendar—theatre, symphony, plan weeks ahead. But I'm very fast in deciding a trip"). Responses to "What does the future mean to you?" were rated from 1 to 3: (1) no future; resignation; (2) live day by day; and (3) future expectation of gratification for self and others.

The SCT time orientation was based on ratings of responses to three stems. The logic of scores is similar to that for the interview time orientation measure with high scores suggesting future extensionality. Rater reliability on ten cases was 93 percent exact agreement. Responses to "An hour is . . ." were rated from 1 to 3: (1) slow, monotonous, or routine; (2) neither fast nor slow; and (3) swift, or, time is valued. "Time is . . ." responses were rated from 1 to 4: (1) means nothing, or slow; (2) something to fill; (3) nice to have; and (4) opportunity, valued, passes swiftly. "I look forward to . . ." responses were rated from 1 to 3: (1) nothing looked forward to; (2) neutral; and (3) gratification for self or others.

The relative weightings of the five measures were: Srole, .45; experiencing, .32; self-esteem, .22; SCT time orientation, .16; and interview time orientation, .12.

Anxiety and Depression. To assess anxiety and depression the Gottschalk, Springer, and Gleser (1961) system was applied to responses to the Sentence Completion Test. The Gottschalk system was originally developed to assess the negative affect expressed in samples of verbal behavior but was readily adapted for responses to the SCT. About half of the responses to the thirty-two stems elicited a negative affect that could be placed into one of the twenty-two categories, grouped into six dimensions by Gottschalk. In adapting his system for use with the SCT, the task was first to determine if the response had a negative quality and, if so, to place the response into one of the twenty-two possible categories. Each "scorable" response was scored for only one category. Where there was a "double-scoring" possibility, the highest level was scored, where the scorer used the listing of categories as a ranking of "negativity" from one to twenty-two. For long responses, only the first "message" was considered for scoring.

A scorable response was one that fit into one of six dimensions, and into one of the categories within these dimensions. For each dimension, there were three to five individual categories. Examples of the types of responses that were considered to illustrate each category are given here.

DESPAIR

Death of Self
I wish I was . . . "dead."
To me, hope means . . . "I would be dead."
If I had my way . . . "I would die."
I can't understand what makes me . . . "to live."
The strongest part of me . . . "my mind, the only thing that keeps me alive."
I would like to be . . . "dead."
There are times when I wish . . . "life would end."

Hopeless
To me, hope means . . . "nothing."

The weakest part of me is . . . "despair."

Each day . . . "is a struggle living."

I would like to think about . . . "good things, but there are no good things."

Sometimes I feel . . . "Is it worth it all?"

I look forward to . . . "nothing."

My past life . . . "is gone."

Time is . . . "without meaning for me now."

Boredom

If I had my way . . . "I wouldn't sit around, but try to occupy my mind."

Each day . . . "is same thing"; "nothing happens"; "Just another day"; "Is a grind."

Time is . . . "very slow"; "hangs heavy on me."

An hour is . . . "a long time when you have nothing to do."

ABANDONMENT

Loneliness

Brothers and sisters . . . "one brother I'm lonely lonesome for"; "wish had them here."

I wish I . . . "could see somebody close to me."

If I had my way . . . "not be so lonesome"; "Have a girl friend"; "wouldn't stay by myself."

I can't understand what makes me . . . "lonesome at times"; "Want to be with people."

I would like to be . . . "in company of a few people could call my friends."

There are times when I . . . "am lonely for Connecticut."

Time is . . . "long when you are alone."

Sometimes I feel . . . "lonely and blue"; "A little lonely for people."

Death of Others

Brothers and sisters . . . "are dead"; "were killed"; "are gone."

My father . . . "is dead."

Our family . . . "is all dead."

My mother . . . "haven't got her"; "Is gone."

Separation (Score for separation from specific others that are introduced. That is, score Category 4, loneliness, if "separation" from people in general or when stem contains an explicit other, such as "brothers and sisters . . . and my mother . . . .

I wish I . . . "could see my children."

If I had my way . . . "be with my kids."

I would like to see . . . "my brother in Europe."

I like to think about . . . "my husband."

If only . . . "my husband were with me."

MUTILATION

Extreme Deterioration

My body's . . . "broken."

When I look at myself in the mirror . . . "I get a shock"; "Get frightened"; "Think I look gruesome."

Strongest part of me . . . "nothing strong."

Pain

I would like to think about . . . "a day without pain."

My body's . . . "hurts me so."

Death is . . . "natural, but I don't want to suffer."

Specific Body Part (also specific disease)

I believe . . . "people should find cure for arthritis."

The weakest part of me . . . "is my legs"; "stomach."

I would like to see . . . "better than I do."

The weakest part of me . . . "is I forget things" (reference to the mind).

Health and Vigor (both of self, including reference to age; and of others)

Self and reference to age of self:

I wish I were . . . "healthy"; "well enough to do things."

I can't understand what makes me . . . "ill"; "sick."

The strongest part of me . . . "is to be well."

Each day . . . "I don't feel well"; "I'm getting older."

When I look at myself in the mirror . . . "I realize how old I am."

Others:

To me, hope means . . . "my children well."

I would like to see . . . "My children should feel well."

ANXIETY AND FEAR

Fear of Death of Self

To me, death is . . . "terrible"; "I'm afraid"; "what can be worse?"

Time is . . . "going *too* fast."

Fear of Death of Self is Denied (respondent introduces fear by saying "not afraid.")

To me, death is . . . "not fearful"; "doesn't mean anything—not afraid to die."

I would like to see . . . "me alive, when the time comes, I'm not afraid."

Signs of Anxiety

Sometimes I feel . . . "irritable."

I can't understand what makes me . . . "nervous."

Diffuse, with Referent

Each day . . . "I wish for better."

There are times, when I . . . "wonder what I'm doing here and why."

My only trouble is . . . "I have so many troubles."

To me, hope means . . . "that I should get in the home already."

If I had my way . . . "like to be living in the home."

If I had my way . . . "my life would be entirely different."

The weakest part of me . . . "I worry too much."

My only trouble is . . . "I worry about my children."

Push of the Past
My past life ... "don't want to think about it"; "don't care to remind myself."

UNHAPPINESS ABOUT SELF

Subjective (direct reference to unhappiness)
There are times when I ... "am a little depressed"; "am a little disappointed in others."
I would like to see ... "a little happiness."
My only trouble is ... "I think too much, I should be satisfied."
People over me ... "have everything and it aggravates me."

Guilt over Impulses (almost always of anger)
Of anger:
The weakest part of me ... "is that I flare up suddenly."
I can't understand what makes me ... "lose my temper"; "mean"; "blow my top sometimes."
Of other impulses:
My mother ... "died in an accident because I was hurt and she died of the shock."
My past life ... "was not appropriately conducted."

Shame and Inadequacy
I wish ... "I could understand them."
To me, hope means ... "to do for self."
If I had my way ... "I would do work."
I can't understand what makes me ... "stop and hesitate"; "so nutty."
I would like to be ... "respected."
The weakest part of me ... "is being a damned fool."

Regret of the Past
My past life ... "was rotten"; "sad memories"; "wasn't always rosy."
If I had my way ... "I would have never gotten married."

If only ... "I could start all over" (implication of doing better).

UNHAPPINESS ABOUT OTHERS

Abused by Others
If I had my way ... "housekeep for self, but children say no."

Other people usually ... "try to decide things for me."

People think of me ... "as good, and some think of me as rotten."

Others as Negative
Brothers and sisters ... "quarrel."

Other people usually ... "gossip"; "are friendly. You think you can trust them?"

Implicit Morality (other people "should do or be")
Brother and sisters ... "should not quarrel."

In using this system, it becomes apparent to the judge that each stem tends to pull a few alternative categories. Thus the stem *My body's* ... tends to pull mutilation responses; and the response is actually being judged regarding one of four mutilation categories. By listing the stem that is scored for each category, it is possible to obtain a "true" distribution of response categories for each stem.

The interjudge reliability of the categorization of stem completions was very high. Two judges categorized the SCTs of fifteen respondents for a total of 480 stems. One judge assessed 220 (or 46 percent) of the responses to have painful messages; the other 203 (or 42 percent). In all, 182 responses were agreed upon by both judges as having painful messages. For those 182 responses, there was exact agreement on placement of 158 (or 87 percent of the common items that were placed in one of the twenty-two categories).

Weightings were then developed for each stem for anxiety and for depression following Gottschalk's logic. The weightings are shown in Table 15. For anxiety, the sample mean before

Table 15. Gottschalk Scoring of the SCT

Dimension	Category	Weighting Anxiety	Weighting Depression
Despair	Death of self	3	4
	Hopeless	0	3
	Boredom	0	2
Abandonment	Loneliness	3	2
	Death of others	2	0
	Separation: specific others	2	0
Mutilation	Deterioration	1	0
	Pain	1	0
	Body part	1	0
	Health and vigor	1	0
Anxiety	Fear: death of self	3	0
	Fear of death denied	1	0
	Signs of fear	3	0
	Diffuse fear	3	0
	Push of the past	3	0
Unhappiness about self	Self: subjective	0	2
	Guilt and anger	3	2
	Shame and inadequacy	3	2
	Regret of the past	0	2
Unhappiness about others	Abused by others	0	2
	Others as negative	0	0
	Implicit morals	0	0

admission was 19.6; the median was 19; and the range, 1 to 48. For depression, the mean was 13.7; the median, 14; and the range, 0 to 35. The two scales correlated .51 with each other.

Body Preoccupation. A separate scale was developed. Responses to twenty of the thirty-two stems were each scored for the presence of a reference to a body part, whether the reference was negative or positive. (Stems *not* used were; 1, 5, 6, 7, 12, 15, 17, 19, 22, 24, 25, and 27.) The mean was 4.4, the median was 4, and the range, 0 to 13. This measure of body preoccupation was essentially unrelated to the anxiety (r = .12) and depression (r = –.09) measures. This result was anticipated because the measure of body preoccupation was based on positive, as well as negative, messages in completions of the stems.

The highest correlation among the measures of emotional states was between the SCT anxiety and depression scales. Depression was more highly associated with the hope index (r =

—.38) and anxiety with LSR ($r = -.22$). LSR and hope results were unrelated.

Area 4: Self-Perceptions

Perception of capacity for self-care was assessed by the Shanas Self-Care Inventory (Shanas, 1962). Because of the admission policy of the homes most respondents reported little incapacity (range, 0 to 15; mean, 2.8; median, 0)—49, or 57 percent, respondents reported complete capacity for self-care on this measure prior to admission.

The Leary (1957) system proved useful for the development of assessments related to the self, particularly the self in interpersonal terms. It also allowed measurement of the range of attributes of self that were consciously perceived by the respondent and could be expressed. In Leary's system, personality is divided into sixteen areas of interpersonal behavior that are systematically related to each other and can be applied to any unit of observed, self-reported, or self-descriptive behavior. These sixteen areas are arranged along a circular continuum in which characteristics and characteristics lying on opposite points of the perimeter represent psychologically opposite characteristics. These areas can then be combined to yield eight interpersonal octants, labeled by Leary as: *competitive-narcissistic, managerial-autocratic, responsible-hypernormal, cooperative-overconventional, docile-dependent, self-effacing/masochistic, rebellious-distrustful,* and *aggressive-narcissistic.* Each octant has several characteristic dispositions or behaviors that can be either self-descriptive or observed. Each of the octants has a moderate and an extreme pole; the moderate pole is adaptive and the extreme pole is pathological.

The eight octants provide a basis for generating two global dimensions: dominance-submission and affiliation-hostility. Formulas for computing these two dimensions are provided by Leary. Simply stated, the dominance-submission dimension is the difference between proportions of managerial-autocratic behaviors and self-effacing/masochistic behaviors, whereas affiliation-hostility is the difference between proportions of cooperative-overconventional behavior and aggressive-sadistic behavior.

(Behaviors within the other four octants are added into Leary's formulas but they have less weight.)

The Self-Sort Task. To assess each of the eight octants of personality, Leary developed an interpersonal checklist consisting of eight statements for each of the eight octants. The respondent is asked to select, from among the sixty-four statements, those that he feels describe himself. The self-selected items represent for Leary an expression of an individual's conscious description of himself and his world. This conscious self-description is distinct from that level of communication that Leary describes as "private symbolization," or that component of the personality tapped by projective instruments that may not be available to conscious awareness.

With some modification in phrasing, to emphasize interpersonal relations, three statements were selected from the original Leary checklist for each of the sixteen categories, or six statements for each of the eight octants. In all, forty-eight statements formed the basis for the Self-Sort Task (see Table 16). This technique consisted of two parts. First, respondents were asked to sort a shuffled deck of cards containing the forty-eight statements into two piles: "like me now" and "not like me now." The second part consisted of asking the respondent to provide an illustration of current interpersonal behavior for those statements in the "like me now" pile.

Statements for each of the sixteen categories, as shown in Table 16, were scaled from 1 to 3 in terms of increasing intensity, having previously been scaled according to Guttman (Rosner, 1968). The theoretical rationale behind Guttman scaling was that if a person chose a highly affective or intense statement as self-descriptive, he was likely to choose other statements within that same category or dimension that were less affect-laden or intense. It was expected, in other words, that if a respondent chose self-descriptive statements at Level 3, he would also choose statements at levels 2 and 1, because there is equivalence of meaning between the statements, but variation in wording and affect-load. Statements were worded for the sorting portion of the Self-Sort Task to allow the respondent a large range for expression of self-concept.

After the respondent selected from among the forty-eight

Table 16. The Forty-Eight Self-Sort Items Grouped by Sixteen Areas and the Intensity (from 1 to 3) of Each Item (in Parentheses are the Weightings of Each Item for Scoring Self-Esteem)

Power

1. (+1) I enjoy being in charge of things.
2. (+2) I am a good leader.
3. (−2) I am somewhat of a dominating or bossy person.

Success

1. (+2) People think well of me.
2. (+1) I believe that I am an important person.
3. (0) I frequently give advice to others.

Narcissism

1. (+2) I am a self-respecting person.
2. (+1) I am an independent and self-confident person.
3. (0) I am proud and self-satisfied.

Exploitation

1. (+2) I am able to take care of myself.
2. (−1) I am a competitive person.
3. (−2) I can be a cold and unfeeling person.

Punitive Hostility

1. (+1) I am firm but fair in my relations with other people.
2. (+1) I can reproach people when necessary.
3. (−1) I am short-tempered and impatient with mistakes other people make.

Pure Hostility

1. (+2) I am frank and honest with people.
2. (0) I am critical of other people.
3. (−1) I frequently get angry with other people.

Unconventional Activity

1. (+1) When necessary, I can complain about things that bother me.
2. (+1) I will argue back when I feel I am right about something.
3. (−1) At times I act rebellious or feel bitter about something.

Deprivation

1. (0) I am frequently disappointed by other people.
2. (−2) I am touchy and easily hurt by others.

3. (−2) It is hard for me to trust anyone.

Masochism

1. (+1) I am able to criticize or find fault with myself.
2. (−1) I am easily embarrassed.
3. (−1) I am rather timid and shy.

Weakness

1. (+1) I can be obedient when necessary.
2. (−1) Usually I give in without too much of a fuss.
3. (−2) Frequently I feel weak or helpless.

Conformity

1. (+1) I am grateful for what other people do for me.
2. (0) I am often helped by other people.
3. (0) I hardly ever talk back.

Trust

1. (+2) I am a trusting person.
2. (−1) I prefer to let other people make decisions for me.
3. (−1) I will believe anyone.

Collaboration and Agreeability

1. (+2) I am a cooperative person.
2. (0) I want everyone to like me.
3. (0) I agree with what everyone says.

All Forms of Pure Love

1. (+2) I am a friendly person.
2. (+2) I am an affectionate and understanding person.
3. (+1) I love everyone.

Tenderness

1. (+2) I am considerate of others.
2. (+1) I am somewhat tender and soft-hearted.
3. (−1) I am too lenient with other people.

Generosity

1. (+1) Generally I can be counted upon to help others.
2. (+1) I often take care of other people.
3. (+3) I spoil people with kindness.

items, he was asked for validating evidence. Because the respondent was asked to select only those items that were currently self-descriptive, it was expected that most of the examples or illustrations given for each of the items would reflect specific interpersonal characteristics of the self-concepts. Respondents could be expected to describe and verbalize some of the feedback or validating experiences derived from interpersonal exchange with others and on which the current image of self was based. Adequacy in using the interpersonal environment to reaffirm the self could therefore be assessed by the percentage of items on which the respondent was able to give current validating examples.

The technique permitted the assessment of the three types variables of interest within the self-concept. It was obviously possible to derive scores for each octant and for the global scores of dominance-submission and affiliation-hostility that could be assessed for change and stability from preadmission to postadmission. It was also possible to derive a self-esteem score for each respondent by weighting each of the items for the extent of positive self-esteem. A third type of variable, that of adequacy in using current information for self-validation, could be assessed from the examples given from the selected items.

Development of the Measure. It was important to establish that the eight octants did indeed tap rather pervasive qualities of the self that were not specific to the Self-Sort Task. Wylie (1961), in her extensive review of the assessment of the self-concept, questions whether the Leary instrument, as typically used, captures dimensions that can be assessed by other measures. In a few studies, investigators have shown the pervasiveness of dimensions of the self by using other instruments for measuring concurrent validation. To assure that the Self-Sort Task tapped dimensions apparent in other instruments, a special study was undertaken. The literature suggested that it might not be possible to derive a stable measure of self-concept using instruments that tapped different levels of personality functioning—both instruments that elicit conscious self-reports as well as instruments of a projective nature that elicit information that may not be available to awareness (Bennet and Klopfer, 1962; Friedman, 1955; Lowe, 1961). The lack of consistency has been attributed to the assumption that projective measures reflect self-qualities that exist at different levels of conscious awareness than those obtained through objective tests, so that, theoretically, the results should be different. Also, it has been the custom, in self-concept research, to use a separate set of scoring criteria or interpretive schema for projective and objective tests, so that additional (and often confusing) inferences must be made about the comparability of the two quite different sources of data.

To determine whether consistency of self-concept across different types of instruments could be demonstrated, Edelhart (1966), using respondents drawn from the available samples, scored each of six measures of self in a consistent manner, using the Leary system. The Self-Sort Task was one of the six instruments included in her study of forty aged people in the community sample and thirty-six aged people in the institutional sample. The other five instruments were: the complete interview, the TAT, the Reitman Stick Figure Test, the Interpersonal Role-Playing Task (which consists of a series of nine simple stories describing conflictual interpersonal situations familiar to an institutional population), and the Revised Cattell 16 Personality Factor Questionnaire.

With the exception of the Self-Sort Task, those words, attitudes, feelings, or motivations that were currently self-descriptive were abstracted and assigned to the most appropriate Leary octant. To allow for the fact that some respondents were more verbal than others, the percentage of the total score in each octant was used in the final calculation. In this way, the respondent's scores could be compared with one another on a particular test regardless of the differences in their total number of responses. For the Self-Sort Task, the proportion of statements selected per octant to the total number of statements chosen comprised the respondent's raw score. For example, if a respondent chose thirty self-sort statements, six of which were from the managerial-autocratic octant, then six out of thirty or 20 percent would be his raw score for that octant. The six instruments were then evaluated in terms of Leary's classification scheme by first computing for each the two global scores, dominance-submission and affiliation-hostility, followed by computing a single summary point that captures the intersection of the two global scores.

Edelhart's major hypothesis was that "there would be a positive relationship among the self-concept scores for any given individual when a uniform system of measuring self-concept was applied to widely varying tasks" (Edelhart, 1966, p. 1). "This can be determined by showing that a heterogeneous group will tend to sort themselves out in terms of their self-concept in the same way on different instruments used to measure self-concept" (Edelhart, 1966, p. 24). By measuring the self-concept presented by respondents on widely different tasks, using a single theoretical model as well as a scoring system derived from that model and applied consistently across the different instruments, Edelhart found that "the self-concept scores on each of the six measures showed a closer correspondence than would be expected by chance ($p = .001$) with all of the other instruments taken as a whole (1966, p. 24). She concluded that the different sources of data significantly tended to sort out people in the same way.

From Edelhart's study, it is possible to draw additional conclusions about the nature of the self-concept and the Self-Sort Task. The first is that the self-concept is, in fact, a usable construct and is not merely an artifact of a particular kind of test data. That is, since *similar* self-concept data can be obtained from *dissimilar* measures, it is reasonable to argue against the presence of unique artifact generated by one instrument and to assume that a uniform phenomenon exists that can be tapped by many different kinds of instruments. The findings of Edelhart thus support the Self-Sort Task as a valid instrument for use in the present investigation; what this instrument tapped regarding the self-concept was also tapped by other instruments previously used to measure the self-concept.

Self-Esteem. To develop a measure of self-esteem, three judges were asked to rate each of the 48 items on a 5-point scale, reflecting from very positive to very negative self-esteem. Of the 48 items rated by three judges there was agreement by all three on 26 items and agreement by two of three judges on

18 items. Thus, on 44 of 48 items (or 92 percent) there was exact agreement by at least two of the three judges. The four items on which all judges disagreed were scored as neutral. The scoring of each of the 48 items is also shown in Table 16.

Adequacy. Five categories were used for scoring the adequacy of each example: an example from the past; from the present; a statement of conviction (that the selected description is valid for him without an actual example); a statement that reflects a wish to be "like that"; and distortion in which self-validation is based on magical fantasy. These five categories were a condensed version of an originally longer list of fourteen that were also ranked from examples in the present to distortion. Rater reliability on the fourteen-category system yielded 79 percent exact agreement and 89 percent one-step agreement.

For an overall score of adequacy, items that were validated with examples in the present or in the past received a weighting of +1; statements of "wish to be" received a weighting of zero; statements of conviction a weighting of −2; and those of distortion, a weighting of −4. To compute the adequacy score, the percentage of these four categories were Z-scored and then multiplied by the appropriate weights.

Focal Concern Using the Earliest Memory

For this analysis, it was assumed that present concerns become incorporated into the reconstruction of the past. If this is indeed the case, then the earliest memory could be used as a projective test to reveal the meanings of loss in people's current lives. The request to reminisce is usually perceived by the aged as an interest in their well-being and recognition of their wisdom. Standard verbal projective tasks, such as the Sentence Completion Test, are often perceived as a mixture of infantilism and threat. Visual projective tasks, such as the Rorschach Ink-blot Test and the Thematic Apperception Test, have the added disadvantage of being contaminated by sensory deficits that limit the subject's ability to perceive and respond. The data gathered by verbal reports of the past are not likely to be limited by sensory deficit nor is the request to reconstruct the earliest memory perceived as an infantilizing or threatening test.

The contemporary view is that the earliest memory reflects the synthesis of a meaningful early event within the context of current environmental transactions. As Schachtel (1947, p. 3) has succinctly stated: "Memory as a function of the living personality can be understood only as a capacity for the organization and reconstruction of past experiences and impressions in the service of present needs, fears and interests." This approach underlies our assumption that current meanings of loss become incorporated into the reconstruction of the earliest memory.

In this measure, the earliest memory of each respondent is placed in one of five categories, which were ranked from "no loss" to "most extreme introduced loss." The positive end of the scale contains no-loss themes, usually of family or peer interaction (Level 1), as well as themes of direct gratifications (Level 2). The next three levels include interpersonal losses or threat of injury (Level 3), personal illness and mutilation themes (Level 4), and deaths, usually of close family members (Level 5). The scale of the most extreme loss introduced into the earliest memory, reproduced below, includes two examples of each level.

The Data. The earliest memory was gathered by asking the question: "What is the first thing you can remember—going back as far as you can?" This question was the lead item of the portion of the interview designed to gather life history data. The earliest memory was operationally defined as the answer to the specific question, which sometimes included more than one memory, as well as the elaboration of the same recollection when given in response to the next question, "What other things can you remember about being very young?"

The Loss Scale. To develop a loss scale that would capture the change in covert affects, a pool of 120 earliest memories was analyzed for dominant themes. This pool of 120 memories consisted of two repeat earliest memories that were collected from sixty respondents at a 6-month interval; 54 memories gathered in two administrations from aged respondents in the community sample while residing in the community; and 66 memories gathered from the study sample when on the waiting list and then again 2 months after institutionalization. This tactic of using two repeat memories of respondents permitted the comparison of a sample in the process of becoming institutionalized to a control sample who had remained in the community for a comparable period of time, a comparison that could be made after "unblinding" the sixty respondents for sample membership (community or study sample) and time of interview (especially pre- or postinstitutionalization for the second sample).

The pool of 120 earliest memories was first analyzed for thematic content. Because many of the earliest memories had several manifest themes, it was apparent that the dominant theme would often be different from the theme reflecting greatest loss. For example, a memory might have both a dominant theme of threat of interpersonal injury and a secondary theme of a greater expression of loss, such as the death of respondent's mother. When earliest memories were sorted separately for dominant theme and highest loss theme it became apparent that fourteen useful categories were employed in making judgments. These fourteen categories were then reduced to five categories to form a 5-point ordinal scale where the low end (a score of 1) represented the least expression of loss and the high end (a score of 5) the highest expression of loss.

After unblinding for sample membership and time of interview, it became evident that scoring by the highest level of introduced loss revealed more change than scoring by the dominant theme. On the scale of the highest level of introduced loss, thirty-three respondents (55 percent) in the pre- and post-institutional sample manifested increased loss over time as compared to only six of the twenty-seven respondents (or 22 percent) in the community sample. The dominant theme appeared to be more stable, but the magnitude of the change on the scale of the highest level of loss suggested the meaningfulness of the latter scale for assessing institutional effects.

To determine the interjudge reliability of ratings, three independent judges rated the pool of 120 earliest memories of the sixty respondents on the 5-point scale. For every memory, at least two judges agreed. For 57 percent of the memories there was exact agreement of three judges, with a third judge disagreeing on the remaining 43 percent of the memories. (For a more complete discussion of the use of the earliest memory as data for research on aging, see Tobin, 1972.)

Level 1. *No-Loss Theme.* Scores of 1 may include guilt, anxiety, and aggressiveness. Themes may vary in level of primitiveness of impulse expression, but all such themes are scored 1 unless there is evidence for scoring 2, 3, 4, or 5. Usual themes are of family or going to school.

Level 2. *No Loss: Loss-Defended Themes.* No direct loss is expressed, but in the theme the respondent is the recipient of direct and primitive gratification. Receiving narcissistic support is the central issue, but overt loss is not introduced. That is, the flagrant wish and seeking for gratification is interpreted as cloaking an underlying fear of deprivation and loss.

Level 3. *Interpersonal Loss Themes.* Losses at Level 3 included: separation, loneliness, and threat of injury.

Level 4. *Injury (or Mutilation) Theme.* In memories where respondent is physically hurt, a score of 4 is given. Themes of illness, being sick, and physical impairment are typical of scores for Level 4.

Level 5. *Death Themes.* Themes of death, usually of close family members, are scored 5. Where respondent focuses on a family member and where the interaction is not one or the other dying, but if in the elaboration there is the discussion of the death of the other, then a score of 5 is given. For example, if respondent talks of playing with a sibling and then adds, "he died 2 years later," the score of 5 is given.

Statistical Analyses. The basic measures tended, as shown in Table 17, not to be highly associated with each other. This result was intended. The four areas were conceptualized to

Table 17. Intercorrelation Among Measures

| | Cognitive Functioning | Affective Responsiveness | | Emotional States | | | | Self- | SS | Self-Perceptions | | |
	Cognitive Sign	Affect Range	Intro- spection	LSR	Hope	SCT Anxiety	SCT Depression	care	Self-Esteem	SS Dominance	SS Affiliation	SS Adequacy
Signs of inadequacy	1.00											
Affect range	-.06	1.00										
Introspection	-.12	.11	1.00									
Life satisfaction (LSR)	-.26	.06	-.06	1.00								
Hope index	-.15	.09	.49	.12	1.00							
SCT anxiety	.20	-.05	-.06	-.22	-.14	1.00						
SCT depression	.16	.04	-.09	.05	-.38	.51	1.00					
Self-care	-.01	.06	.12	-.26	-.15	.20	.16	1.00				
SS self-esteem	-.26	.01	.07	.47	.50	-.18	-.19	.07	1.00			
SS dominance	-.16	-.03	-.02	.53	.30	-.12	-.22	-.10	.68	1.00		
SS affiliation	.23	.00	-.08	.08	.17	.08	.14	.13	.08	.04	1.00	
SS adequacy examples	-.31	-.15	.29	.00	.12	.22	.05	.02	-.09	-.10	-.06	1.00

be distinct, as were the variables within each area. The highest correlations were between measures within the same area that used the same data source, such as SCT anxiety and depression (r = .5) and Self-Sort self-esteem and dominance (r = .68). Across dimensions, there was little or no association among measures.

Data Analysis. The matched-pair t-test was used to assess the significance of the change over time on individual measures. When the t-test revealed changes not likely to be due to chance, one source of explanation other than the effect of the reloca-tion was consistently explored. This "source of error" was the change related to repeat measurement.

Because control samples were available, who were also fol-lowed over time with repeat measurements, it was possible to determine if the mean shift on each measure reached statistical significance for all three samples. Where significant shifts did occur in all samples, they could not be attributed to the inter-vening events that had occurred to the study sample; rather, they were interpreted as a function of a second experience with a previously administered question or task. For example, con-trol sample had a statistically significant mean change on the Pascal scores of the Bender Gestalt Test, reflecting the like-lihood of an increased ability to reproduce the design at the second exposure. Three control samples were used for this assessment of practice effects: the community control sample for which there was repeat data on twenty-three respondents; the institutional control sample for which there also was repeat data for twenty-three respondents; and a waiting-list control sample composed of seventeen respondents who had been inter-viewed twice over a 6-month period while they remained on the waiting list. A practice effect—in the sense of an improvement in performance for the control groups—was only found for the Bender Gestalt Test.

In addition to the matched-pair t-tests, data were concur-rently analyzed using a multivariate analysis of variance pro-gram, MESA 97, developed by Bock (1963, 1966). The program permitted contrasts between the waiting-list and initial adjust-ment phases, as well as the initial adjustment and adaptation phases, and of the trend from the waiting-list phase to the initial adjustment to the adaptation phase. The MESA 97 program also permitted the analyses of covariants, such as age, sex, and living arrangements while on the waiting list, to determine if significant changes transcended these covariates. The findings of these analyses are not reported here, but were used in assessing the meaning of mean changes generated by the matched-pair t-test statistic. Multivariate analysis by means of other statistical programs was also used in the prediction studies using age, sex, and living arrangements as covariates.

References

Adams, B. N. *Kinship in an Urban Setting.* Chicago: Markham, 1968.

Aldrich, C. K., and Mendkoff, E. "Relocation of the Aged and Disabled: A Mortality Study." *Journal of the American Geriatrics Society,* 1963, *11,* 185-194.

Ames, L. B. "Age Changes in the Rorschach Responses of a Group of Elderly Individuals." *Journal of Genetic Psychology,* 1960, *97,* 257-285.

Ames, L. B., Learned, J., Metraux, R., and Walker, R. *Rorschach Responses in Old Age.* New York: Hoeber-Harper, 1954.

Anderson, O. W. "The Sick Aged and Society: Some Dismal Implications for Public Policy." Paper presented at the annual meetings of the American Public Health Association, New Orleans, May 1974.

Bender, L. "A Visual Motor Gestalt Test and Its Clinical Use." *American Orthopsychiatry Association Research Monograph,* 1938, *3,* 117-125.

Bennet, G. F., and Klopfer, W. G. "Levels of Awareness in Projective Tests." *Journal of Projective Techniques,* 1962, *26,* 34-35.

Bennett, R. "The Meaning of Institutional Life." *The Gerontologist*, 1963, *3*, 117-125.

Billingslea, F. "The Bender-Gestalt Test: An Objective Scoring Method and Validating Data." *Journal of Clinical Psychology*, 1948, *4*, 1-28.

Birren, J. E. (Ed.) *Handbook of Aging and the Individual.* Chicago: University of Chicago Press, 1959.

Blenkner, M. "Environmental Change and the Aging Individual." *The Gerontologist*, 1967, *7*, 101-105.

Blenkner, M. "The Normal Dependencies of Aging." In R. A. Kalish (Ed.), *The Dependencies of Old People.* Ann Arbor, Michigan: Institute of Gerontology, 1969.

Blenkner, M., Bloom, M., and Nielsen, M. "A Research and Demonstration Project." *Social Casework*, 1971, *52*, 483-499.

Block, J. *The Q-Sort Method in Personality Assessment and Psychiatric Research.* Springfield, Ill.: Charles C Thomas, 1961.

Bock, R. D. "Programming Univariate and Multivariate Analysis of Variance." *Technometrics*, 1963, *5*, 95-117.

Bock, R. D. *A Computer Program for Univariate and Multivariate Analysis of Variance, in Proceedings of the IBM Scientific Computing Symposium on Statistics, October 21-23, 1963.* White Plains, N.Y.: IBM Data Processing Division, 1966.

Bortner, R. W. "Test Differences Attributable to Age, Selection, Processes, and Institutional Effects." *Journal of Gerontology*, 1962, *17*, 58-60.

Bowlby, J. *Maternal Care and Mental Health.* Geneva: World Health Organization, 1952.

Brody, E. M. "Follow-Up Study of Applicants and Non-Applicants to a Voluntary Home." *The Gerontologist*, 1969, *9*, 187-196.

Butler, R. N. "The Life Review: An Interpretation of Reminiscence in the Aged." *Psychiatry*, 1963, *26*, 65-76.

Caird, W. K., Sanderson, R. E., and Inglis, J. "Cross-Validation of a Learning Test for Use With Elderly Psychiatric Patients." *Journal of Mental Science*, 1962, *108*, 386-470.

Camargo, O., and Preston, G. H. "What Happens to Patients Who are Hospitalized for the First Time When Over Sixty-Five?" *American Journal of Psychiatry*, 1945, *102*, 168-173.

Carp, F. M. "The Impact of Environment on Old People." *The Gerontologist*, 1967, *2*, 106-108.

Cattell, R. B. *Handbook Supplement for Form C of the Sixteen Personality Factor Test* (2nd ed.). Champaign, Ill.: Institute for Personality and Ability Testing, 1962.

Cavan, R. S., Burgess, E. W., Havighurst, R. J., and Goldhamer, H. *Personal Adjustment in Old Age.* Chicago: Science Research Associates, 1949.

Chalfen, L. "Leisure-Time Adjustment of the Aged: II. Activities and Interests and Some Factors Influencing Choice." *Journal of Genetic Psychology*, 1956, *88*, 261-276.

Chown, S. "Rigidity—A Flexible Concept." *Psychological Bulletin*, 1959, *56*, 195-223.

Coe, R. M. "Self-Conception and Institutionalization." In A. M. Rose and W. A. Peterson (Eds.), *Older People and Their Social World.* Philadelphia: F. A. Davis, 1965.

Cosin, L. R. "Organizing a Geriatric Department." *British Medical Journal*, 1947, *2*, 1044-1046.

Costello, J., and Tanaka, G. "Mortality and Morbidity in Long-Term Institutional Care of the Aged." *Journal of the American Geriatrics Society*, 1961, *9*, 959-963.

Cumming, E., and Henry, W. E. *Growing Old.* New York: Basic Books, 1961.

Dana, R. H. "Proposal for Objective Scoring of the TAT." *Perceptual and Motor Skills*, 1959, *9*, 27-43.

Davidson, H. H., and Kruglov, L. "Personality Characteristics of the Institutionalized Aged." *Journal of Consulting and Clinical Psychology*, 1952, *16*, 5-12.

Dörken, H., Jr. "Personality Factors Associated with Paraplegia and Prolonged Hospitalization: A Clinical Note." *Canadian Journal of Psychology*, 1951, *5*, 134-137.

Edelhart, G. "Consistency of Self-Concept and Across Instruments." Unpublished master's thesis, University of Chicago, 1966.

Eicker, W. F. "Age-Related Differences in Behavioral Rigidity, Level of Aspiration, and Adjustment in a Veterans Administration Domiciliary Population." Unpublished doctoral dissertation, University of California, Los Angeles, 1959.

Eidelberg, L. (Ed.) *Encyclopedia of Psychoanalysis*. New York: The Free Press, 1968.

English, H. B., and English, A. *A Comprehensive Dictionary of Psychological and Psychoanalytic Terms*. New York: David McKay, 1958.

Erikson, E. H. *Identity and the Life Cycle*. New York: International Universities Press, 1959.

Fink, H. "The Relationship of Time Perspective to Age, Institutionalization, and Activity." *Journal of Gerontology*, 1957, *12*, 414-417.

Fogel, E. J., Swepston, E. R., Zintek, S. S., Vernier, C. N., Fitzgerald, J. F., Marnocha, R. S., and Weschler, C. H. "Problems of Aging: Conclusions Derived from Two Years of Interdisciplinary Study of Domiciliary Members in a Veterans Administration Center." *American Journal of Psychiatry*, 1956, *112*, 724-730.

Foster, G. *Traditional Cultures and the Impact of Technological Change*. New York: Harper & Row, 1962.

Fox, C. "The Intelligence of Old Indigent Persons Residing Within and Without a Public Home for the Aged." *American Journal of Psychology*, 1950, *63*, 110-112.

Frankl, V. E. *Man's Search for Meaning*. New York: Washington Square Press, 1963.

Fried, M. "Grieving for a Lost Home." In L. J. Duhl (Ed.), *The Urban Condition: People and Policy in Metropolis*. New York: Basic Books, 1963.

Friedman, U. "Phenomenological, Idea, and Projective Concepts of Self." *Journal of Abnormal and Social Psychology*, 1955, *51*, 611-615.

Friedsam, H. J. "Reactions of Older Persons to Disaster-Caused Losses: An Hypothesis of Relative Deprivation." *The Gerontologist*, 1961, *1*, 34-37.

Gaynes, N. "A Logic to Long-Term Care." *The Gerontologist*, 1973, *13*, 277-281.

Gendlin, E. T. and Tomlinson, T. M. "The Process Conception and Its Measurement." In C. Rogers (Ed.), *The Therapeutic Relationship and Its Impact.* Madison: University of Wisconsin Press, 1967.

Gitlitz, I. "Morbidity and Mortality in Old Age. Parts I-V." *Journal of the American Geriatrics Society,* 1956, *4,* 543-59, 708-21, 805-22, 896-908, 975-97.

Gitlitz, I. "Morbidity and Mortality in Old Age. Parts VI-VII." *Journal of the American Geriatrics Society,* 1957, *5,* 32-48, 299-305.

Goffman, E. *Asylums: Essays on the Social Situation of Mental Patients and Other Inmates.* Garden City, N.Y.: Doubleday, 1961.

Goins, A. "Rigidity-Flexibility: Toward Clarification." *Merrill-Palmer Quarterly,* 1962, *8,* 41-61.

Goldfarb, A. "The Psychodynamics of Dependency and the Search for Aid." In R. A. Kalish (Ed.), *The Dependencies of Old People.* Ann Arbor, Michigan: The Institute of Gerontology, 1969.

Goldfarb, A. "Predictors of Mortality in the Institutionalized Aged." In E. Palmore and F. C. Jeffers (Eds.), *Prediction of Life Span.* Lexington, Mass.: Heath Lexington Books, 1971.

Goldfarb, A. "Minor Adjustments of the Aged." In S. Arieti and E. Brody (Eds.), *American Handbook of Psychiatry.* Vol. 3: *Adult Clinical Psychiatry.* New York: Basic Books, 1974.

Goldfarb, A., Fish, M., and Gerber, I. E. "Predictors of Mortality in the Institutionalized Aged." *Diseases of the Nervous System,* 1966, *27,* 21-29.

Goldfarb, A., Shahinian, S., and Turner, H. "Death Rates in Relocated Aged Residents of Nursing Homes." Paper presented at the annual meeting of the Gerontological Society, New York, November 1966.

Gottschalk, L. A., Springer, K. H., and Gleser, G. C. "Experiments With a Method of Assessing the Variations in Intensity of Certain Psychologic States Occurring During the Psychotherapeutic Interview." In L. A. Gottschalk (Ed.),

Comparative Psycholinguistic Analysis of Two Psychotherapeutic Interviews. New York: International Universities Press, 1961.

Greenfield, N. A., Roosaler, R., and Crosley, A. P. "Ego Strength and Length of Recovery from Infectious Mononucleosis." *Journal of Nervous and Mental Disease,* 1959, *128,* 125-134.

Gunderson, E. K. E. "Personal History Characteristics of Antarctic Volunteers." *Journal of Social Psychology,* 1964, *64,* 325-332.

Gutmann, D. "An Exploration of Ego Configurations in Middle and Later Life." In B. L. Neugarten (Ed.), *Personality in Middle and Later Life—Empirical Studies.* New York: Atherton Press, 1964.

Haberland, H. W. "Psychological Dimensions of Hope in the Aged: Relationship to Adaptation, Survival, and Institutionalization." Unpublished doctoral dissertation, University of Chicago, 1972.

Hacker, S., and Gaitz, C. "The Moral Career of the Elderly Mental Patient." *The Gerontologist,* 1969, *9,* 120-127.

Hall, G. H., Mathiasen, G., and Ross, H. A. *Guide to Development of Protective Services for Older People.* Springfield, Ill.: Charles C Thompson, 1973.

Hammerman, J. "The Role of the Institution and the Concept of Parallel Services." *The Gerontologist,* 1974, *14,* 11-14.

Hanway, J. "An Earnest Appeal for Mercy to the Children of the Poor." In D. B. Horn and M. Ransome (Eds.), *English Historical Documents.* London: Eyre and Spottiswoode, 1957. Chapter by Hanway originally published in 1756.

Heyman, D., and Jeffers, T. "Observations on the Extent of Concern and Planning by the Aged for Possible Chronic Illness." *Journal of the American Geriatrics Society,* 1965, *13,* 152-159.

Hilgard, E. R. "Human Motives and the Concept of the Self." *American Psychology,* 1949, *4,* 374-382.

Hill, R., Foote, N., Aldous, J., Carlson, R., and Macdonald, R. *Family Development in Three Generations.* Cambridge, Mass.: Schenkman, 1970.

Hochschild, A. R. *Unexpected Community.* Englewood Cliffs, N.J.: Prentice-Hall, 1973.

Hutt, M. *A Tentative Guide for the Administration and Interpretation of the Bender-Gestalt Test.* Washington, D.C.: U.S. Army, Adjutant General's School, 1945.

Inglis, J. "A Paired-Association Learning Test for Use With Elderly Psychiatric Patients." *Journal of Mental Science,* 1959, *105,* 440-443.

Isaacs, B., Livingstone, M., and Neville, Y. *Survival of the Unfittest.* Boston: Routledge and Kegan Paul, 1972.

Jackson, B. "Who Goes to Prison: Caste and Careerism in Crime." *Atlantic Monthly,* 1966, *1,* 52-57.

James, R. L. *Edmonton Senior Residents Survey.* Edmonton, Alberta: Edmonton Welfare Council, 1964.

Janis, I. L. *Psychological Stress.* New York: Wiley, 1958.

Jasnau, K. F. "Individualized Versus Mass Transfer of Nonpsychotic Geriatric Patients from Mental Hospitals to Nursing Homes, With Special Reference to the Death Rate." *Journal of the American Geriatrics Society,* 1967, *15,* 280-284.

Josephy, H. "Analysis of Mortality and Causes of Death in a Mental Hospital." *American Journal of Psychiatry,* 1949, *106,* 185-193.

Kahana, E. "Matching Environments to Needs of the Aged: A Conceptual Scheme." In J. Gubrium (Ed.), *Late Life-Communities and Environmental Policy.* Springfield, Ill.: Charles C Thomas, 1974.

Kahana, E., and Coe, R. "Staff and Staff Conception of Institutionalized Aged." *The Gerontologist,* 1969, *9,* 264-267.

Kahn, R. L. "Psychological Aspects of Aging." In I. Rossman (Ed.), *Clinical Geriatrics.* Philadelphia: Lippincott, 1971.

Kahn, R. L., Pollack, M., and Goldfarb, A. I. "Factors Related to Individual Differences in Mental Status of Institutionalized Aged." In P. H. Hoch and J. Zubin (Eds.), *Psychopathology of Aging.* New York: Grune & Stratton, 1961.

Kaplan, J. "The Institution as the Cornerstone for Alternatives to Institutionalization." *The Gerontologist,* 1974, *14,* 5.

Kaplan, S. *Report on Services to the Aged.* Chicago: Jewish Federation of Metropolitan Chicago, 1966.

Kasl, S. "Physical and Mental Health Effects of Involuntary Relocation and Institutionalization on the Elderly—A Review." *American Journal of Public Health,* 1972, *62,* 377-384.

Kastenbaum, R. "While the Old Man Dies: Our Conflicting Attitudes Toward the Elderly." In S. Schoenberg, A. C. Carr, D. Peretz and A. H. Kutscher (Eds.), *Psychosocial Aspects of Terminal Care.* New York: Columbia University Press, 1972.

Kastenbaum, R., and Candy, S. "The Four Percent Fallacy: A Methodological and Empirical Critique of Extended Care Facility Population Statistics." *International Journal of Aging and Human Development,* 1973, *4,* 15-21.

Kay, D., Norris, V., and Post, F. "Prognosis in Psychiatric Disorders of the Elderly." *Journal of Mental Science,* 1956, *102,* 129-140.

Killian, E. C. "Effects of Geriatric Transfers on Mortality Rates." *Social Work,* 1970, *3,* 19-26.

Kleban, M., Brody, E., and Lawton, M. "Personality Traits in the Mentally Impaired Aged and Their Relationship to Improvements in Current Functioning." *The Gerontologist,* 1971, *11,* 124-133.

Kleemier, R. "The Use and Meaning of Time in Special Settings." In R. Kleemier (Ed.), *Aging and Leisure.* New York: Oxford University Press, 1961.

Klopfer, W. "Personality Patterns of Old Age." *Rorschach Research Exchange,* 1946, *10,* 145-166.

Komarovsky, M. *Blue-Collar Marriage.* New York: Random House, 1964.

Kosberg, J. I., and Tobin, S. S. "Variability Among Nursing Homes." *The Gerontologist,* 1972, *12,* 214-219.

Kounin, J. S. "Experimental Studies of Rigidity, I & II." *Character and Personality,* 1941, *9,* 251-282.

Kubler-Ross, E. *On Death and Dying.* New York: Macmillan, 1969.

Kuypers, J. "Elderly Persons En Route to Institutions: A Study of Changing Perceptions of Self and Interpersonal Relations." Unpublished doctoral dissertation, University of Chicago, 1969.

Lakin, M. "Formal Characteristics of Human Figure Drawings by Institutionalized and Non-Institutionalized Aged." *Journal of Gerontology*, 1960, *15*, 76-78.

Lakin, M., and Eisdorfer, C. "Affective Expression Among the Aged." *Journal of Projective Techniques*, 1960, *24*, 403-408.

Laverty, R. "Nonresident Aid—Community Versus Institutional Care for Older People." *Journal of Gerontology*, 1950, *5*, 370-374.

Lawton, M. P. "Assessment, Integration and Environments for Older People." *The Gerontologist*, 1970, *10*, 38-46.

Lazarus, R. S. *Psychological Stress and the Coping Process.* New York: McGraw-Hill, 1966.

Leary, T. *Interpersonal Diagnosis of Personality.* New York: Ronald Press, 1957.

Lecky, P. *Self-Consistency: A Theory of Personality.* New York: Island Press, 1951.

Lecky, P. "The Personality." In C. E. Moustakas, *The Self: Explorations in Personal Growth.* New York: Harper & Row, 1956.

Lepkowski, J. R. "The Attitudes and Adjustments of Institutionalized Aged and Non-Institutionalized Catholic Aged." *Journal of Gerontology*, 1956, *2*, 185-191.

Le Shan, L. L. "A Basic Psychological Orientation Associated with Malignant Diseases." *Psychiatric Quarterly*, 1961, *35*, 314-330.

Levisohn, H. G. "A Study of Adjustment in Old Age." Unpublished master's thesis, University of Chicago, 1942.

Lieberman, M. A. "Relationship of Mortality Rates to Entrance to a Home for the Aged." *Geriatrics*, 1961, *16*, 515-519.

Lieberman, M. A. "Psychological Correlates of Impending Death: Some Preliminary Observations." *Journal of Gerontology*, 1965, *20*, 181-190.

Lieberman, M. A. "Institutionalization of the Aged: Effects of Behavior." *Journal of Gerontology,* 1969, *24,* 330-340.

Lieberman, M. A. "Some Issues in Studying Psychological Predictors of Survival." In E. Palmore and F. C. Jeffers (Eds.), *Prediction of Life Span.* Lexington, Mass.: Heath Lexington Books, 1971.

Lieberman, M. A. "Relocation Research and Social Policy." *The Gerontologist,* 1974, *14,* 494-501.

Lieberman, M. A., and Lakin, M. "On Becoming an Institutionalized Person." In R. H. Williams, C. Tibbits, and W. Donahue (Eds.), *Processes of Aging.* Vol. 1: *Social and Psychological Perspectives.* New York: Atherton Press, 1963.

Lieberman, M. A., and Tobin, S. S. Crises of Late Life: *Predicting Adaptation to Change, Loss and Death.* New York: Basic Books, in press.

Lieberman, M. A., Tobin, S. S., and Slover, D. "The Effects of Relocation on Long-Term Geriatric Patients." Final Report to the Department of Mental Health, State of Illinois, Project #17-328, 1969.

Lissitz, S. "Theoretical Conceptions of Institutional and Community Care." *The Gerontologist,* 1970, *10,* 298-304.

Lowe, C. M. "The Self-Concept: Fact or Artifact?" *Psychological Bulletin,* 1961, *58,* 325-336.

Lowenthal, M. F. *Lives in Distress: The Paths of the Elderly to the Psychiatric Ward.* New York: Basic Books, 1964.

Lowenthal, M. F., and Haven, C. "Interaction and Adaptation: Intimacy as a Critical Variable." In B. L. Neugarten (Ed.), *Middle Age and Aging.* Chicago: University of Chicago Press, 1968.

Mangan, G., and Clark, J. W. "Rigidity Factors in the Testing of Middle-Aged Subjects." *Journal of Gerontology,* 1958, *13,* 422-425.

Markson, E. W., and Hand, J. "Referral for Death: Low Status of the Aged and Referral for Psychiatric Hospitalization." *Aging and Human Development,* 1970, *1,* 261-272.

Mason, E. P. "Some Correlates of Self-Judgments of the Aged." *Journal of Gerontology,* 1954, *9,* 324-337.

Montgomery, J. E. "Living Arrangements and Housing of the Rural Aged in a Central Pennsylvania Community." *Patterns of Living and Housing of Middle Aged and Older People, Public Health Service No. 1496.* Washington, D.C.: U.S. Government Printing Office, 1965.

Morris, R. *Alternatives to Nursing Home Care: A Proposal.* Washington, D.C.: U.S. Government Printing Office, 1971.

National Center for Health Statistics. "Hospitalization in the Last Year of Life: United States." Series 22, No. 1, 1965.

Neugarten, B. L., and Associates. *Personality in Middle and Late Life.* New York: Atherton Press, 1964.

Neugarten, B. L., Havighurst, R. J., and Tobin, S. S. "The Measurement of Life Satisfaction." *Journal of Gerontology,* 1961, *16,* 134-143.

Newman, N. C. "Institutionalization, Interaction, and Self-Conception in Aging." Unpublished master's thesis, University of Minnesota, 1964.

Office of Nursing Home Affairs. *Long Term Care Facility Improvement Study.* Washington, D.C.: U.S. Government Printing Office, 1975.

Palmore, E., and Jeffers, F. C. (Eds.) *Prediction of Life Span.* Lexington, Mass.: Heath Lexington Books, 1971.

Pan, J. "A Study of the Influence of Institutionalization on the Social Adjustment of Old People." *Journal of Gerontology,* 1948, *3,* 276-280.

Pascal, G. R., and Suttell, B. J. *The Bender-Gestalt Test: Quantification and Validity for Adults.* New York: Grune & Stratton, 1951.

Perlman, L. W., Hammerman, J., and Tobin, S. S. *Social Casework—Fieldwork Training in a Geriatric Institutional Setting: Review of a Five-Year Experience.* Chicago: American Public Welfare Association, 1969.

Pincus, M. A. "Toward a Conceptual Framework for Studying Institutional Environments in Homes for the Aged." Unpublished doctoral dissertation, University of Wisconsin, 1968.

Pollack, M., Karp, E., Kahn, R. L., and Goldfarb, A. I. "Perception of Self in Institutionalized Aged Subjects. I. Response Patterns to Mirror Reflection." *Journal of Gerontology,* 1962, *17,* 405-408.

Pollack, W. *Cost of Alternative Care Settings for the Elderly.* Washington, D.C.: The Urban Institute, 1973.

Prados, M., and Fried, E. "Personality Structure in the Older Age Groups." *Journal of Clinical Psychology,* 1947, *3,* 113-120.

Reitman, F., and Robertson, J. P. "Reitman's Pin-Man Test: A Means of Disclosing Impaired Conceptual Thinking." *Journal of Nervous and Mental Disease,* 1950, *112,* 498-510.

Rogers, C. R. *Client-Centered Therapy.* Boston: Houghton Mifflin, 1951.

Rosen, J., and Neugarten, B. L. "Ego Functions in the Middle and Later Years: A Thematic Apperception Study." In B. L. Neugarten (Ed.), *Personality in Middle and Late Life —Empirical Studies.* New York: Atherton Press, 1964.

Rosenthal, R. "The Adjustment of Old People in an Old Age Home." Unpublished master's dissertation, University of Chicago, 1942.

Rosner, A. "Stress and the Maintenance of Self-Concept in the Aged." Unpublished doctoral dissertation, The University of Chicago, 1968.

Rosow, I. *Social Integration of the Aged.* New York: The Free Press, 1967.

Roth, M. "The Natural History of Mental Disorders in Old Age." *Journal of Mental Science,* 1955, *101,* 281-301.

Saunders, C. "A Therapeutic Community: St. Christopher's Hospice." In F. Schoenberg, A. C. Carr, D. Peretz, and A. H. Kutcher (Eds.), *Psychosocial Aspects of Terminal Care.* New York: Columbia University Press, 1972.

Schachtel, E. "On Memory and Childhood Amnesia." *Psychiatry,* 1947, *10,* 1-26.

Schaie, K. "Rigidity—Flexibility and Intelligence." *Psychological Monographs,* 1958, *72,* 1-25.

Shanas, E. *Family Relationships of Older People.* National

Opinion Research Center, University of Chicago: Health Information Foundation, Research Series 20, 1961.

Shanas, E. *The Health of Older People: A Social Survey.* Cambridge: Harvard University Press, 1962.

Shanas, E., Townsend, P., Wedderburn, D., Friis, H., Milhøj, P., and Stehouwer, M. *Old People in Three Industrial Societies.* New York: Atherton Press, 1968.

Shore, H. "Alternatives to Institutional Care: Fact or Fancy." *Journal of Long Term Care Administration,* 1973, *2,* 23-36.

Shrut, S. D. "Attitudes Toward Old Age and Death." *Mental Hygiene,* 1958, *42,* 259-66.

Slover, D. L. "The Relationship Between Rigidity and Adaptation to the Stress of Institutionalization Among the Aged." Unpublished master's thesis, University of Chicago, 1967.

Snygg, D., and Combs, A. W. *Individual Behavior.* New York: Harper & Row, 1949.

Sommer, R., and Osmond, H. "Symptoms of Institutional Care." *Social Problems,* 1961, *8,* 254-262.

Spitz, R. A. "Hospitalism—An Inquiry into the Genesis of Psychiatric Conditions in Early Childhood." *Psychoanalytic Studies of the Child,* 1945, *1,* 53-74.

Srole, L. "Social Integration and Certain Corollaries: An Exploratory Study." *American Sociological Review,* 1956, *21,* 707-716.

Stotsky, B. A. "A Controlled Study of Factors in the Successful Adjustment of Mental Patients to Nursing Homes." *American Journal of Psychiatry,* 1967, *123,* 1243-1251.

Swenson, W. M. "Attitudes Toward Death in an Aged Population." *Journal of Gerontology,* 1961, *16,* 49-52.

Tobin, S. S. "The Earliest Memory as Data for Research." In D. Kent, R. Kastenbaum, and S. Sherwood (Eds.), *Research, Planning and Action for the Elderly: Power and Potential of Social Science.* New York: Behavioral Publications, 1972.

Tobin, S. S. "Social Health Services for the Future Aged." *The Gerontologist,* 1975, *15,* 32-37.

Tobin, S. S., and Etigson, E. C. "Effects of Stress on the Earliest Memory." *Archives of General Psychiatry*, 1968, *19*, 435-444.

Tobin, S. S., Davidson, S. M., and Sack, A. *Models for Effective Service Delivery: Social Services for Older Americans.* Final report to the Administration on Aging. Project No. 90-A-366, 1975.

Tobin, S. S., Hammerman, J. and Rector, V. "Preferred Disposition of Institutionalized Aged." *The Gerontologist*, 1972, *12*, 129-133.

Townsend, P. *The Last Refuge—A Survey of Residential Institutions and Homes for the Aged in England and Wales.* London: Routledge and Kegan Paul, 1962.

Triers, T. R. "A Study of Change Among Elderly Psychiatric In-Patients During their First Year of Hospitalization." *Journal of Gerontology*, 1968, *23*, 354-362.

Troll, L. *Early and Middle Adulthood.* Monterey: Brooks/Cole, 1975.

Tuckman, J., and Lorge, I. "The Effect of Institutionalization on Attitudes Toward Old People." *Journal of Abnormal and Social Psychology*, 1952, *47*, 337-444.

Tuckman, J., and Lorge, I. "Somatic and Psychological Complaints of Older People in Institutions and at Home." *Geriatrics*, 1953, *8*, 274-79.

Turner, B. F. "Psychological Predictors of Adaptation to the Stress of Institutionalization in the Aged." Unpublished doctoral dissertation, University of Chicago, 1969.

Turner, B. F., Tobin, S. S., and Lieberman, M. A. "Personality Traits as Predictors of Institutional Adaptation Among the Aged." *Journal of Gerontology*, 1972, *27*, 61-68.

Twente, E. E. *Never Too Old: The Aged in Community Life.* San Francisco: Jossey-Bass, 1970.

Vernon, D. A., Foley, J. M., Sipowicz, R. R., and Schulman, J. L. *The Psychological Responses of Children to Hospitalization and Illness: A Review of the Literature.* Springfield, Ill.: Charles C Thomas, 1965.

Vital Statistics of the United States, 1967. Vol. 2: *Mortality.*

Washington, D.C.: National Center for Health Statistics, 1969.

Webb, M. A. "Longitudinal Sociopsychologic Study of a Randomly Selected Group of Institutionalized Veterans." *Journal of the American Geriatrics Society,* 1959, *7,* 730-740.

Weinberg, J. "Personal and Social Adjustment." In J. Anderson (Ed.), *Psychological Aspects of Aging.* Washington, D.C.: American Psychological Association, 1956.

Whittier, J. R., and Williams, D. "The Coincidence of Constancy of Mortality Figures for Aged Psychotic Patients Admitted to State Hospitals." *Journal of Nervous and Mental Disease,* 1956, *124,* 618-620.

Wolf, S., and Ripley, H. A. "Reactions Among Allied Prisoners of War Subjected to Three Years of Imprisonment and Torture by the Japanese." *American Journal of Psychiatry,* 1947, *104,* 130-193.

Wylie, R. Z. *The Self-Concept: A Critical Review of Pertinent Research Literature.* Lincoln: University of Nebraska Press, 1961.

Index

297